6995
70C

GENDER AND THE POLITICS OF THE CURRICULUM

Have girls been free agents in their choice of subjects to pursue at school? Will a compulsory national curriculum promote greater gender equality?

This book uses detailed case studies of two secondary schools to examine the relationship between curriculum choice and gender identity among fourteen-year-old pupils making their first choices about what subjects to pursue at exam level. It reveals a two way process. Pupils' decisions on what subjects to take are influenced by how they perceive themselves in gender terms, and the curriculum once chosen reinforces their sense of gender divisions. Sheila Riddell looks at the influences on pupils at this stage in their lives from peers, family and the labour market as well from teachers. She argues that the belief in freedom of choice and school neutrality espoused by many teachers can become an important factor in the reproduction of gender divisions, and that unless the introduction of the national curriculum is accompanied by systematic efforts to eradicate sexism from the hidden curriculum it will fail in its aim of creating greater equality of educational opportunity among the sexes.

Sheila I. Riddell is a lecturer in education at Stirling University. She taught in comprehensive schools for six years before moving into higher education and her publications include work in the area of learning difficulties as well as numerous articles on gender and education.

GENDER AND THE POLITICS OF THE CURRICULUM

Sheila I. Riddell

London and New York

First published 1992
by Routledge
11 New Fetter Lane, London EC4P 4EE

Simultaneously published in the USA and Canada
by Routledge
a division of Routledge, Chapman and Hall, Inc.
29 West 35th Street, New York, NY 10001

Typeset in Palatino by Witwell Ltd, Southport
Printed and bound in Great Britain by
Biddles Ltd, Guildford and King's Lynn

British Library Cataloguing in Publication Data

Riddell, Sheila I., 1953–
Gender and the politics of the curriculum.
I. Title
376

ISBN 0-415-04813-3

Library of Congress Cataloging in Publication Data
ISBN 0-415-048133

CONTENTS

FIGURES AND TABLES

FIGURES

TABLES

FIGURES AND TABLES

FIGURES AND TABLES

FIGURE AND TABLES

FIGURES AND TABLES

ACKNOWLEDGEMENTS

I owe many thanks to the staff, pupils and parents of Millbridge and Greenhill schools, who so willingly answered my questions and shared aspects of their lives with me.

Whilst working on this research, colleagues at Bristol, Edinburgh and Stirling Universities have generously shared ideas with me. In particular, I would like to thank Sandra Acker who supervised my doctoral thesis on which this book is based.

Janet Siltanen and Judith Fewell provided useful comments on an earlier draft of this book and I am grateful to both of them.

This book is dedicated to Ken Sorbie and my daughters Annie and Bella, who sustained me with their love at times when I felt this book would never be completed.

INTRODUCTION

The central concern of this study is the role of the school, the family and pupils' construction of femininity and masculinity in the production of gender divisions within the curriculum. A recurring motif is that of change across a number of interconnecting dimensions, in particular the school curriculum, the culture of femininity and the labour market. Let us briefly consider the first of these. In all cultures the curriculum is informed by social values, in the sense that it is an expression of the knowledge and skills deemed necessary for young people to acquire in order to prepare them for their future adult role. It is also a dynamic entity, influenced not only by the changing requirements of the economy and shifting ideologies of political masters, but also by the consciousness of those who teach and learn. At the time of writing, the national curriculum is in the process of being introduced in England and Wales, with very different predictions being made concerning its potential to alter the nature of gender divisions within the curriculum. As well as addressing the question of the effects of this particular curriculum innovation, I also consider more fundamental issues concerning the relationship between curriculum choice and change and the formation of gender identity. This is envisaged as a two-way process whereby pupils' struggle to establish an appropriate gender identity influences their orientation towards particular areas of the curriculum, which in turn furthers the process of gender identity formation. It might well be argued that the interests of girls and women have generally been of only peripheral concern to curriculum planners. Here, I attempt to reverse this precedent by placing these interests at the centre of my analysis.

1

Although the central focus here is the school, it is important to recognise that the changing backcloth of the labour market inevitably affects pupils' educational experiences and their conception of what it means to be male or female. Schools in the 1990s continue to produce pupils who are ready, if not willing, to take their place in a labour market sharply stratified along lines of both gender and class (Martin and Roberts, 1984; Dex, 1985). But while this pattern of gender stratification persists, changes are occurring in the labour market, with women's participation increasing at a time when male unemployment has grown (Mitchell, 1986; Coyle and Skinner, 1988). In some ways, it would appear that women's and men's roles in the labour market are becoming more similar, with most households now having two wage earners rather than just one. However, the nature of the work carried out by women and men is still very different, with the majority of women undertaking part-time work in the service sector. Although areas such as financial services enjoyed a boom period in the 1980s, there has been only minimal progress towards the equal representation of women in managerial positions (Ashburner, 1988). The present recession coupled with the introduction of new technology has shown that women's jobs in the service sector are highly vulnerable. Women's average weekly earnings are still only two-thirds of the average male wage despite the passage of the equal opportunities legislation of the mid-1970s. So despite the fact that more women than ever before are working, their position in the labour market is still one of disadvantage, since they continue to be concentrated in areas of low pay and low status, deprived of access to positions of power. This book asks questions about the school processes which contribute to this outcome and whether there are any signs of change in girls' gender identity and the choices they are currently making about their future education and working lives.

The book focuses, then, on the interrelationship between the curriculum and the process of gender identity construction which ultimately leads to unequal roles for women and men in both the private and the public spheres. These relationships defy simple causal explanations, but are, none the less, worth exploring in order to understand the process of change taking place in schools at the present time, spreading out into the wider society.

The layout of the book is as follows. Part I sets the scene in terms of the research questions, the theoretical background and the physical setting. In Part II I discuss a number of aspects of school life which tend to reinforce traditional gender divisions. Among these, I critically examine the idea that pupils operate as free agents in selecting their subject options. Part III of the book shifts the focus away from institutions and individual teachers towards pupils and parents, and considers whether constructions of masculinity and femininity appear to challenge or reinforce the gender code of the schools.

I return to the theme of the curriculum and gender divisions in Part IV, considering the possible impact of present curricular developments. Some commentators have suggested that the national curriculum, introduced into schools in England and Wales under the terms of the Education Reform Act 1988, might have the effect of promoting more progressive versions of masculinity and femininity by preventing girls from prematurely rejecting areas of the curriculum perceived as masculine. I consider whether this is indeed likely to be the case, and also consider the counter argument that even if more girls do continue to study science for longer, other damaging aspects of sexism in school may persist untouched by curricular reforms.

Throughout the book, I attempt to convey a sense of the interaction between gender and class codes, although I am very aware of the complexity of these relationships and the inevitability of providing only a partial account. (A more detailed technical account of the research is available in my doctoral thesis, Riddell, 1988.) My central emphasis is on the experience of girls (working-class girls in particular) who are the major victims of the option choice system. Much work clearly remains to be done in unpicking the dynamic relationship between gender and class.

Part I

SETTING THE SCENE: THE PHYSICAL AND THEORETICAL CONTEXT OF THE STUDY

Social research does not occur in a vacuum, but is a complex result of the researcher's initial interests and motivation, theoretical and methodological preferences, and the various influences encountered whilst undertaking the fieldwork. Burgess (1984) reminds us that knowing something of the biographical as well as the technical background to the research is likely to be extremely helpful in allowing the reader to make a fair evaluation of its authenticity. In Chapter 1 of this book I set the scene of the study by providing the reader with some insight into the concerns which initially prompted my interest in gender and education, the research strategy I adopted and the research questions I developed. I also discuss the theoretical background which has informed the study from the initial shaping of the research design to the final analysis and interpretation of the findings. The methods which I selected were suggested both by my theoretical concerns and my political position as a feminist. Chapter 2 attempts to convey a sense of the physical location of the study, the classroom, staffrooms, towns and villages where pupils, parents and teachers generously offered me insight into their lives. I hope that from these early chapters, the central themes of the study will begin to emerge and take shape.

1

RESEARCHING GENDER AND CURRICULUM CHOICE

Theory, methods and research role

INTRODUCTION

The research which I describe here is rooted in my experience as a comprehensive school teacher in a county lying to the south west of England which I call Westshire. During the period of my life spent in the classroom between 1976 and 1983, I became fascinated by the significance of both the overt and the covert curriculum. Qualifications in particular subjects clearly acted as passports to various areas of work and higher education but also, at a more subtle level, the culture of each subject, even its physical location in the school, ranging from the factory atmosphere of the 'heavy craft' areas through to the cosy domesticity of the home economics room, carried powerful symbolic messages about the appropriate spheres of activity of women and men, working-class and middle-class pupils. In the early 1980s, when I began my research, at a national level the 'gender spectrum' in subject option choice was extremely marked. This is reflected, for example, in the secondary schools studied by Pratt, Bloomfield and Seale (1984), as well as in national statistics of gender differences in examination presentation (DES, 1981). Similar divisions were also apparent at Millbridge School in Westshire, a rural area in the south west of England where I was then working.

Along with many other comprehensives at the time, Millbridge offered a cafeteria style of option choice, where, within certain limits, pupils in their third year of secondary schooling were permitted to select their own curriculum from a wide range of subjects on offer. In view of this, the question of why so many pupils made such sex-stereotyped choices appeared even more puzzling, since at least at one level some degree of freedom of action appeared to be possible. Indeed, one of the remarkable things about the option choice system was the smoothness with which the whole process seemed to operate. Particular courses were offered by the school and were generally filled with approximately the right number and 'type' of pupils. But was the whole process as unproblematic as it might at first sight appear? An art teacher commented:

> Makes you a bit suspicious, doesn't it? The way that all the courses get filled up with the right number of pupils year after year.

It was the desire to investigate this puzzle which inspired me to embark on the research project which I describe here.

CENTRAL QUESTIONS OF THE RESEARCH

Many interesting studies in the sociology of education start out by asking questions which at first sight appear naive, but on reflection reveal important insights into how schools function within wider social systems. Willis (1977), for instance, begins by asking questions about why working-class kids get working-class jobs. More recently, Stanley (1989) introduces her study of comprehensive schooling by asking why fourth- and fifth-year pupils persevere with examinations designed to fail 40 per cent of them. In the same way, the starting point of my research was the following question: Why do girls, and working-class girls in particular, continue to opt for a school curriculum which is likely to lead to their long term disadvantage in the labour market?

Clearly, in order to make sense of gender differentiation in the curriculum, it is necessary to understand both the ways in which pupils are actively engaged in the process of gender identity construction and also the filtering system constructed by the school through which they pass. A range of questions were thrown up by these considerations. Did girls still generally subscribe to traditional notions of femininity and did this account for the traditional choices which they made? Further, was there any evidence of change in the gender identity they were constructing, reflecting the changing nature of the labour market and more radical notions of femininity deriving from the women's movement? Did the management of the option choice system by the school channel them, perhaps unwillingly, in conventional directions? In the context of the introduction of the national curriculum, was there likely to be a reduction in gender differentiation, or was the establishment of male and female curricula likely to continue in a relatively unimpeded manner? Further questions arose with regard to the influence of parents. Did these powerful figures subscribe to versions of masculinity and femininity which were broadly in line with those officially espoused by the school or were points of conflict likely to emerge and if so how were pupils to resolve these conflicting messages from home and school? With regard to individual teachers, could it be assumed that they would all support similar constructions of masculinity and femininity and how might divergent views be conveyed to pupils? By addressing these questions I hoped to discover whether pupils' apparent compliance in the process could be accepted at face value, or whether the underlying reasons for the outcome of option choice required a more subtle explanation.

THEORETICAL BACKGROUND

My concern, then, was to analyse the part played by option choice in the cultural reproduction of gender and class and I was aware of the attempts made by earlier analysts to come to terms with these issues. In the 1970s, the most frequently offered explanations were variations of social or cultural reproduction theory. Althusser (1971) and Bowles and Gintis (1976) offered explanations of the way in which the school prepared young people to fit neatly into predefined work roles necessary for the capitalist economy. Bourdieu (1977) and Bernstein (1975) approached the issue of reproduction from a slightly different angle, examining how dominant class values, essential to the perpetuation of capitalist society, were reproduced. Researchers such as Willis (1977) rejected the view that the school merely rubber-stamps children in preparation for a particular position in the social formation. Arguing that pupils' culture represents a vital ingredient in the process of social reproduction, Willis claimed that the lads featuring in his study were far from passive observers of their own destiny. Clearly, there were strong pressures on them to follow their fathers' footsteps into hard manual labour, but at the same time it was essential to their sense of pride to feel that they were actively choosing this role for themselves and their adamant rejection of all things educational signified anything but passive compliance. Combining feminist understandings with the type of neo-marxist analysis employed by Willis, Anyon (1983) discusses how the culture of femininity is used by girls in school to both accommodate and resist aspects of the dominant ideology. According to Arnot and Whitty (1982), by stressing the transformative potential of the school, she avoids some of the deterministic pitfalls of neo-marxist analysis. Movement away from traditional marxist accounts of social reproduction theory is also evident in the work of Connell *et al.* (1982) who provide a rich sense of the scope for individual action which exists within structural constraints.

More recently, commentators such as Weis (1990) have gone even further in questioning the validity of social reproduction theory. She points out that the deindustrialisation of western societies has made it no longer useful for schools to produce boys ready to slot into traditional male working-class jobs of the hard manual variety and girls anticipating a lifetime of domesticity. Given the rapidly changing nature of the labour market, reproduction theory fails to describe adequately the processes at work in school or the wider society. Citing Touraine (1981), she suggests that it is no longer appropriate to envisage the struggle between labour and capital as the fundamental pivot of society. Rather, society is best understood as 'a dynamic set of social movements – as the material accomplishment of conflicting groups struggling for control of the field of historical cultural action' (p. 10). Although noting that it is not yet clear how the traditional working class is to define itself in relation to the rapid process of de-industrialisation currently occurring in the USA, Weis suggests that outcomes may be far less firmly circumscribed than they were in the past. In view of these changes, the task should now be to understand the nature and form of the production of self engaged in by young people in school. To investigate the 'new ideology' of the white working class she utilises a social action perspective.

The theoretical approach which I adopt here incorporates aspects of both social reproduction and social action perspectives. I explore the nature of actors' rational decisions and the context within which these are made, whilst acknowledging the very powerful constraints on their actions. Pupils' culture is clearly very important in the formation of group and individual identities and the way in which social movements impinge on the process of identity formation is also important. However, whilst acknowledging that individual identities and outcomes are not entirely predetermined, I feel that a danger of the social action perspective is that it loses sight of the structural constraints on action. For example, an important aspect of girls' access to a wider range of jobs is a recognition that there is nothing inherent preventing them from working as a mechanic or an electrician or an engineer. But unless jobs are available in these areas, their aspirations cannot be fulfilled. It is also the case that some interactionist work underplays the importance of class, Although there are undeniably major changes currently taking place in the nature and identity of the working class linked to the erosion of the manufacturing base in Britain and many other western societies, this does not imply that class has lost all its power as an explanatory tool. In the following chapters I attempt to shed light on actors' own accounts of their decisions, but also show how these diverge significantly along lines of gender and class.

At this point it is worth commenting briefly on the definition of gender and class which I have used. Oakley (1972) clarified the distinction between sex and gender, pointing out that whereas sex refers to biological differences between males and females, gender is a socially constructed category which may vary in different cultures and different historical periods. Recently, some commentators have suggested that women's experience is now so diverse as to call into question whether the category 'woman' continues to be meaningful (Delmar, 1986). My aim in this book is to explore both the common ground and the differences which characterise the experiences of girls and women.

Since class is one of the major factors differentiating female experience, I have attempted to incorporate it into my analysis where appropriate. The definition I have used is broadly in line with the Registrar General's classification of occupation, but takes mother's as well as father's occupation into account. Thus if one parent reported a middle-class occupation, then the family was defined as middle class. Further details are reported in the Appendix. This clearly differs from the view of class taken by Connell *et al* (1982). Although acknowledging that some state schools may contain a significant proportion of children from business or professional backgrounds, Connell *et al*. defined all the state schools in their study as working class because this was their predominant character. The private schools, on the other hand, were described as ruling class. Within the context of the Westshire schools where I was conducting my research, this classification would have been too simplistic, and I decided that it was appropriate to distinguish between working-class and middle-class families, although I do recognise that the Registrar General's classification is something of a rough instrument. However, the importance of including some measure of class is underlined by Mitchell (1986). She comments that when she started her research in education in 1962, it was impossible to find data on gender; everything was broken down by class. Today, she says, precisely the reverse is the case. In so successfully focusing attention on the importance of gender, the women's movement may have been complicit in official attempts to conceal the importance of social class. Although the major focus of this study is on gender and subject choice, I have attempted to indicate the salience of social class in influencing the different educational outcomes of girls and boys from different social backgrounds. In many parts of the country the links between race and gender also demand exploration, but in the Westshire schools, the minority ethnic population was almost non-existent, and so this does not feature as a major focus of analysis.

PREVIOUS WORK ON GENDER AND CHOICE IN SCHOOLS

Turning from the macro- to the micro-theoretical background, this section explores the literature on schools and subject choice. My initial survey of the literature suggested that some studies of subject choice offered important insights into the way in which comprehensive schools continued to operate a system of social as well as educational selection, but concentrated on class rather than gender divisions (Woods, 1976; Ball, 1981). Other studies, such as Pratt *et al*. (1984); focused on the operation of option choice systems within schools and failed to look in depth at wider aspects of social reproduction in the classroom and the family.

Some feminist researchers, on the other hand, had come much closer to conceptualising curriculum choice in ways which took acount of both the social constraints on action and the propensity of individuals to take meaningful actions within these boundaries. Gaskell (1985), for instance, in her study of Canadian teenagers and 'tracking', pointed out that an analysis of the mechanisms by which young people negotiate their future paths within the school curriculum brings us to the heart of a major problem in social theory. It is not simply a matter of deciding whether pupils choose or are coerced in different situations, but rather of understanding the relation-ship between individual agency and social structure. Pointing to the work of Giddens (1979), Gaskell reminds us that even subordinate groups have some social power and are more than helpless pawns in a pre-decided game. Applying these under-standings to the context of gender differentiation and option choice, I decided that my objective should be to understand the external forces which were shaping girls' lives, also their perception of these constraints and the rational and creative strategies with which they responded.

Within the field of gender and education, it would appear that whilst earlier studies tended to reflect rather rigid notions of the overwhelming power of sex-role socialisation, implicitly adopting a deficit model to describe the behaviour of pupils and parents, more recent studies paid greater attention to the role of teachers, the school and education policies in general (Acker, 1987). Kelly (1987) describes the shift in the analysis of girls' relative absence from science classes, arguing that recent work:

> locates the fault at least partly within science, within schools or within society at large. These institutions must change to accommodate girls. Science is not an immutable 'thing', it is a socially constructed process which is pro-duced in schools and laboratories in accordance with societal norms.
>
> (Kelly, 1987 p. 1)

Reports of the GIST study (Whyte, 1986) and Kelly (1985) provide some fascinating insights into the potential of teachers to sabotage or facilitate equal opportunities initiatives, and I felt that there was a need for further exploration of teachers' attitudes to gender equality policies.

In deciding that subject option choice should be the starting point for my investigation of gender identity construction, it also struck me that I would learn very little from sticking too narrowly to an analysis of what happened at a discrete point in time when pupils filled out their option choice forms, in many cases making decisions which would significantly alter the shape of their future working lives. The choices that pupils made here seemed to me to be a reflection of an ongoing process of identity construction involving the young person themselves and their interaction with parents, friends and school. Since pupils' subject choices appeared to diverge along axes of gender and class (statistics from the two schools where I carried out research confirmed this – see Chapter 3), I was interested in exploring the extent to which their personal curriculum represented a statement of their gender and class identity. Arnot's (MacDonald, 1980; Arnot, 1982) notion of gender code was useful here in helping me to refine this idea. She uses the term 'gender code' to refer to the messages concerning appropriate models of masculinity or femininity which pupils both receive and transmit. The notion of gender code thus encompasses the cluster of behaviours, attitudes, and emotional responses judged appropriate for one sex or the other. Codes 'have varying degrees of boundary strength and insulation between categories of masculinity and femininity' (Arnot, 1982). Pupils are actively involved in interpreting the gender code of the school and also bring with them into the classroom competing gender codes derived from their own and their parents' culture.

At this point it is also worth drawing attention to my use of the term ideology during the course of the book. Ideology refers to the network of beliefs, values and assumptions which individuals draw on in making sense of the world. My use of the term reflects the view that an ideology tends to conceal the interests of particular power groups in maintaining a set of beliefs. For example, an ideology of femininity may well encompass the belief that male dominance over women is natural rather than socially constructed (Deem, 1981).

15

RESEARCH METHODS

Clearly, the task of examining the relationship between gender codes and subject choice was not something which could be dealt with satisfactorily by a speedily administered questionnaire, but demanded a longer term and more detailed approach. In the early stages of planning the research, I decided that it would be necessary to carry out parallel studies in two schools. Since I had worked in one of the schools where I was to conduct the research, I was interested in drawing comparisons with another school where I was an unknown entity. Further, the literature on school effectiveness (Reynolds, 1982; Rutter *et al.* 1979; Mortimore *et al.* 1988 has alerted us to the importance of the ethos of individual schools in affecting educational outcomes. I was interested in observing whether either school was markedly more successful in fostering an attitude conducive to gender equality.

The ethos of Millbridge Upper School was generally liberal and democratic, characterised by an absence of uniform for pupils and a relaxed dress code for staff. The headmaster had an unobtrusive presence, even handing over the chairing of staff meetings to other teachers. Although great emphasis was placed on meeting the needs of individual pupils, many local parents felt that stronger discipline was required. Greenhill Upper School, twice the size of Millbridge, was much more formal and bureaucratic in style. Among staff, lines of management were clearly defined and strict dress codes were observed by both teachers and pupils. Greenhill was also much more conscious of its public image, ensuring that all school activities were well publicised in the local press. In the local community it was generally regarded as a 'good school'.

What I actually found was that although there were differences between the schools in many respects, the ethos in both institutions with regard to the predominant gender code was remarkably similar. Neither considered gender equality as a high priority, and there were no formal policies in either school or in the local authority with regard to equal opportunities. For this reason, it was not necessary to treat the schools as entirely separate cases in the writing up of the research.

In order to gain some degree of insight into how pupils' curricular paths were charted through the gradual establish-

16

ment of their gender identities, I felt it would be necessary to spend considerable time observing their daily interaction with their peers and teachers in the classroom, over a period of months rather than weeks. In this way, I hoped to be able to shed light on the central problem of why girls and boys apparently consented to a process which would be to the long-term detriment of many, and was likely to be particularly damaging to working-class girls. I also decided it would be necessary to carry out detailed in-depth interviews with pupils, parents and teachers in the two schools so that my observations could be cross-checked against the pupils' own account of events. However, as well as generating data which would be sensitive to participants' lived experiences, I also required some means of exploring the connections between key variables. I therefore took the decision to administer questionnaires to parents and pupils. School documents and records provided a further source of data. Ultimately, I hoped to use the various types of data in a complementary way to provide a rounded view of the social world. (See Sieber (1973) and Denzin (1970) for arguments in favour of using a range of research methods.)

In deciding on the research methods I would use, I was also influenced by debates on feminist methodology (Duelli Klein, 1983; Scott, 1985; Stanley and Wise, 1983). Broadly speaking, I attempted to adhere to the principle of reflexivity, making explicit my political and theoretical position and their impact on the process of data collection. I believe that this is necessary to allow the reader to judge the validity of the research account. A further hallmark of feminist research is its insistence on respect for the subjects of the research and an overall concern for the democratisation of the research relationship, with the subjects having the opportunity to at least comment on the researcher's interpretation of the data. Mies (1983), in her work with battered women in West Germany, developed a model of feminist action research, where the women who were the subjects of the research were involved in analysing the findings and writing the final report. Although it was not possible for me to engage in such closely collaborative work with the pupils, parents and teachers with whom I worked, it was part of the research contract that I should feed the findings back to the schools, which I did. I also discussed the data with interested teachers and pupils and incorporated their ideas as much as possible into the analysis. I have written in greater detail elsewhere about the ethics of feminist educational research (Riddell, 1989).

THE RESEARCH ROLE ADOPTED IN THE TWO SCHOOLS

Since the purpose of carrying out research in two schools was to investigate whether similar findings were produced, it is extremely important to be clear about the role which I adopted and how this influenced the nature of the data which emerged. The obvious advantage of starting the research at Millbridge, where I had previously taught, was that I brought with me a knowledge of the layout, timetable and key personalities, thus it was possible to avoid the frustration, experienced by many researchers, of spending a whole lesson in a corridor having failed to locate a particular class. Another advantage of familiarity was being able to sit unobtrusively in a staffroom and overhear conversations. Similarly, because my interests and concerns were already known, I did not have to be quite socircumspect in discussing my interest in gender as well as option choice. At first, I thought that teachers might be reluctant to share their honest opinions with me if they felt that I might not approve. However, this was not the case, as I think the interview data in Chapter 4 make clear. Relationships with pupils at Millbridge proved more problematic, since most remembered me as a teacher. They were still inclined to address me rather suspiciously as 'Miss' and I quickly realised that attempts to chat with them in social areas at lunch time would not be welcomed. Rather than foisting myself upon them, I decided to concentrate on observation in the classroom and the staffroom.

At Greenhill, my original strategy was to present myself in as neutral a way as possible to the staff, emphasising the subject choice rather than the gender aspect of the study, to try to ensure that they were not simply responding to me as a feminist. Generally, relationships with this group of teachers were less comfortable than with my former colleagues at Millbridge. First, I had the tricky task of dealing with the various gatekeepers, one of whom I felt was constantly shadowing me, asking for an account of what I had discovered that day. It was more difficult for me to gain access to various records and documents, which would have been automatically available to me at Millbridge. Further, I felt that I was always regarded as a potential critic, partly due to the fact that the period of fieldwork at Greenhill coincided with the teachers' industrial action, which caused major divisions to emerge in the staffroom. Some teachers clearly resented the fact that I was apparently able to walk round the school observing and gossiping with pupils without any of the responsibility of teaching. One maths teacher, Mr Johnson, expressed his views thus:

> There's never any feedback from research. People make their careers out of it, but things just carry on in school anyway. Like the HMI Report we've just had. They tell you what's wrong, but not what you can do about it.

Relationships with at least some of the teachers at Greenhill improved considerably once I relaxed enough to talk more about the main purpose of my research. A general discussion in the staffroom over dress codes for women teachers opened up a wider discussion about gender issues in the school. The conversation stemmed from the fact that I was wearing trousers, and one of the women remarked that these were not considered an acceptable form of female dress, since they signalled a generally rebellious attitude. By taking part in this discussion I could no longer pretend to be detached and impartial but the incident was ultimately beneficial because it was after this that a number of women teachers talked to me openly about their experiences.

By way of contrast, relationships with pupils at Greenhill were on a more equal footing than they had been at Millbridge. After I had spent several weeks following a group of pupils to their lessons, I realised that I had been accepted as a sympathetic visitor who was certainly not a teacher when I heard one girl telling her friend not to swear, to which she replied:

> It's all right, we can say what we like to her. She's not a teacher.

However, my easy relationship with the pupils in itself constituted something of a threat to some of the teachers. Pupils would sometimes remark deliberately loudly to me:

This is the lesson which I hate most in the week. I always forget my book.

Or they would offer as an excuse when told to be quiet:

We can't work quietly because the lady keeps on asking us questions.

In general, I found that relationships with girls and women were more open than with boys and men, which confirms what other feminist researchers have reported about their experience of interviewing women (Oakley, 1981; Finch, 1984). However, I had to be careful not to exploit their willingness to talk by asking for more information than they might wish to divulge. At both schools I respected the right of the girls to decide how much insight they wished to give me into their lives. When they wished for privacy, they generally politely broke off the conversation. McRobbie and Garber comment that:

girl culture is so well insulated as to effectively exclude not only other undesirable girls – but also boys, adults, teachers and researchers.
(McRobbie and Garber, 1976, p. 222)

I did not feel as totally excluded as this statement implies, but was very conscious of the limits which the girls placed on my participation in their culture.

Two main points emerge from this reflection on my research role in the two schools. The first is that my status as teacher or non-teacher made a significant difference to my interaction with teachers and pupils in the two schools, allowing me to be closer to the teachers and more distant from the pupils at Millbridge and vice versa at Greenhill, and I think this emerges from the data which I present in the following chapters. The second point is that I found it impossible to maintain a neutral identity whilst undertaking the research. At Millbridge this was impossible from the start, but at Greenhill cultivating an appearance of neutrality formed part of my early strategy. In practice, this simply caused me anxiety, and it was not until I became more open myself that my relationship with teachers here improved. Clearly there are problems in having a theoretical position and a clear identity in a research environment, but it is difficult for me to conceive of gathering meaningful data whilst cultivating a bland and unresponsive persona. Maybe those who claim that neutrality is the ideal are either dishonest or naive.

CONCLUSION

This study draws on the tradition of social reproduction theory, since the central focus is the way in which option choice is used by the school to bring about traditional gender divisions in the curriculum. The work is also informed by the concerns of social interactionists, who see people's understandings of social situations as crucial in determining particular outcomes. My concern was not simply to describe the pattern of subject choice, but to explore the meaning attached to particular courses of action by pupils, parents and teachers. The desire to understand subjective meanings and at the same time to make comparisons beween groups informed my decision to collect both quantitative and qualitative data. Further, my identity as a former teacher and a feminist undoubtedly influenced the nature of the data I collected, in ways which I try to make explicit in the following chapters.

2

THE PHYSICAL LOCATION OF THE STUDY

INTRODUCTION

As I have already commented, the 1980s has been a decade of rapid change in the structure of the national economy, with manufacturing industry suffering a marked decline and with sporadic growth in the service sector. At the same time, there have been marked changes in women's and men's economic roles as women have increasingly moved into the public sphere of employment, although generally on worse terms than their male counterparts. The structure of the labour market in Westshire in the mid-1980s was clearly influenced by this national pattern, although the area had not been subjected to the rapid process of deindustrialisation common in the north. This chapter provides an overview of the local economy and its impact on social relations, in turn strongly influencing the nature of schooling. I argue that these shifting economic and social relations are important factors in understanding the complex mixture of conservatism and desire for change which characterise Westshire girls' attitudes to education and work and their sense of identity more generally.

WESTSHIRE – AN OVERVIEW OF THE AREA

Westshire is set in the south west of England and is a predominantly rural area with a few small towns and many villages. The only large centre of population is on the eastern margin, where there is a conurbation, Upton and Mere, with a population of 325,000. This is one of the most rapidly expanding urban areas in the country, its growth stimulated by the

22

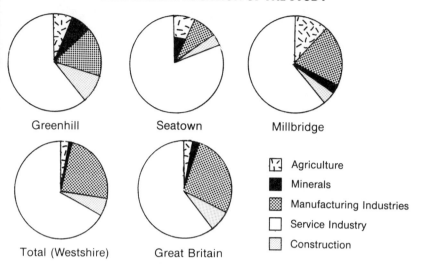

Greenhill   Seatown   Millbridge

Total (Westshire)   Great Britain

- Agriculture
- Minerals
- Manufacturing Industries
- Service Industry
- Construction

Source: Department of Environment, September Census, 1981

Figure 2.1 Employment structure by main sectors, 1981

mushrooming of financial and service industries during the 1980s. Because of its beautiful countryside and coastline, the county is also popular as a retirement area and the age profile of the population is skewed towards the elderly. In Westshire as a whole, the vast majority of people (67.5 per cent) work in the service sector. This is even higher than for Great Britain as a whole, where 58.7 per cent of people work in this sector (see Figure 2.1 and Table 2.1). In the two local employment areas where the research was carried out, Millbridge (population 4,500) and Greenhill (population 8,000), the percentage of employees in the service sector was 57.5 per cent and 58.5 per cent respectively. A much smaller proportion of the population worked in agriculture, 14.2 per cent of the Millbridge population and 8.4 per cent of the Greenhill population. This compares with a national average of 1.7 per cent. From this, it can be seen that although farming employs considerably more people than the national average, it is still a relatively small employer, and the number of people working in this sector has continued to fall over the last decade. The other major areas of employment are construction, minerals and light manufacturing.

National patterns of sex segregation in the labour market also pertain in Westshire, and at this point it is perhaps useful

Table 2.1 Employment structure by main sectors, 1976 and 1981 (percentages)

Local office	1976 % of all employees					1981 % of all employees				
	Agriculture	Minerals	Manufacturing	Construction	Service Industry	Agriculture	Minerals	Manufacturing	Construction	Service industry
Millbridge	14.2	—	21.7	6.6	57.5	11.2	—	21.0	4.0	63.7
Seatown	7.3*		3.6	3.7	85.4	5.4*		7.7	3.1	83.5
Greenhill	8.4	5.2	18.7	9.2	58.5	7.0	5.4	18.4	8.1	61.1
	3.2	0.3	23.8	5.2	67.5	2.7	0.3	23.0	4.8	69.1
Total	1.7	1.6	32.2	5.8	58.7	1.7	1.6	28.2	5.3	63.1

Source: 'Abstract of statistics for Westshire 1986', Westshire County Council (based on Department of Employment statistics)
Notes: *These figures are given for the combined categories of agriculture and minerals to avoid indicating the level of employment in individual enterprises

decades, there has been a continuous growth in women's participation in waged work. Thus by 1986, women represented 44.5 per cent of the labour force, but many were in part-time rather than full-time jobs. During the recession of 1979–1986, women's representation in the labour market increased by 3 per cent, whilst male economic activity rates decreased from 58.6 per cent to 55.5 per cent. However, although women are now more active in the labour market, many commentators argue that their conditions of work and pay are still less favourable. Coyle comments that:

> It is the combination of occupational segregation and part-time working which has enabled women's pay to be determined at levels significantly lower than men's.
>
> (Coyle, 1988, p. 6)

Weis, discussing the situation of women in Freeway, a deindustrialising steel town in the north west of the USA, also comments on the pattern whereby women increasingly participate in the labour market, but do not enjoy equally favourable working conditions:

> Thus, the move towards post-industrial society has meant that a higher proportion of females is employed in the labor force relative to earlier years, but that females increasingly earn relatively lower wages than males.
>
> (Weis, 1990, p. 25)

A further distinctive feature of Westshire, which may well have an impact on the nature of social relations, is the presence of the military. In the North Westshire district, where the town of Millbridge is situated, 4.3 per cent of the population was employed in the armed forces, and in the Welbourne district where Greenhill is situated, the military employed 8 per cent of the population. This compares with 0.9 per cent for England and Wales as a whole. Unemployment in the Millbridge area and in the Greenhill and Seatown areas is shown in Table 2.2. At 10.4 per cent for Millbridge and 8.3 per cent for Greenhill and Seatown in August 1986, unemployment was slightly lower than the national average. In Millbridge, more women were unemployed than men, and in Greenhill and Seatown the reverse was true. This is probably due to the fact that the service sector is a bigger employer in the Greenhill area, and many women are employed in temporary jobs connected with the tourist industry. It should also be remembered that the actual number of women seeking employment is probably substantially higher than this, since married women whose husbands are working often do not register as unemployed.

The pattern of employment in Westshire, then, is very different from those areas in Britain and elsewhere which have experienced a rapid process of deindustrialisation. The decline in agricultural employment has been offset by growth in service industries, particularly those associated with tourism and light industry. Young people who are not able to find work in the small towns travel to the nearby conurbation of Upton and Mere.

There is considerable debate over whether such a thing as a rural school exists and how it might be defined. Comber *et al.* (1981), a team of researchers based at Aston University exploring the effect of primary school closures on local communities, defined rural schools as those 'located in areas of scattered developments as well as free-standing hamlets, villages and small towns with a population of 10,000 or less.' Within this definition, Millbridge and Greenhill schools could certainly be defined as rural, but this blanket term tends to conceal the complexity and diversity of the local communities. Within Westshire, there are vast differences in experiences and values between, for instance, the small minority who work in agriculture and the far larger number who live on new estates in villages or small towns and commute to work in the nearby conurbation. In the accounts which I report in the following chapters, I hope that a sense of the diversity of pupils and parents emerges, rather than a false sense of a uniform rural character. This is in line with general developments in rural sociology. Work in the community studies tradition (Cohen, 1982: Lynd and Lynd, 1964) stressed the social solidarity of rural communities. Later research (Newby, 1977, 1980 and Newby *et al.* 1978) emphasised the economic conflict which underlay farmworkers' deference and farmers' paternalism. The idea that gender and class conflict are peculiar to urban areas, a view propounded by the community studies school, would receive little support today.

Table 2.2 Unemployment rates, September 1985 to August 1986 (percentages)

Travel to work area	1985 Sept	1985 Oct	Nov	Dec	Jan	Feb	Mar	1986 Apr	May	June[2]	July	Aug
Males												
Millbridge	10.4	10.5	11.0	10.7	11.5	11.4	10.9	10.4	10.1	10.2	10.3	10.1
Greenhill and Seatown	9.2	9.6	10.6	11.1	11.3	11.0	10.5	10.2	9.6	8.3	8.5	8.6
Westshire	13.0	13.2	13.5	13.8	14.6	14.4	14.0	13.6	13.2	12.3	12.4	12.2
South West	13.5	13.5	13.6	13.8	14.5	14.3	14.0	13.8	13.4	10.6	10.6	10.6
Great Britain	16.0	15.7	15.7	15.9	16.5	16.4	16.2	16.1	15.8	13.3	13.3	13.3
Females												
Millbridge	11.6	10.6	10.3	10.3	10.8	11.8	10.1	10.6	10.3	10.1	10.5	10.9
Greenhill and Seatown	9.8	10.4	10.8	11.0	11.3	11.9	10.8	9.4	8.7	7.8	7.9	7.9
Westshire	9.1	9.2	9.4	9.5	9.9	9.9	9.4	9.2	8.9	8.3	8.6	8.6
South West	10.3	10.2	10.3	10.3	10.8	10.7	10.3	10.1	9.9	8.6	8.9	9.1
Great Britain	10.4	10.1	10.0	9.9	10.3	10.2	9.9	10.0	9.9	9.0	9.3	9.4
Persons												
Millbridge	10.9	10.5	10.7	10.5	11.2	11.2	10.6	10.5	10.2	10.1	10.4	10.4
Greenhill and Seatown	9.4	9.9	10.7	11.0	11.3	11.4	10.6	9.9	9.2	8.1	8.3	8.3
Westshire	11.3	11.4	11.7	11.9	12.5	12.4	12.0	11.6	11.3	10.5	10.7	10.6
South West	12.1	12.1	12.2	12.3	12.9	12.8	12.4	12.2	11.9	9.7	9.9	10.0
Great Britain	13.6	13.4	13.3	13.4	13.9	13.8	13.6	13.6	13.3	11.5	11.7	11.7

Source: 'Abstract of statistics for Westshire, 1986', Westshire County Council (based on Department of Employment statistics)
Notes: (1) The basis of compilation of this data changed at March 1986; the effect was to lower rates, (2) The basis of compilation of this data for the South West and Great Britain changed again in June 1986, the effect was again to lower rates.

THE SCHOOLS AND THE TOWNS

In the mid-1980s, the comprehensive upper school at Millbridge catering for pupils aged from 13 to 19 had 770 pupils on roll. Constructed in the 1960s on the site of the former grammar school, its buildings are state-school utilitarian style. The metal window frames are draughty and ill-fitting, and many of the pre-fabricated panels are leaky. A visitor has to walk to the back of the school to find the main entrance, past maths rooms where the curtains hang in shreds but have not been replaced because some work is about to be done to replace the front facade of the school building. When the visitors' lobby is reached, very little of the pupils' work is on display, and the general atmosphere is rather unwelcoming. Dingy as the school may be, the view from the playing fields is very striking. Broad meadows in which horses graze sweep down towards the river which runs through the town, and on the opposite bank a deciduous wood surrounds the Victorian Gothic buildings of a well-known and expensive public school. The contrast between the two schools is immediately obvious. Social divisions are also apparent in the town centre, where some shops obviously cater for the needs of the upper middle class. There are, for example, two old-fashioned shops selling horse tack and shooting and fishing equipment, an expensive boutique, a wholefood shop and a delicatessen. These rub shoulders with the supermarket and a shop selling 'seconds' clothing. Apart from the Georgian buildings in the centre, much of the housing in Millbridge consists of small Victorian terraces. There is also a large modern housing estate begun in the 1960s which is still expanding. The Victorian brewery producing the local beer dominates the eastern side of the town and is still one of the largest employers of unskilled labour.

Greenhill Upper school is generally smarter than Millbridge. Opened in 1974, it was one of Westshire's show-piece purpose-built comprehensives, amalgamating the grammar and secondary modern schools of Greenhill and Seatown, a small seaside resort (population 8,500), 10 miles from Greenhill. In the mid-1980s, approximately 1,400 pupils were enrolled. Like Millbridge, it has a well-equipped sports centre and houses the local youth club. The school faces a busy roundabout, and there are open fields beyond. The visitors' entrance to the school is extremely well maintained, with glass cases full of trophies and pupils' art and pottery work on display. On the first floor, the offices of the headmaster and deputy heads lead off a corridor which is not open to pupils and an official visitor to the school in this part of the building would think that there were no pupils present at all. This contrasts with the bustle and crush of other parts of the school, particularly the technology department and the youth centre, which are set well back from the main entrance.

The buildings in the centre of Greenhill, like Millbridge, are Georgian or Victorian, and there are many low-roofed cottages. The shops have a slightly unused feel and it is clear that for many inhabitants the main shopping centre is in Upton or Mere (the large conurbation referred to earlier). The proximity of the larger urban centre, only 10 minutes away by train, means that Greenhill is much less of a self-contained community than Millbridge, and it appears to be in the process of transformation into a dormitory town. Again, like Millbridge, a large estate containing some council but mainly private housing has been expanding since the 1960s. The other small town which feeds the school, Seatown (population 8,500), is much more of a holiday and retirement centre than an agricultural market town. It has a traditional seaside front, with mainly Victorian hotels, and there is little even in the way of light industry. The Isle of Welbourne, lying between Greenhill and Seatown, with its heathland and hills, is a conservation area, and attracts many visitors in the summer. Because of its position on the tip of the Welbourne peninsula, a ferry service connects it with Mere, and this used to be a main line of communication. Now, it is much quicker to travel between Mere and Seatown by road.

The villages surrounding Millbridge and Greenhill, from which pupils travel to the schools, have grey stone or brick cottages, sometimes with thatched roofs. Some of these are damp and crumbling, lived in by old people who have spent all their lives there. Many of these buildings have now been done up and are well beyond the means of the locals. There is a marked contrast between the cottages, with their Laura Ashley and Habitat style decoration, and the council houses – often on small estates at the edge of villages. Favoured building materials here are concrete and pebble-dash, and financial rather than aesthetic considerations have clearly been in the forefront of the planner's mind. Here, rural poverty is very much in evidence. Government policy on the sale of council houses has also affected the nature of Westshire village life. The most desirable houses quickly moved into the private market, making the prospect for young people of achieving a home in the locality even more remote.

During the course of the interviews which I carried out with Millbridge and Greenhill parents, many working-class women living outside the towns talked about the restrictions which were placed on their lives through isolation and lack of work opportunities. Mrs Rennick, who lived outside Greenhill, felt that her life was lonely and boring:

> When you're stuck down here it's lonely – you don't see anyone all day. There's a woman who's moved in next door and they're so busy at the moment getting the house up together, but I say give her a year and she'll be looking for something else. Just being here and having to make your husband's tea – it's dead boring.

Mrs Turner lived in a small village to the north of Millbridge, overlooked by a huge hill. The setting was very beautiful but as far as Mrs Turner was concerned, the advantages were definitely outweighed by the disadvantages:

> These days unless you've got your own transport and a good wage, about £20 a week spare money, there's no advantage at all to being in the country apart from country air. I mean that – it's the only advantage, because public transport is very scarce, so if you haven't got your own transport you're stuck.

Often she did not even bother going into Millbridge for shopping because when she had priced it she had found that Keymarket was only fifty pence cheaper for a weekly shop, so it was not worth lugging the stuff back on the bus.

Mrs Little, who also lived on a rural council housing estate to the north of Greenhill, emphasised how important it was to have independent transport and how being able to drive had made a difference to her life:

> You need a car. I wasn't happy until I could drive, that's what, six years ago. You can feel quite cut off out here . . .

So if I didn't have a car, no, I wouldn't be happy. You get one bus a week, that's Thursday and it goes into Greenhill about quarter to ten and it comes back about half eleven. And you're expected to do the whole week's shopping. There's no shops here, you've got to do everything, bank and that. I mean when I first moved out here we used to live in a caravan up the road, there used to be buses every day, and then of course people drove and it sort of dwindled. You do really need a car.

The question of transport was clearly crucial, not simply to get out to see people, but also to have access to employment. Mrs Little was about to take up a job as a dinner lady at Greenhill School, but without her own transport this would have been impossible. It is interesting to note that in the 1981 census, 25 per cent of households in Westshire did not own a car.

Girls who lived outside the towns talked of the restrictions in their lives in similar terms. This was partly due to the lack of basic amenities like youth centres and other meeting places. Catherine Thomas, whose father was a dairyman at the time of the interview, lived in a remote cottage 7 miles from the nearest hamlet and described her life thus:

You just sit there and watch TV and get square eyes or else read. I'm a bookaholic. You can't go out . . . You don't have any self will to do anything . . . I've just sat at home and vegetated.

Middle class girls like Bernardette Coles, daughter of a country doctor, also complained of boredom and loneliness:

There's only one other girl in the village who's my age and she goes to a private boarding school and I don't get on very well with her anyway. So apart from my two little brothers, I'm all by myself and it gets really boring during the long winter evenings.

As the comments of Westshire women and girls illustrate, life was far from the rural idyll which some earlier commentators might have led us to believe. Rather, as Newby and his colleagues (1977, 1978, 1980) have pointed out, social and economic conflicts are as real here as anywhere else. And as Chamberlain (1983) and Whitehead (1976) make clear, patriarchy is certainly not a phenomenon restricted to urban areas. Indeed, Rosenfeld *et al.* (1985), writing in the US context, argue that even though very few people are now directly employed in farming, the remnants of traditional rural patriarchal relations may continue to affect a wider population.

CONCLUSION

Overall, Westshire is an area which may still be described as rural, but with the recognition that this term certainly does not denote a closed and cohesive community with a shared value system. Traditional rural working-class and middle-class people now live alongside newcomers who are either elderly retired people or middle-class people working in the service sector, often travelling into Upton or Mere to work. The traditional rural working-class is increasingly having to seek work in service, construction or light manufacturing industries and the escalation of house prices and shortage of council housing means that it is difficult for young working-class people to find accommodation in the area. Interview data suggest that women and girls living outside the towns suffered from boredom and isolation, and the existence of rural poverty amidst the affluence was very evident. The distance from London has meant that Westshire has not become a general commuter area to the same extent as parts of Berkshire and Hertfordshire; however, the general population drift to the south of England has certainly changed its population and local economy. The conservatism which pervades the area is informed both by Thatcherite entrepreneurial values as well as old fashioned beliefs in paternalism and deference. Westshire is clearly undergoing major changes, and those who move into the area expecting to find a timeless haven from the modern world would be sorely disappointed.

Part II

SCHOOL ORGANISATION AND THE CONSTRUCTION OF THE GENDERED CURRICULUM

This section deals with the part played by aspects of school organisation and by teachers in the reconstitution of gender divisions within the curriculum. I begin by analysing the way in which girls' and boys' curricular paths diverge after passing through the option choice system. A number of writers have considered the way in which the entire fabric of school life is pervaded by particular messages concerning appropriate forms of masculinity and femininity. Kessler *et al.* (1985) have termed this the school's gender regime and have discussed the central part played by the school in arbitrating between different forms of masculinity and femininity. Arnot (1982), as noted earlier, uses the term gender code to refer to the particular form of masculinity and femininity legitimated by the school. I examine the nature of the gender code transmitted to pupils through the presentation of particular subjects and the treatment meted out to pupils and parents during the course of subject choice. I also seek to analyse the educational ideologies rooted in the option choice system, in particular that of free choice which, I argue, acts as a legitimating device for differing educational outcomes. This is particularly significant for working-class girls, whose future life chances are particularly limited by their choice of subjects. I also consider the view of equal opportunities which is reflected to pupils and their parents through official documents and public statements.

Weiner (1986) suggests that two distinctly different perspectives on gender and equal opportunities may be discerned in school practice. The equal opportunities perspective 'identifies inequality as a pedagogical problem of equal importance to girls and boys' whilst the anti-sexist perspective 'regards the under-representation and under-achievement of girls in schools as part of a far broader pattern of female subordination'. As the following analysis will demonstrate, to the extent that any clear perspective could be discerned, it was certainly of the more limited equal-opportunities variety, based firmly on a notion of female deficiency.

Commentators in Britain and Australia have disagreed on the impact of feminist ideas in schools. Acker (1987) takes the pessimistic view that: 'In a situation where neither government dictates nor conventional teacher ideologies nor conditions of work promote and support anti-sexist innovation, feminist futures seem grim'. Connell (1986), on the other hand, writing from an Australian perspective, presents a very different view. He argues that: 'Feminism has had a significant impact on teachers' outlooks; conversely, teachers have become an important vehicle for feminism' (p. 189). This disagreement perhaps reflects not only differences in the nature and outlook of the teaching profession in the two countries but also different degrees of public awareness of feminist ideas and government support for them. The final chapter in Part II assesses the validity of each of these views in the light of the culture of Westshire teachers and the way in which they mediated the schools' position on equal opportunities to the pupils. I consider the possibility that individual teachers might adopt a more radical perspective on gender issues than that reflected by the general ethos of the school, as well as the alternative possibility that teachers might minimise further the already lukewarm attitude towards equal opportunities. My findings in fact suggest that the latter was more likely to be the case, and I discuss the range of ideologies and operating principles which appeared to underlie their resistance to the pursuit of equal-opportunities policies. I also draw attention to the diversity of teachers' attitudes to gender equality and the determination of a minority of women teachers who identified strongly with the ideas of the women's movement and struggled to ensure that discussion of equal-opportunities issues entered and remained on the official agenda.

3

THE MANAGEMENT AND MEANING OF OPTION CHOICE

INTRODUCTION

The purpose of this chapter is twofold. First, I provide a picture of the outcome of option choice in the two schools and, second, I explore the way in which the process of option choice was managed by the schools in order to promote an ideology of free choice and open access whilst at the same time selecting pupils on to particular courses on the basis of sex, class and achievement. Both schools also attempted to nod in the direction of equal opportunities, although I argue that the messages conveyed reveal a weak understanding of the issues, and amount to no more than tokenism. In order to analyse the precise nature of the ideological messages conveyed to pupils through the process of option choice, I examined the official brochures handed out to pupils at the beginning of their third year and attended occasions when parents were invited into the school to discuss their child's choice of subjects.

Much of the debate in the literature on subject choice has focused on whether the school actively channels pupils in particular directions when they make their subject choices or whether the process is one of self-selection. Ryrie *et al* (1979) and Whyte (1986) place greater importance on the capacity of pupils to internalise the school's expectations, whereas Ball (1981) and Pratt *et al.* (1984) place more emphasis on direct intervention on the part of the school in terms of rejecting less able pupils from higher status courses. Woods (1976) and Ball (1981) suggest that middle-class parents are more actively involved and more successful than working-class parents in negotiating their children's entry to higher status courses.

Some studies which have addressed the issue of gender and option choice have tended to adopt a female deficit model in searching for reasons to explain why girls have opted out of science and technology. As I pointed out in Chapter 1, only recently have researchers like Gaskell (1985) begun to explore this problem from the perspective of the girls themselves, taking class as well as gender into account, and seeing girls' subject choices as a logical response to perceived external circumstances. In this chapter, having considered the curricular divisions which emerged as a result of subject choice, I go on to explore the extent to which the school is centrally involved in shaping the pattern of option choice through the ideological messages which it conveys. In later chapters, I consider parents', pupils' and teachers' understandings of the process of option choice.

THE PATTERN OF OPTION CHOICE AT MILLBRIDGE AND GREENHILL

At both Millbridge and Greenhill, the subjects chosen by pupils were analysed by sex and class, and at Greenhill further analysis was carried out by achievement. (Definitions of class and achievement levels used throughout this book are given in Appendix 1.) Tables 3.1 – 3.4 provide detailed analysis of the pattern of option choice at the two schools, and in both cases clear-cut sex and class differences emerged. In general terms, more girls featured in languages, biology, commercial subjects and domestic crafts: boys predominated in physical sciences and technical craft subjects. At Greenhill, it was interesting that pre-catering, a specifically vocationally orientated course, was taken mainly by boys, whereas home economics, textiles and home and family studies, which did not have this vocational bias, remained firmly in the female domain. The way in which sex and class intersected was very interesting. At Greenhill, working-class girls predominated in home and family studies, a course which was presented as equipping girls for a future domestic role, and at Millbridge, needlework, a course unlikely to have high exchange value in the labour market, was taken mainly by working-class girls. Middle class girls, on the other hand, were likely to opt for a second language. Despite the fact that many young women no longer envisage their future in terms of life-long financial dependency and most will return to work after a short break for child-rearing, it appears that such changes have not yet permeated through to the curriculum. Here, a culture of femininity rooted in the past continues to be propagated.

Class as well as sex differences were apparent in the takeup of science courses, with middle-class pupils clustering in pure science subjects and working-class pupils opting for the general science course. Physics is possibly the most elite subject on the curriculum, being taken almost exclusively by middle-class boys. At Greenhill, subjects were also analysed by pupils' achievement level. Subjects where more middle-class pupils were found were also those where there were significantly more above-average-achieving pupils. These tended to be languages, physics, chemistry, biology, geography, economics and political affairs and music. It would appear that teachers' exclusion of pupils defined as lower achieving from particular courses also has the effect of excluding working-class pupils, whether this is intended or not.

Subjects on the Greenhill curriculum were grouped into areas, and an analysis was carried out to see whether there were any significant differences in the overall pattern of choice. The categories were as follows: sciences; humanities; languages; applied science and technology; domestic crafts and office skills; aesthetic subjects. The aim was to investigate whether there were any differences with regard to sex, class or achievement between pupils not taking any subject in a particular area, those taking a non-academic subject in this area, those taking one academic subject in the area and those taking two or more academic subjects in the area. (Non-academic refers to those subjects which offered only a restricted grade at CSE or did not lead to any public examination. Academic refers to those subjects leading to CSE or 'O' level examinations.) Table 3.4 gives a list of the subjects included in each area and a summary of data.

The analysis revealed that all pupils took some form of science and more boys than girls took two academic sciences, although this was not at the level of significance. The vast majority of pupils doing two academic sciences were middle class. In the humanities area, a higher percentage of boys than girls were doing two academic subjects and all pupils in the non-academic option were working class. In the area of

Table 3.1 Percentages of pupils opting into different subject areas by sex and class at Millbridge in 1983 and results of chi-square test

Subject	Total	Per cent girls	Per cent boys	Per cent working class	Per cent middle class	Results of Chi-square test by sex	Results of Chi-square test by class	Group more likely to choose subject
French	78	71	29	68	32	$\chi^2 = 13.13$ df1 p < .001	ns	Girls
German	36	73	27	50	50	$\chi^2 = 7.1$ df1 p < .01	$\chi^2 = 5.04$ df1 p < .05	Middle-class girls
Biology	92	79	22	68	32	$\chi^2 = 13.59$ df1 p < .001	ns	Girls
Social and Economic history	49	78	22	70	30	$\chi^2 = 14.87$ df1 p < .001	ns	Girls
Commerce	57	83	27	84	16	$\chi^2 = 14.75$ df1 p < .001	ns	Girls
Typing	50	96	4	89	11	$\chi^2 = 21.16$ df1 p < .001	$\chi^2 = 6.32$ df1 p < .05	Working-class girls
Pottery	20	85	15	85	15	$\chi^2 = 9.8$ df1 p < .01	ns	Girls
Art	75	64	36	78	22	$\chi^2 = 5.88$ df1 p < .05	ns	Girls
Parentcraft	14	14	0	80	20	$\chi^2 = 7.0$ df1 p < .01	ns	Girls
Needlework	14	14	0	100	0	$\chi^2 = 7.0$ df1 p < .01	$\chi^2 = 8.2$ df1 p < .01	Working-class girls
Home economics	41	91	9	75	25	$\chi^2 = 13.28$ df1 p < .001	ns	Girls
Physics	59	29	71	44	56	$\chi^2 = 5.3$ df1 p < .05	$\chi^2 = 13.26$ df1 p < .001	Middle-class boys

Subject								
Computer studies	39	24	76	63	37	$\chi^2 = 11.30$ df1 p < .001	ns	Boys
Electronics	11	0	100	63	37	$\chi^2 = 11.00$ df1 p' < .001	ns	Boys
Rural studies	19	6	94	88	12	$\chi^2 = 15.21$ df1 p < .001	ns	Boys
Technical drawing	70	10	90	58	42	$\chi^2 = 22.4$ df1 p < .001	ns	Boys
Woodwork	31	0	100	75	25	$\chi^2 = 31.0$ df1 p < .001	ns	Boys
Metalwork	49	0	100	48	52	$\chi^2 = 49.0$ df1 p < .001	ns	Boys
Combined technical course	13	0	100	86	14		ns	Boys
Chemistry	81	51	49	48	52	ns	$\chi^2 = 13.5$ df1 p < .001	Middle class
Science	60	42	58	87	13	ns	$\chi^2 = 5.30$ df1 p < .05	Working class
20th-century history	100	42	58	72	28	ns	ns	
Geography	117	50	50	70	30	ns	ns	No group preference shown for these subjects
Community service	15	47	53	90	10	ns	ns	
Use of English	14	4	10	88	12	ns	ns	
Religious education	9	78	22	67	33	ns	ns	
Music	18	50	50	64	36	ns	ns	

Notes: (1) The total number of pupils is 208, of whom 49 per cent are boys and 51 per cent are girls- 70 per cent of these pupils are working class and 30 per cent are middle class. (2) Science is a limited grade CSE and Use of English is a non-examination subject.

Table 3.2 Percentages of pupils opting into different subject areas by sex and class at Greenhill in 1985 and results of chi-square test

Subject	Total	Per cent girls	Per cent boys	Per cent working class	Per cent middle class	Results of Chi-square test by sex	Results of Chi-square test by class	Group more likely to choose subject
Drama	22	75	25	86.4	13.6	$\chi^2 = 10.53$ df1 p < .001	ns	Girls
Music	8	62.5	37.5	0	100	ns	$\chi^2 = 12.21$ df1 p < .001	Middle class
French	51	54.9	45.1	48.4	51.6	ns	$\chi^2 = 9.92$ df1 p < .01	Middle class
German	33	63.6	36.4	60.9	39.1	ns	ns	
Latin	3	66.7	33.3	0	100	ns	ns	Middle class
Secretarial studies	14	100	0	70	30	$\chi^2 = 14.41$ df1 p < .0001		Girls
Computer studies	30	33.3	66.7	81	19		ns	
Religious studies	2	100	0	0	100	ns	ns	
Community service	7	71.4	28.6	100	0	ns	ns	

Subject	N							Group
History	51	58.8	41.2	63.6	36.4	ns	ns	
Geography	69	46.4	53.6	76.9	23.1	ns	ns	
Geology	5	0	100	100	0	ns	ns	
Economic and public affairs	15	20	80	27.3	72.7	$\chi^2 = 4.29$ df1 p $<.05$	$\chi^2 = 9.28$ df1 p $<.001$	Middle-class boys
Humanities	9	0	100	100	0	$\chi^2 = 7.13$ df1 p $<.01$	ns	Boys
Biology	47	68.1	31.9	51.5	48.5	$\chi^2 = 10.04$ df1 p $<.001$	$\chi^2 = 7.99$ df1 p $<.01$	Middle-class girls
Chemistry	46	50	50	44.8	55.2	ns	$\chi^2 = 12.19$ df1 p $<.001$	Middle-class
Physics	48	18.7	81.2	61.3	38.7	$\chi^2 = 24.86$ df1 p $<.0001$	ns	Boys
Science	39	48.7	51.3	89.7	10.3	ns	ns	Working-class
Art	32	50	50	71.4	28.6	ns	ns	
Pottery	19	15.8	84.2	91.7	8.3	$\chi^2 = 8.03$ df1 p $<.01$	ns	Boys
Art textiles	21	100	0	80	20	$\chi^2 = 24.14$ df1 p $<.001$	ns	Girls
Electronics	10	0	100	100	0	$\chi^2 = 8.19$ df1 p $<.01$	ns	Boys
Woodwork	14	0	100	100	0	$\chi^2 = 12.65$ df1 p $<.001$	ns	Boys
Metalwork	10	0	100	88.9	11.1	$\chi^2 = 8.19$ df1 p $<.01$	ns	Boys
English Technology	14	0	100	80	20	$\chi^2 = 12.65$ df1 p $<.001$	ns	Boys
Applied engineering	8	0	100	100	0	$\chi^2 = 6.08$ df1 p $<.01$	ns	Boys
Technical graphics	20	0	100	80	20	$\chi^2 = 19.96$ df1 p $<.001$	ns	Boys

Notes: (1) N = 132. 51 per cent are boys and 49 per cent are girls; 71 per cent are working class and 29 per cent are middle class. (2) Science is a limited grade CSE subject.

Table 3.3 Percentages of pupils opting into different subject areas by achievement at Greenhill in 1985 and results of chi-square test

Subject	Number	% High achievement	% Above average achievement	% Below average achievement	% Low achievement	Level of significance	Group more likely to choose subject
Drama	3,2	3.1	40.6	34.4	21.9	ns	High achievement
Music	8	50.0	25.0	25.0	0	$\chi^2 = 11.869$ df3 p < .01	High achievement
French	51	21.6	54.9	21.6	2.0	$\chi^2 = 22.301$ df3 p < .0001	Above average achievement
German	33	18.2	66.7	15.2	0	$\chi^2 = 19.541$ df3 p < .001	High achievement
Latin	3	66.7	33.3	0	0	$\chi^2 = 9.035$ df3 p < .05	
Secretarial studies	14	0	57.0	42.9	0	ns	
Computer studies	30	3.3	30.0	50.0	16.7	ns	
Religious studies	2	0	100	0	0	ns	
Community service	7	0	0	42.9	57.1	$\chi^2 = 16.334$ df3 p < .001	Low achievement
History	51	13.7	35.3	37.3	13.7	ns	
Geography	69	8.7	46.4	39.1	5.8	$\chi^2 = 8.069$ df3 p < .05	Above average achievement

Subject	N					Statistic	Achievement
Geology	5	0	20.0	60.0	20.0	ns	High achievement
Economic and public affairs	15	55.3	26.7	20.0	0	$\chi^2 = 27.688$ df3 $p < .0001$	Low achievement
Humanities	9	0	0	44.4	55.6	$\chi^2 = 20.293$ df3 $p < .0001$	High achievement
Biology	47	21.3	44.7	34.0	0	$\chi^2 = 14.317$ df3 $p < .00001$	High achievement
Chemistry	46	28.3	43.5	26.1	2.2	$\chi^2 = 22.928$ df3 $p < .0001$	High achievement
Physics	48	29.2	43.7	22.9	4.2	$\chi^2 = 25.672$ df3 $p < .0001$	High achievement
Science	39	0	20.5	46.2	33.3	$\chi^2 = 34.305$ df3 $p < .0001$	Low achievement
Art	32	6.3	37.5	43.7	12.5	ns	
Pottery	19	0	31.6	47.4	21.1	ns	
Art textiles	21	0	42.9	52.4	4.8	ns	
Electronics	10	0	20.0	60.0	20.0	ns	
Woodwork	14	7.1	21.4	35.7	35.7	$\chi^2 = 8.879$ df3 $p < .05$	Low achievement
Metalwork	10	0	20.0	50.0	30.0	ns	
Engineering technology	14	14.3	42.9	28.6	14.3	ns	
Applied engineering	8	0	0	50.0	50.0	$\chi^2 = 15.028$ df3 $p < .01$	Low achievement
Technical graphics	20	10.0	45.0	30.0	15.0	ns	

Note: N = 132

Table 3.4 Chi-square test applied to Greenhill pupils not taking a subject in a particular area, taking a non-academic subject, taking one academic subject or taking two or more academic subjects (by sex, class and achievement)

	% Boys	% Girls	Results of chi square test	% Working class	% Middle class	Results of chi square test	% above average achievement	% below average achievement	Results of chi square test
Science									
Doing non-ac. sub.	29.4	29.7		39.4	11.1		11.6	49.2	
Doing 1 ac. sub.	35.3	46.9	ns	47.0	37.0	$\chi^2 = 5.865$	46.4	34.9	$\chi^2 = 20.610$
Doing 2/3 ac. subs.	35.3	23.4		13.6	51.9	df1	42.0	15.9	df1
	100	100		100	100	p < .01	100	100	p < .001
Languages									
Not doing	54.4	34.4	$\chi^2 = 4.574$	60.6	18.5	$\chi^2 = 11.958$	18.8	73.0	$\chi^2 = 36.940$
Doing 1 ac. sub.	39.7	53.1	df1	34.8	66.7	df1	63.8	27.0	df1
Doing 2 ac. subs.	5.9	12.5	p < .05	4.6	14.8	p < .01	17.4	0	p < .0001
	100	100		100	100		100	100	
Humanities									
Not doing	5.9	12.5		6.5	0	$\chi^2 = 4.653$	11.6	6.3	
Doing non-ac. sub.	11.8	0	ns	10.6	0	df1	0	12.7	
Doing 1 ac. sub.	54.4	70.3		60.6	77.8	p < .05	63.8	60.4	ns
Doing 2 ac. subs.	27.9	17.2		19.7	22.2		24.6	20.6	
	100	100		100	100		100	100	

Applied Science and Technology									
Not doing	20.6	84.4	$\chi^2 = 48.851$	40.9	74.1	$\chi^2 = 6.471$	65.2	36.5	$\chi^2 = 8.653$
Doing non-ac. Sub.	1.5	0	df1	1.5	0	df1	0	1.6	df1
Doing 1 ac. sub.	39.7	15.6	$p < .0001$	33.3	18.5	$p < .05$	21.8	34.9	$p < .01$
Doing 2 ac. subs.	38.2	0		24.3	7.4		13.0	27.0	
	100	100		100	100		100	100	
Domestic/office									
Not doing	83.8	17.2	$\chi^2 = 53.383$	43.9	59.3	ns	53.6	49.2	ns
Doing non-ac. sub.	0	1.6	df1	1.5	0		0	1.6	
Doing 1 ac. sub.	16.2	35.9	$p < .001$	28.8	18.5		23.2	28.6	
Doing 2 ac. subs.	0	45.3		25.8	22.2		23.2	20.6	
	100	100		100	100		100	100	
Aesthetic									
Not doing	50.0	39.1	ns	42.4	51.9	ns	56.6	31.7	$\chi^2 = 7.206$
Doing 1 ac. sub.	38.2	46.9		47.0	37.0		30.4	55.6	df1
Doing 2/3 ac. subs.	11.8	14.0		10.6	11.1		13.0	12.7	$p < .01$
	100	100		100	100		100	100	

Notes: (1) N=132. (2) Science = physics, chemistry, biology and science at work (non-academic); humanities = geography, geology, history, economic and public affairs, religious studies and humanities (non-academic); languages = German, French and Latin; applied science and technology = electronics computer studies, woodwork, metalwork, engineering technology, technical graphics and applied engineering (non-academic): domestic/office = home economics, textiles, art textiles, secretarial studies, keyboarding, home and family studies; aesthetic = music, pottery, art and drama. (3) Non-ac. sub. = non-academic subject (i.e. non-examination or restricted grade CSE); Ac sub. = academic subject (i.e. leading to CSE or 'O' level).

aesthetic subjects, there were no class or sex differences between pupils but 56 per cent of above-average-achieving pupils, compared with 32 per cent of below-average-achieving pupils were not doing any subject in this area. Perhaps the most interesting contrasts emerged in the analysis of applied science and technology and office subjects and domestic crafts. Apart from the expected sex differences, significant class and achievement differences were found in the applied science and technology area, with 74 per cent of middle-class pupils and 65 per cent of above-average-achieving pupils taking no subject in this area. By way of contrast, there were no significant class and achievement differences between pupils in domestic and office subjects. This suggests that middle-class and higher-achieving boys are being channelled out of applied science and technology, whereas the same is not true to the same extent for middle-class and higher-achieving girls in domestic crafts and office skills. This finding confirms data gathered from observation of option choice interviews at Millbridge, where even the highest-achieving girls were given strong encouragement to do home economics. The school's stated policy that all pupils should take a craft and aesthetic subject in order to have a balanced curriculum was clearly not being universally enforced.

From this discussion, it is clear that at both schools the option choice system was operating in a highly selective way, creating divisions along class, sex and achievement lines, and producing an elite group of middle-class boys likely to gravitate in the future towards the most prestigious jobs in science and technology. Earlier discussion of changing patterns of employment alerts us to the fact that it is no longer appropriate for working-class boys to anticipate spending their lives engaged in traditional hard manual labour, and girls to expect to spend most of their adult lives as wives and mothers outside the labour market. However, patterns of option choice at Millbridge and Greenhill in the mid-1980s certainly did not indicate that the curriculum followed by girls and boys was responding to these new conditions of employment. The intriguing question which needs to be addressed is the extent to which the school was directly responsible for producing these divisions, or whether they resulted from the gender and class culture of parents and pupils. The following discussion considers whether pupils were indeed being channelled into sex and class stereotyped areas of the curriculum through gender codes implicit in the school's management of option choice or whether more overt forms of coercion were taking place. I begin by analysing the messages conveyed in the presentation of subjects to pupils and go on to consider the implicit understandings of the nature and function of choice itself.

THE PROCESS OF OPTION CHOICE AT MILLBRIDGE AND GREENHILL

At both schools, the process of option choice was treated as one of the key events of the school year. Documents were distributed to all pupils explaining the nature of the curriculum and the content of particular courses, and parents were invited into the school for formal meetings with teachers. Both schools attempted to communicate their concern that all pupils should select just the right course for them as individuals. There were some organisational differences between the two institutions. For instance, at Millbridge, a cafeteria style system operated, whereby pupils were free to choose any subject, with the recommendation that all pupils should study one subject from the sciences, humanities, creative arts and design subject areas. The school prided itself on its ability to timetable almost any combination of subjects. In addition, pupils were advised to continue with a modern language if they were making reasonable progress with it. At Greenhill, on the other hand, subjects were offered in specific groups, and some combinations of subjects were impossible. Pupils who took secretarial studies were particularly restricted. Since this took up three options, it was impossible to fulfil the school's advice to take a science, a humanity, a modern language and a craft or aesthetic subject.

A number of unifying themes ran through the process of option choice in the two schools. First, a great deal of emphasis was placed on pupils' own responsibility for deciding which subjects they wanted to study and accepting the consequences of their choice. Every pupil was treated as an atomised individual, free from the influence of school, parents or peer group. At the same time, it was apparent from the official documents and the various formal meetings with pupils and parents that in reality both schools were exercising a guiding influence. Indeed, it was apparent that the schools had very clear ideas about which pupils they wished to see in which areas, and their task was to convey this in such a way as to make the message apparent but not so overt as to undermine the ideology of free choice. In the following section, I will first illustrate how a selective process based on sex and achievement, closely connected with class, operated through the official presentation of particular subjects. I will then consider how, simultaneously, an ideology of free choice was communicated to pupils and parents. Finally, I will note how both schools paid lip-service to the rhetoric of equal opportunities, whilst failing to formulate any clear and consistent whole school policy. Clearly, these messages are grossly inconsistent, and I point out moments at which the contradictions became apparent.

SELECTIVE PROCESSES OPERATING THROUGH THE PRESENTATION OF SCHOOL SUBJECTS

We have already seen, through the analysis of patterns of option choice, how some subjects attracted particular groups of pupils with regard to sex, class and achievement. Since science subjects were markedly divided along these lines, it is worth considering the extent to which this may stem from the way in which they were presented to pupils. At both Millbridge and Greenhill, physics in particular was characterised as an abstract, mathematical subject connected essentially with a mechanistic view of the world. Thus, in the Millbridge options booklet it was described as the study of 'heat, light, sound, electricity, mechanics, waves, radioactivity and atomic physics'. In the Greenhill booklet, it was presented as 'a detailed study of energy and their relationships one with the other'. We know from the work of Harding and Sutoris (1987) and others that girls are more likely to be attracted to science if it appears to have a clear human and social dimension, but no attempt at either school was being made to highlight these aspects of the physics curriculum. Its vocational applications were presented in similarly masculine terms. The subject was said to be an important qualification for technical apprenticeships, medicine or engineering, all of which, with the possible exception of medicine, are likely to be regarded as male areas of work. No attempt was made to explain the usefulness of physics in traditionally female areas of work, which girls might be considering at this stage. At both schools, it is interesting to note that chemistry was described in far less abstract terms and its practical applications in, for example, food production and processing, were stressed. This might provide a clue as to why it was not rejected to the same extent by girls. Biology, the science subject in which girls predominated at both schools, was not described as requiring mathematical ability, and its concern with living things was emphasised. So despite the fact that the science departments claimed to operate an equal-opportunities policy, the presentation of these courses undermined this objective.

Craft subjects, too, were presented in terms which were likely to encourage traditional patterns of enrolment. At both schools, the description of domestic craft subjects made no concession to the notion of gender neutrality, and whilst not actually stating that these courses were for girls only, constantly emphasised their traditional feminine concerns. For example, the CSE course, always referred to as 'hostess cookery' but named rather incongruously 'host/hostess' cookery in the options booklet, was said to emphasise 'entertaining, personal grooming, clothes and fabric care'. The entire course description was rather reminiscent of the contents of a traditional women's magazine and was scarcely designed to encourage equal numbers of girls and boys into the subject. Needlework and textiles courses focused on the traditional female domestic craft of home dressmaking from printed patterns, rather than the design or production aspects of clothing and furnishing. The only home economics course which was orientated towards the acquisition of work-related rather then domestic skills was the pre-catering course at Greenhill, a vocational course aimed at and taken almost exclusively by, working-class boys. This course dealt with food technology and preparation in commercial settings and it was interesting that one middle-class girl was dissuaded from taking it on the grounds that it was not sufficiently academic. Her reason for rejecting the 'O' level home economics class was that it was 'all to do with families and babies', whereas she was interested in the world of work. It is interesting that both data from observation of option-choice interviews and from statistical analysis of the subjects which different pupils actually took show that whereas higher-achieving and middle-class boys were less likely to be taking craft subjects than lower-achieving and working-class boys, the same was not true for girls. The domestic role of higher-achieving and middle-class girls seems to be considered just as important as it is for their working-class sisters. Given the changing structure of the labour market, it is surprising that schools should continue to foster this culture of domesticity in such an overt form.

Traditionally masculine craft areas tended to provide fairly straightforward descriptions of the skills which would be covered in the course, and stated that they were open to both sexes. This was despite the fact that at both schools pupils were forced to choose their craft subjects for the third year at the middle school, before having had any experience of the secondary school subject, thus effectively pre-empting any later decision. This is a clear example of the way in which equal-opportunities policies were conveyed in a confused and inconsistent manner, a point discussed further in a later section of this chapter.

Overall, then, in key subject areas it appeared that subjects were presented in such a way as to ensure that gender boundaries would be maintained. There is clearly a marked discrepancy between the cultural understandings inherent in these subject descriptions and the more radical aspirations of some of the girls which emerged from the interviews and questionnaires.

With regard to differentiation on the basis of achievement levels, it was clear that both schools were involved in a sifting process, signalling that some courses were suitable for 'O' level pupils, some for CSE pupils and others for those deemed incapable of attempting any examination at all. However, since this ran counter to the much vaunted principle of free choice and open access, it had to be conveyed in a reasonably subtle way. Occasionally, as in the case of computer studies at Millbridge, a subject was described bluntly as 'not suitable for the least able'. More usually, as in the science-at-work option at Greenhill, vaguer terms were used such as 'this course is intended to meet the real needs of youngsters'. At an open meeting held for parents at Greenhill, the discomfort of the staff was apparent when they were asked questions by confused parents about the content of the large range of science and technology courses on offer. The deputy head addressing the meeting became almost lost for words when asked to spell out which courses were intended for which pupils. Mr Dewey, the head of technology, was less reticent in his explanation of the content of the various technology options. Engineering technology, he said, was intended for 'the apprentice of the future', whereas applied engineering 'is meant in the same way as home and family studies for the girls. It's meant for those who couldn't cope with the exam.' Staff at Millbridge were briefed at a special meeting about the minimum-achievement groupings for which each course was designed, and some were very unhappy about the covert selection process. A female art teacher commented:

> Anyone would think we were still running a grammar school – what exactly are these other poor kids meant to be doing? It seems like they need to be 'O' level material even to do a typing course.

OPTING FOR SUBJECTS – THE IDEOLOGY OF FREE CHOICE

At the start of the summer term at Millbridge, each third-year pupil and his or her parents were invited to the school to meet the tutor and a senior member of staff to discuss future studies. Each interview lasted between 15 and 30 minutes, and I sat in on the interviews of all the third-year pupils in two mixed-ability tutor groups. Tutor groups at Millbridge were organised vertically, and there were eleven third-year pupils in the groups I selected. The fact that the groups were mixed ability ensured that I observed an approximately equal number of interviews with girls and boys and higher- and lower-achieving pupils. Because these interviews provided such useful insights into the subtle processes which produced such neat and predictable outcomes, I discuss a number in depth. Table 3.5 provides a brief summary of the interviews as a whole.

The function of the option choice system as a means of controlling potentially disruptive pupils through the ideology of free choice was apparent in the interviews of Emma Martin and Keith Howells, both of whom were identified as troublemakers. Throughout these interviews, both members of staff repeatedly used such phrases as, 'Now you must show

Table 3.5 Brief summary of data gathered at pupils' option choice interviews held at Millbridge Upper School, June 1983

Pupil's Name	Interviewers	Parents present	Pupil's stated career intention	Subjects provisionally chosen	Level of achievement	Summary of observation
Aimee Smith	Female deputy head and male chemistry teacher	Mother and father	Something to do with science	Chemistry; biology; physics; computer studies; French; twentieth-century history. Reserve: pottery	High	Rather vague about career intentions; says she does not like home economics, but deputy head tries to persuade her to develop manual dexterity; no mention made of technology; no aesthetic subject.
Martin Thorp	Female deputy head and male chemistry teacher	Mother and father	Science and particularly meteorology	Computer studies; geography; physics; chemistry; technical drawing; French. Reserve: pottery	Above average	Very clear about career intentions; given much encouragement, despite fact that science grades are only slightly above average; no aesthetic subject.
Ruth Thomas	Female deputy head and male chemistry teacher	Mother and father	Nursing	Use of English; biology or science; social and economic history; home economics; community service. Reserve: pottery	Low	Discouraged from doing academic sciences; discouraged from nursing; no alternative jobs suggested; mother thinks home economics very important whether she gets married or not.

Name	Interviewers	Parent present	Career idea	Subjects chosen	Exam level	Notes
Keith Howells	Female deputy head and male chemistry teacher	Mother only	Engineer	Metalwork; technical drawing; physics; chemistry; twentieth-century history; combined technical course	Below average	Turns up without list of subjects; shows boredom throughout interview; very clear about the job he wants; suggestion by deputy head that he might do home economics treated as joke by everybody present; teachers stress that he has chosen subjects and therefore must work at them.
Clare Murdoch	Female deputy head and male chemistry teacher	Mother only	No idea	Social and economic history, biology; chemistry; home economics; needlework; parentcraft Reserve: typing French	Above average	Painfully shy throughout interview, nods or shakes head rather than replying; no idea what she wants to do – nothing suggested; chemistry teacher advises against home economics, needlework and parentcraft; mother says she would like her to do French.
Louise Mellor	Male head of house and Male physics teacher	Mother only	No idea – likes looking after children	Community services; use of English; twentieth-century history; science	Low	Louise has hearing and speech defects; no suggestion made about possible job she might do; mother advised not to expect exam success; mother wants her to do home economics for when she gets married.

Table 3.5 Continued

Pupil's Name	Interviewers	Parents present	Pupil's stated career intention	Subjects provisionally chosen	Level of achievement	Summary of observation
Sarah Ballard	Male head of house and male physics teacher	Mother and father	Secretary or bank work; but not really sure	Commerce; typing; German; French; geography; biology or general science; Reserves: home economics; twentieth-century history	Above average	Father talked a lot during interview; says daughter is no good in science (but she has grade B in biology); wants her to do languages and history because he likes the subject himself; Sarah and mother both very worried about making wrong choice; IQ testing decided upon
Michael Brown	Male head of house and male physics teacher	Mother only	Mechanical engineering	Physics; chemistry; technical drawing; metalwork; twentieth century history; french.	Above average	Great emphasis on only choosing subjects which will help him in job he wants to do; mother concerned about unemployment and need for right qualifications; physics teacher says grades rather low to do two sciences, but research shows boys' performance improves with age.

Name	Careers guidance	Parental situation	Career choice	Subjects chosen	Ability	Comments
Emma Martin	Male head of house and male physics teacher	Mother only	Hairdressing	Art; biology; history; geography; typing; home economics. Reserve: commerce	Above average	Very clear about what she wants to do – says she has apprenticeship arranged; tension between her and mother – mother says she thinks Emma really wants to go to art college; great emphasis on need to settle down and work because she has chosen subjects voluntarily
Karen Jones	Male head of house and male physics teacher	Mother and father	Hairdressing	Biology; social and economic history; art; typing; commerce; chemistry. Reserves: geography; pottery	Above average	Asked if she has carefully considered career choice, but no other possibility suggested; father says almost as a threat that she will have to work for him doing typing if she cannot get hairdressing job
Stewart Hubbard	Male head of house and male physics teacher	Mother only	Bricklayer	Use of English; rural studies; general science; pottery; woodwork; twentieth-century history. Reserves: combined technical course; music	Low	Very clear idea of what he wants to do – go to college and then be a bricklayer; only doing history because he could not think of anything else – warned that he has chosen it so he must work at it

commitment to these subjects because you have chosen to study them, no one's forcing you.' Keith conveyed a strong sense of scepticism by refusing to make eye contact with anyone and providing monosyllabic answers to the questions which he was asked. Emma looked angry throughout her interview and there appeared to be considerable tension in the relationship with her mother. Mrs Martin said that Emma might be thinking of going to art school, which Emma promptly contradicted. At this point, Mrs Martin said that she thought her daughter was under pressure from her friends with regard to smoking, drinking and wearing a lot of make-up, and she thought that girls generally had too much freedom. Meanwhile Emma was sighing and raising her eyes to the ceiling, as if to signal complete boredom. Both Keith and Emma had chosen stereotypically masculine and feminine areas of the curriculum and sex-stereotyped occupations, with Emma saying she wanted to be a hairdresser and Keith an engineer. Keith was asked by the female deputy head if he had considered home economics, but this suggestion was accompanied by laughter, as if it was not to be taken seriously. Emma's choice of home economics was not questioned at all. Neither pupil was asked why they had chosen the particular job which they said they wanted when they left school, and if they had considered any alternatives.

During both these interviews, I had a strong sense that the real interests and concerns of these pupils were not being dealt with. The aim seemed to be to slot them into a conventional curriculum package with the minimum of fuss, whilst at the same time persuading them to take full responsibility for the outcome. I suspected that neither of these pupils was going to accept the deal unquestioningly but, none the less, it appeared that the ideology of free choice was being used as a means of controlling these two potentially deviant pupils, and, of course, this raises interesting questions with regard to the national curriculum. If free choice, of however dubious a nature, is no longer to be available as a means of legitimating curricular divisions, then it is likely that schools may have a harder task in controlling their disenchanted pupils. This issue is discussed in more detail in Chapter 10, but it is interesting to note that, recently, more emphasis has been placed on the possibilities for free choice within the national curriculum.

The cases of Sarah Ballard and Michael Brown illustrated the way in which pupils' subject choices and educational and occupational aspirations were accepted unquestioningly when these were in line with traditional gender stereotypes. Sarah had mainly B grades and, although she mentioned an interest in office or bank work, it was clear that she did not have a firm idea of the direction she would like to follow. Despite this uncertainty, the interview proceeded on the assumption that Sarah wanted to do office work. Sarah's father took up a lot of the talking time in the interview, and it was he who said that she did not want to carry on with science because it was a bit of a grey area for her. In response to the teacher's question, 'Is it Sarah's considered decision to rule out science?' it was actually Mr Ballard rather than Sarah herself who replied that it was. He and the two interviewers agreed that science at work (the non-academic option) would probably be a better bet than biology. Mr Ballard also said that he would like to see her carrying through her languages and history. 'I'd like her to take history', he said, 'You know how keen your dad is on history.' Before the end of the interview, Sarah's mother expressed anxiety about the whole process: 'I don't want her to end up like me, full of "I should have done this, that and the other".' Finally it was decided that some IQ testing should be carried out but despite this it was clear that repeatedly expressed fears about sinking into some unfulfilling job were not dealt with at all by the two male interviewers. The promise of IQ testing seemed to hold out the hope that something was being done, but the inertia of the system was clearly propelling Sarah towards some sort of low-status clerical work, despite her relatively high level of achievement.

Michael Brown's interview was in sharp contrast with Sarah's. Although his grades were lower than hers, he was very clear about the work he wanted to do, which was mechanical engineering. The entire interview focused around the qualifications he would need for this job and, despite his rather low grades, mostly Cs and Ds, his choice of two sciences was approved. The argument used by the male physics teacher conducting the interview was a very clear example of how boys' performance in science may be aided by beliefs about their natural ability in this area. Michael was told by the physics teacher:

Your grades are a bit low at the moment to be doing two sciences, but research shows that boys tend to be a bit behind girls at this stage and then catch up later, so you should be all right.

Buswell (1984) describes a similar incident in which a sixth-form boy's poor performance was attributed to laziness and lack of motivation rather than lack of ability.

The contrast in the emphasis given to future work was even more apparent in the interviews of lower-achieving boys and girls. Stewart Hubbard, who had mainly D and E grades, said that he wanted to be a bricklayer and go to college, and his subjects were all chosen with a view to the craft and technology background which he would find useful in his future work. Ruth Thomas and Louise Miller also had low grades in all subjects, but their interviews focused much more on choosing subjects to prepare them for their future domestic role rather than their future working lives. Home economics was seen as a priority in both cases. To quote Mrs Thomas: 'Domestic science is a good thing all girls should learn whether they get married or not.' The interviewers appeared to be in firm agreement with this comment.

It would appear, then, that some channelling by the school was taking place during the course of the option choice interviews, but there was little evidence of parents or pupils actively resisting. The extent to which further manipulation went on behind the scenes was not altogether clear. I asked the deputy headmistress responsible for option choice how often she had to guide pupils away from unsuitable choices. She replied that this did not happen very often because most pupils seemed to have a realistic idea of their own capabilities. This would appear to support the findings of Ryrie et al. (1979) that generally little direct intervention takes place, since pupils have already effectively internalised the school's expectations of their future performance. In my analysis of the process at Millbridge, there was little evidence of teachers intervening to persuade pupils to alter their choice of subject, although some degree of persuasion clearly was used. In interviews, the majority of pupils confirmed that they were able to study the subjects they originally chose.

To summarise, then, despite the rhetoric of free choice, a

process of selection based on both sex and achievement, the latter associated with class, was at work during the option choice interviews. All the boys, whatever their level of achievement, were encouraged to choose subjects in relation to the area of work they claimed they were aiming for in the future. They were also encouraged to take courses which were likely to stretch them, since teachers anticipated that their current levels of performance were going to improve rather than stabilise or decline. The boys themselves all had clear ideas of what they wanted to do. The girls tended to be much vaguer in this respect, or else suggested sex-stereotyped jobs such as hairdressing, and no attempt was made to encourage them to think of alternatives. With regard to non-academic subjects, it was taken for granted that boys would go into technology and girls into domestic craft subjects or office skills. Statistical analysis of option choice data discussed earlier in this chapter shows that the schools' insistence on a balanced curriculum for everybody, which should include a craft and aesthetic subject, was more likely to be reflected in the option choices of girls than boys and of lower-achieving than higher-achieving pupils. This finding was reinforced by evidence from the option choice interviews.

A further major theme which emerged was the use of the ideology of free choice as a means of exerting control over unruly pupils and of legitimating different curricular paths more generally. Reynolds and Sullivan (1981) have identified the individualistic nature of timetabling in comprehensive schools as one of the means by which working-class pupils are prevented from developing a sense of class solidarity. Instead of spending all day with the same group of pupils, they experience the confusion of moving into a different group for each lesson. Because of the fragmentary nature of these encounters, they are prevented from developing a sense of social-class identity and solidarity. Thus the option choice system might well be a means of causing working-class pupils to accept class divisions within the curriculum as manifestations of their own free choice rather than products of the education system. In the same way, pupils may very well find it hard to recognise and challenge gender divisions within the curriculum if they believe that a system of choice rather than selection is at work. They are likely to feel personally responsible for their own failure to break away from the gender divisions of the labour market, instead of recognising these as structural features of society.

OPTION CHOICE AND EQUAL OPPORTUNITIES

The preceding discussion illustrates the way in which the management of the option choice system in both schools tended to reinforce traditional gender stereotypes. However, although neither school had a formalised equal-opportunities policy, some teachers were aware that this was an issue which they could not entirely ignore. This may have been, in part, because of an awareness of the requirements of the Technical and Vocational Educational Initiative (TVEI) in which both schools were participating, which specified equal opportunities as one of its key criteria of success. My overall impression was of a very limited understanding of the issue which was unlikely to lead to any real progress. In the Greenhill options booklet, for instance, physics was specifically described as a course for girls and boys, followed by a course description which emphasised its masculine concerns. As we noted earlier, metalwork, woodwork and technical drawing were described as equally suitable for boys and girls, but with no indication of any practical support to help girls make up for the earlier experience which almost all had missed.

In the various talks given to pupils at the two schools on the subject of options, a female deficit model underpinning the understanding of equal opportunities was clearly apparent. For example, Mr Lill, who was in charge of subject choice at Greenhill, spoke to the assembled third year about the danger of selecting a sex-stereotyped curriculum. As far as he was concerned, there were many opportunities there, and girls were simply not taking them up:

> We know that if a girl had earned equal grades with a boy, the employer would take the girl because if the pressure's on them and they've got that far they must be good. Heathland (a nearby atomic energy research establishment) is crying out for girls as technical and electrical apprentices. We try to encourage girls every year but it falls on stony ground. You can do it but you think you can't. Again, go and ask the teachers.

He then went on to tell the boys that they should not reject the idea of doing home economics and textiles:

> There is not one hotel in London where the top cook is a woman. There are only three top female hair stylists – the rest are men. This is London fashion week – most of the stylists there are men. Boys say they would be called a poof if they did a job like that. I wouldn't mind being called a poof if I was being paid two and a half million pounds a year for it.

While girls and their parents are characterised as narrow-minded and conservative, teachers and the school are seen as generally progresssive and keen to encourage girls and boys into non-traditional areas of the curriculum.

A deficit model of girls' behaviour was also implicit in other comments made by staff on the subject of option choice. Peter Johns, a young softly-spoken woodwork teacher, who gave the impression that he was genuinely concerned about the male dominance of the technology department, ended his talk to pupils on future options in the technology department with a special plea to the girls 'to be a bit more adventurous and choose a boys' subject. Don't have a blinkered view of it.' As an afterthought he added: 'And, of course, the boys might want to think about home economics.' Like Mr Lill, he was blaming the girls for their lack of enterprise in sticking to traditional subjects, without offering them any help in breaking away from this pattern or offering an anlysis of the structural constraints in the school and the labour market. Reactions from pupils to these talks suggested that girls recognised the female deficit model which informed the school's conception of equal opportunities and resented it. For instance, after Mr Lill's talk Bernadette Coles commented: 'They don't make the boys do needlework, so why should we be made to do physics?'

It was also interesting to note how traditionally female subjects were presented in a substantially different light to encourage boys to consider them. Mrs Hankin, the female deputy head at Greenhill, told parents that there was no reason why boys should not do the secretarial course:

> We've had some very successful young gentlemen doing

it. If they want to set up their own business, for instance,
it gives them a very useful background.

Girls opting for secretarial studies were certainly not told that
it was a subject generally leading to low-paid office work, but
neither were they offered the promise of their own business as
a reason for taking it. In general, then, when the issue of equal
opportunities was mentioned, it was in the context of either
criticising girls for their limited horizons, or urging boys to
move into traditionally female areas where they would soon
outstrip their female competitors. This was certainly not an
empowering message for the girls who received it, and may
account for some of their reluctance to abandon female
curriculum ghettoes.

CONCLUSION

Analysis of subjects taken in both schools showed that selection
processes were evident in the option choice system, dividing
pupils according to class, sex and achievement. Interestingly,
even though the two schools ran slightly different option
choice systems, Millbridge offering an entirely free choice and
Greenhill requiring pupils to choose from specific groups of
subjects, the results in terms of curricular divisions along sex
and class lines were very similar. Pratt *et al.* (1984) suggest that
entirely free option choice is likely to lead to less sex stereotyping, but in the case of Millbridge this certainly did not seem to
be true. However, the fact that pupils were required to choose
their craft subjects before they left their middle schools, thus
pre-empting subsequent choice of subjects, undoubtedly con-
tributed to the sex-stereotyping of these areas.
   The various talks to pupils and parents and the option choice
booklets stressed the openness of the curriculum to all pupils,
and the necessity of choosing a properly balanced curriculum.
However, further analysis of interviews, talks and printed
material revealed the existence of a sifting process based on sex
and achievement. Although class did not form an overt basis
for selection, the strong association between class and achievement in both schools meant that by discouraging pupils who
were below average in their level of achievement from taking
certain subjects, working-class pupils were also being discour-

aged. The option choice interviews at Millbridge also played a key role in this selection process and appeared to be used to promote an ideology of free choice which might ultimately serve to legitimate differential educational outcomes.

There is evidence, then, to suggest that option choice procedures are centrally involved in the production of gender, class and achievement divisions. However, this cannot be regarded as the only, or even necessarily the most important, mechanism involved. What is interesting is how little evidence there is, in, for example, the Millbridge option choice interviews, of parents questioning or resisting the channelling processes. (Parents' roles are discussed in more detail in Chapter 8.) Key teachers at both schools maintained that direct intervention was not often necessary because pupils had a good idea of their own abilities, and pupils supported this view. Subsequent chapters focus on possible reasons for parents' and pupils' acquiescence in a process which appeared to be against the interests of many girls and working-class pupils.

4

TEACHERS' CONSTRUCTIONS OF MASCULINITY AND FEMININTY

INTRODUCTION

The previous chapter argued that a conservative gender code was reflected in the schools' management of option choice, with firm boundaries maintained between masculine and feminine areas of the curriculum. I wanted to examine whether the gender codes of individual teachers were equally conservative or more progressive than the general ethos of the school, and therefore undertook an extensive series of interviews and observation. Both schools claimed to support the principle of equal opportunities, although no policy statements had ever been drawn up, and I was particularly interested to see how teachers actually interpreted and mediated this policy.

Neo-marxist accounts of schooling, produced in the 1970s, accorded very little power to teachers for good or ill, since they were regarded as the hapless pawns of the capitalist system (Bowles and Gintis, 1976; Althusser, 1971). This view of relatively impotent teachers has been radically revised since then. Connell (1986), for instance, argues that: 'it is teachers' work as teachers that is central to the remaking of the social patterns investing education' (p. 4). Despite the fact that teachers have now been elevated to the status of 'bearers of educational change' (Kelly *et al.*, 1985), it is only relatively recently that researchers have begun a systematic investigation of their attitudes to issues of gender equality (Pratt *et al.* 1984, Kelly *et al.* 1985, Connell, 1986). In the first part of this chapter, I explore teachers' explanations of why pupils make sex-stereotyped option choices and in the second part I focus more closely on teachers' construction of femininity as revealed by their attitudes towards the sexual hierarchy of the school. My hope is to gain an increased understanding of what Acker (1987) has described as the puzzle of teachers' resistance to gender-equality policies, which may take the form of hostility or inactivity.

TEACHERS' EXPLANATIONS OF THE PROCESS OF GENDER DIFFERENTIATION

In this section I focus on Millbridge teachers' responses to questions concerning the tendency of girls and boys to make different option choices, and whether positive action to encourage non-traditional option choices could be taken by the school. The purpose of these questions was to see whether teachers attributed the production of a gender-differentiated curriculum at the end of the third year to the transmission by the school of a dominant gender code, or to the extra-school environment. Ultimately, I was interested in the extent to which teachers' perceptions of such issues might themselves play a reproductive role in creating gender divisions. Detailed analysis of patterns in teacher responses to the two questions above is restricted to Millbridge teachers, although Greenhill teachers gave very similar replies.

When Millbridge teachers were asked why they thought girls and boys chose different subjects, their responses tended to fall into one of two categories. The first category attributed different patterns of option choice to factors outside the school's control, for instance girls' and boys' differing abilities, parental pressure, peer group pressure, early childhood socialisation, traditions in a rural area. The second category of responses attributed differences between girls' and boys' option choices to within-school factors – including teacher attitudes, curriculum content, school ethos and organisational procedures. What follows is an analysis of the teachers' responses, which seemed to be influenced by three variables, namely age, sex and position within the school hierarchy. Subject taught also seemed to have some connection with teacher attitudes, although the pattern here was not as clearcut. It is important to note that all teachers felt that the school should treat girls and boys equally, offering them open access to all subjects.

THE OLDER GROUP OF TEACHERS

Seven teachers over 40 were interviewed, all of whom were members of the school hierarchy. In this particular school, the hierarchy, or senior management team, consisted of four heads of house, three deputy heads, the director of studies and the headmaster. There were four men and three women. All the teachers in this group placed a great deal of emphasis on socialising forces outside the school. Particular emphasis was placed on the traditional roles of parents in a rural area. Mr Broughton, a male head of house who taught woodwork, had this to say:

> A lot of it is role learning from early on, attitudes of parents . . . I suppose there are traditional things that men do to earn a living and women do to earn a living or cope with the home. A lot of them still don't view the woman as going out to work. They still seem to me to think of the girl being equipped for life in terms of spending time in the home, which to me is wrong.

These teachers seemed to be influenced strongly by models of social learning according to which, traditional gender identities are formed at a very early age. Mr Spiller, the director of sixth-form studies who taught commerce and economics said:

> In terms of craft skills, very few girls are given Meccano or Lego to play with at pre-school level, and it's at pre-school level that it matters. By the time they're at primary school it's too late. The prejudices are already formed in the child's mind.

When asked to consider the role of the school in the encouragement of non-traditional option choices, the older group of teachers often cited the strength of environmental socialising forces as the main reason why the school could do very little to break these long-established patterns. Mr Spiller, the director of studies, felt that nothing could be done because:

> the constraints aren't in the school's provision . . . You're fighting parental prejudice, very strong, and for the school to try and change that would simply be counter-productive. So I think in terms of school policies you have

to tread in this area extremely softly. The other area you're treading on is employers' expectations.

Connell (1986) discusses the way in which teachers tend to use the notion of the 'bad home', often synonymous with the working-class home, to account for the problems which schools experience in educating and controlling children. He comments 'this yields an image of the school as a kind of a middle-class lifeboat adrift in a sea of proletarian roughness' (p. 170). Clearly, this view of the pathological family is at the forefront of teachers' minds in accounting not only for class divisions, but also gender divisions.

Pupil peer groups were also seen as a major factor in preventing boys from making non-traditional option choices, as suggested by Mr Ginger, deputy head at Millbridge and teacher of mathematics:

I think boys regard cooking as slightly . . . not the sort of thing you want to tell your friends you're doing at 14 or 15.

Two of the teachers said that the first and middle schools were responsible for enforcing gender stereotypes, and a further three talked in terms of differing abilities or stages of development among male and female pupils. The inference from some teachers was that these differences were innate:

It's also stages of development. You will find so often that a girl will work industriously and produce pages of writing that looks most impressive and when they get higher up the school you look at it and it isn't so impressive, and the boys come on and the ideas are there.
(Miss Maple, deputy head, teaching mathematics)

When it comes to using language, girls score much higher, they enjoy apparently greater success; even though boys may be just as good they don't work . . . A lot of girls shy away from workshop type things because it involves physical skills, it involves three-dimensional perception at which a lot of girls seem to be rather bad.
(Mr Spiller, director of studies)

It is interesting to note that none of these teachers was willing to accord any degree of responsibility to the school for the perpetuation of gender differences in the curriculum, and in this they differed markedly from the younger group of teachers.

All of the older teachers placed a great deal of importance on the idea of pupils freely choosing the subjects they wanted to study and were concerned that if the school were to become over-active in discouraging sex-stereotyped option choices it would be guilty of undermining this freedom. Mr Appleyard, the headmaster of Millbridge who taught mathematics, said:

> I think to take over a child and tell it it ought to do something, that's just not the business of the school . . . If you try to turn the whole lot upside down then you would be pushing people to do things differently. It's not the school's job to push, it's to make opportunities available.

Miss Maple, the deputy head, made similar points:

> It's difficult once you start selling subjects . . . I would hate to generate anything in school which is artificial and push youngsters to doing things they don't actually want.

The most radical suggestion they made in terms of what the school could actually do to encourage non-traditional option choices was to appoint male and female teachers to areas of the curriculum normally associated with the opposite sex. This policy was endorsed by both the headmaster and the female deputy head, who said they were very pleased to have appointed a female woodwork teacher at the end of 1983:

> It's rather nice we were able to appoint a female teacher in the engineering department. She was a very good candidate. I don't think there's any point in appointing a female candidate just for the sake of it – but it will help to confirm there's no reason why women shouldn't be appointed in that department as much as anywhere else. (Mr Appleyard, Headmaster and maths teacher)

The headmaster made it clear that he was expecting this woman to take the entire responsibility for encouraging girls to take technology, and did not consider that any official policy statement was necessary to support her. Overall, Mr Appleyard felt that everything that the school could do in terms of intervention was already being done:

In careers lessons people are shown all the things that are available. Notices are up showing particular opportunities for girls in engineering. If that's intervening, yes, we do intervene.

Mrs Lovell, the female head of house who taught English, also had a very restricted view of action which the school could take to bring about change. She said she did not agree with the idea of an official equal-opportunities policy within the school. If such a policy were to be implemented at all, it would have to be 'by an individual teacher on a personal basis – or perhaps a department might be prepared to push it'.

Teachers' attitudes towards option choice exemplify a number of what Connell (1986) has termed the 'operating priciples' which govern teachers' approach to their work. One of these operating principles is the desire to be seen as moderate and value-free, certainly not at the hub of any radical reform which might cause the wrath of conservative parents to descend. A second operating principle which appears to be at work here is the need to limit the impact of educational innovations as a labour saving device. To quote Connell again: 'no matter how attractive a proposal is in principle, if it makes it more difficult for you to manage a classroom, if it increases the emotional pressure on you, if it adds to the workload, then you do not do it' (p. 181). The strategy of sticking up a few posters and claiming that equal-opportunities policy has been fulfilled, is clearly in line with this principle.

These teachers also clearly found themselves in a paradoxical position with regard to the issue of free choice. On the one hand, they were emphasising the weight of environmental pressures shaping pupils' option choices, indicating that these choices were very far from free. On the other hand, they were asserting that the school should do nothing to influence these choices in any way, because this would be to interfere with the pupils' right to make independent decisions. Pratt (1985) found similar contradictions in teachers' attitudes and criticises the notion that the school should do nothing to challenge the problem of sex-stereotyping in subject selection. He argues that 'neutrality' means simply allowing the many and powerful pressures on pupils to operate untrammelled upon them. He is also critical of the teachers who point to 'the pervasiveness and power of the external environment'. They are right, he says, 'only in the sense that they – and pupils – need to know of its existence, but by accepting its power the teachers are making decisions for the pupils, the antithesis of education'.

At least in its early conception, the national curriculum, currently in the process of being implemented in England and Wales, challenged many cherished beliefs with regard to the importance of pupils' voluntarily selecting their subject options, and, implicitly, their future destinies. As I argued in Chapter 3, the ideology of free choice has been used as a means of persuading individual pupils to accept responsibility for educational outcomes which are in reality due to structural forces beyond their control. In Chapter 9 I return to the discussion of the implications of the national curriculum for the principle of voluntarism within course selection, and suggest that the function of free choice as a mechanism of control had not been fully appreciated by the original architects of the national curriculum. The government's later insistence that there will be plenty of opportunity for choice within the national curriculum represents a belated recognition of the dangers of replacing apparent choice with overt coercion.

The stress on the determining forces outside the school led these teachers to ignore some blatant examples of the manipulation of pupils' option choices by the school. For instance, while they were still at their middle schools, pupils were asked to choose their design subjects for the following year. Not surprisingly, most opted for the security of following their friends into traditional areas of the curriculum, which then restricted their choice at the end of the third year of the upper school. All of these teachers justified this practice on administrative grounds. Mr Spiller, for instance, said:

> Well, it's a question of resources. To make it possible for everbody to do all of the areas, we would need at least one more workshop, one more home economics room, and we would need extra staffing to give you the extra opportunities and times.

On the question of curriculum content, there was again a tendency to accept what was being taught in each subject area as given and unalterable. Miss Maple, for instance, could see no way in which needlework could possibly be of any interest to the boys:

> I mean the boys don't do needlework. They're scared stiff of it. It's all making soft toys and learning to use a machine at that age, and it's just not a boy's thing.

Despite their stated commitment to equality of access, then, these teachers were all involved in defending the status quo in various ways. It is also interesting to note that the majority of teachers in this group were maths teachers, and researchers such as Pratt *et al.* (1984) and Kelly *et al.* (1985) have also found that teachers of traditionally masculine subjects such as science, maths and technology have more conservative attitudes to gender issues.

THE YOUNGER GROUP OF TEACHERS

In the younger group of teachers I have included all those whom I interviewed who were under 40, and I found greater variety in their responses. There were seven women and six men. Of the women, seven were on Scale 2 and three were on Scale 1. Of the men, two were on Scale 3, one was on Scale 2 and one was on Scale 1. Not only in this sample, but in the school as a whole, women were concentrated on Scales 1 and 2, and men tended to occupy more senior positions. In 1983, out of twelve head-of-department positions at Millbridge, only two, home economics and French, were held by women. Subjects taught by the group of teachers I interviewed were sex-typed – the men teaching physics, chemistry, biology, maths and geography, and the women teaching English, physical education, religious education, needlework and typing.

Like the senior members of staff, the younger group of teachers believed that environmental pressures played an important part in determining the gender-differentiated pattern of pupils' option choices, although men tended to describe these influences in much greater detail. Parents' role models were also seen as an important influence, as were the media, peer groups and first and middle schools. Mr Tiller, the head of maths, and Mrs Marshwood, an English teacher, talked about pupils' perception of the labour market:

I think one thing is they look at the careers these subjects lead to and you see that the careers that there are tend to be mainly staffed by men. And in biology they see that there are a great deal of women working in that area. I'm sure that some of them see biology as working with animals and think that's nice as well. But really it is this careers thing to a great extent.

Mrs Stonecroft, an art teacher who saw herself as a feminist, felt that sex-stereotyping in the curriculum was related to the construction of masculinity and femininity in western culture:

I think it's not very well accepted in our society that we all have masculine and feminine qualities within us – we are all masculine and feminine . . . In western cutures it's denied and I think a lot of problems arise from denying part of ourselves – I think it works like that for both boys and girls. Particularly in education that part is denied, so we have to reinforce what we happen to be, whether a boy or a girl – we almost have to prove our masculinity or femininity.

Although both women and men mentioned environmental factors in determining option choice, it is interesting that men talked about these factors at far greater length than women, whereas women placed greater emphasis on pressures within school. Only two of the men but five of the women said that they thought the school was actively involved in channelling pupils into sex-stereotyped areas of the curriculum.

The two feminist teachers were the most categorical about the overriding importance of influences within the school, particularly the importance of teacher attitudes:

Certainly there's very much the attitude that typing and needlework will be good for the girls and it's almost unthinkable that boys should do needlework . . . I think the craf department is very male orientated and the men definitely encourage the boys rather than the girls.

(Mrs Marshwood, English teacher)

This was in interesting contrast to two of the men who specifically denied that teacher attitudes had any influence at all:

> I don't think we give physics a male image at all. That is already there in the minds of the pupils.
>
> (Mr Mottram, head of physics)

> I don't know why girls tend to do biology rather than physics because there's no pressure put on them from the department in any way.
>
> (Mr Jones, head of biology)

Mrs Stonecroft felt that curriculum content was of crucial importance in attracting pupils to particular subject areas:

> In this school I think it's got a lot to do with the way the subject's actually presented. At my last school, the people who taught home ec. had broken down that barrier where it was seen as a subject for the girls. There was the multi-ethnic side – the home ec. was to do with a dietary thing and world-wide food distribution and the idea that we are what we eat.

This teacher disagreed with the idea that peer group pressure was an important influence on the sex-stereotyping of option choices:

> We reinforce the stereotypes as adults rather than students themselves. Particularly round about 13 or younger, if they have fun doing it, they'll do it. I don't think it comes from them unless teachers foster it in the first place.

Both the younger and the older group of teachers, then, felt that environmental influences played an important part in the production of a gender-differentiated curriculum, but the younger group, particularly women teachers who identified themselves as feminists, placed much greater emphasis on the importance of within-school factors.

In answer to the question of whether the school should take an active role in encouraging non-traditional option choices, a wide range of views was expressed. In general, those who emphasised the power of environmental forces were pessimistic about the school's potential to initiate reform. Mr Jones, who talked at great length about the importance of parental role models, felt that the school could do little to bring about social change:

I was talking with Gareth Wood (teacher at a middle school) about how we teach sex education and he was saying that even at 11, 12, there is already the stereotyping that the boys are out for what they can get and it's up to the girls to say no . . . and if you've got that sort of stereotyping at that age then I'm sure it applies to all spheres of activity and you're naive to think the school can change that very dramatically.

Two of the men felt that the school was already involved in counteracting sex-stereotyping in the curriculum. Mr Mottram, the head of physics, said they did make a conscious effort to make the subject relevant to girls, although perhaps his words suggest a rather superficial understanding of the issue:

When we're talking about speed increasing gears instead of getting a hand drill I always get an egg whisk or what have you. In some ways you could say it was a sop to the ladies. Having said that, there's no reason why girls should say machines and mechanics aren't for me. It's just an idea that's in their minds.

Whereas all the older teachers had defended the practice of pupils choosing design options while still at the middle school, all the younger teachers apart from one opposed it.

Women made a variety of suggestions about how the school could encourage non-traditional option choices. Miss Jenkins, an RE (religious education) teacher, said that girls were often placed in RE classes not because they had any particular interest in the subject but because the class needed filling, and it was felt that girls would make less of a fuss about it than boys. According to Mrs Marshwood, not only formalistic equality but real enthusiasm from the teachers was necessary for changes to be made. This would probably involve changing curriculum content and subject presentation:

I think there should be a positive sales technique for the subjects boys are choosing like craft subjects. They should be positively sold to the girls, perhaps with displays and talks, and there should be a policy of positive discrimination to make sure you get a class which is half girls. I mean nationally I'd like to see a policy introduced in schools to make sure that boys and girls have equal opportunities in all subjects, not just on paper.

She also felt there was a need to challenge the overwhelmingly male atmosphere of the metalwork and woodwork areas and redistribute scale points more equably. This teacher had clearly moved beyond the liberal concern for equality of access and was arguing that equality of outcome was vitally important. Connell (1986) perhaps rather dismissively refers to teachers' brand of feminism as being that of the married woman, and argues that it is limited in that it does not relate to the experience of working-class girls. Data presented in Chapter 7 do suggest that there was a lack of sympathy between girls who were rejecting traditional constructions of femininity and their female teachers. None the less, it is important to recognise the courage of feminist women teachers like Mrs Marshwood who were quietly insisting that gender equality was an issue which the school had to address.

To summarise, all teachers placed great emphasis on the power of socialisation to determine the outcome of subject option choice. Teachers in the older age group denied that the school had any control over this outcome because of the power of socialisation forces, and they also tended to place some of the blame on innate differences in developmental patterns between girls and boys. Younger teachers were generally more critical of the role of the school in producing a gender-differentiated curriculum, but it was only the teachers who explicitly identified themselves as feminists who were in favour of the school taking positive action to change this outcome. Among the older group of teachers, women were just as reluctant as men to endorse the idea of radical change in the school, suggesting that becoming members of the school hierarchy makes women less critical of the institution and more willing to defend the status quo. There was also an overall tendency for teachers of arts subjects to be more in favour of positive moves towards gender equality than teachers of maths and technology, but since few teachers in the hierarchy taught arts subjects, it was difficult to separate out the variables of position within the school and subject taught. One of the female heads of house, who taught English, had extremely traditional views on issues of gender equality, and perhaps this again gives some indication that once teachers occupy positions of power within a school they are less likely to criticise its practices. Another possibility is that it is women with less challenging views who tend to get promoted in the first place. I will now go on to explore the significance of certain teacher ideologies in producing an environment unsympathetic to the implementation of equal-opportunities policies.

There is evidence, not just in Westshire but elsewhere in the country too, that teachers react with hostility or reluctance to anti-sexist intervention strategies (Payne *et al.*, 1984) and, outside progressive local education authorities, the implementation of equal opportunities policies seems to be left to isolated individual teachers. Data from Millbridge and Greenhill teachers indicated that teacher ideologies relating to both education and gender were implicated in sustaining a school ethos which was essentially hostile to gender equality. In the following sections I explore the nature of these ideologies in creating an atmosphere in which it is difficult for positive attitudes towards gender equality to flourish.

RESISTANCE TO GENDER EQUALITY DERIVING FROM IDEOLOGIES OF SCHOOLING

Perhaps the major factor blinding teachers to the role of the school in the production of gender divisions within the curriculum was their overwhelming belief in environmental determinism. This led to scepticism about the power of school intervention strategies to have any impact on received views. At Greenhill, for instance, the WISE (Women Into Science and Engineering) initiative was remembered as having had very little effect. Mick Savage, a physics teacher at Greenhill, commented:

> Well, I'm rather suspicious of active policies. Things like this WISE, as far as I'm aware has been a tremendous flop. It's something the school should be aware of and make some efforts. But I think it's a much wider problem, it's society, the parents and television, the lot.

Mrs Alcott, a teacher of English at Greenhill in her late forties, was also puzzled by the lack of impact of such initiatives:

78

In feminist years they were almost urged to do science and technology by the media. There were programmes on the media saying, 'You can do this, you can build bridges, you can be a civil engineer. I remember that very attractive lady talking about bridge building, civil engineering, she was flying to Saudi and things like this. 'And you too can do this girls!' It doesn't seem to have any effect, does it?

She concluded that forces of socialisation, coupled with differences in development, were such powerful shaping forces that there was very little the school could do.

Another danger of socialisation theories is that they tend to blame girls and their parents for the perpetuation of sex-stereotyped attitudes rather than the school. Wolpe (1974) and Deem (1981) have explored the way in which the assumption of the differing educational needs of girls and boys was a central part of the thinking behind post-war educational reports such as the Norwood Report (1943), the Crowther Report (1959) and the Newsom Report (1963). Many teachers, however, seemed to think that girls themselves were entirely responsible for the gender-divided curriculum, and saw the problem entirely in terms of changing girls' attitudes instead of looking at the structures which produced those attitudes. Reynolds and Sullivan (1981) have argued that teachers' world views represent a significant barrier to social change, in that they emphasise the immense power of socialisation forces and deny that the school has any autonomy. Instead they argue that the school does have relative autonomy and is able to influence educational outcomes within certain structural parameters. There would appear to be much evidence to suggest that teachers' preference for explanations based on deterministic socialisation theories are likely to discourage them from putting radical policies into practice.

Although belief in environmental determinism was the most common educational ideology used to explain gender differentiation in the curriculum, genetic determinism also featured as a likely causal mechanism. There was a tendency to revert to this type of explanation when intervention strategies were perceived to have failed. Commenting on the failure of WISE, Mike Savage commented that this suggested to him that biological explanations were probably 'lurking in the background'. Kelly (1986) encountered similar reactions to the GIST project. Some teachers, she says, reacted to a report in *The Times Educational Supplement* that the project had failed to alter teachers' attitudes and behaviour by concluding that 'since GIST was unsuccessful in altering girls' options, the sex differences were clearly genetic, and no more action should be taken to counteract girls' underrepresentation in the physical sciences'. Kamin (1974) points out that the apparent failure of compensatory education programmes in the 1960s provided ammunition for those who favoured genetic explanations of the educational failure of black children. It is interesting to note that in the area of gender differentiation, the apparent failure of intervention programmes may be used to support theories of biological determinism.

Teachers' hostility towards equal opportunities policies was also rooted in their belief that the job of the school was to provide a value-free environment for pupils to exercise freedom of choice. Many teachers at both schools talked about the motivational advantages of allowing pupils this freedom, and clearly felt that there were advantages in getting pupils, rather than the school, to take responsibility for any limitations which might arise later.

Belief in the virtues of child-centred education was used to justify teachers' reluctance to pursue equal-opportunities policies actively. Normally associated with primary education (King, 1978; Carrington and Short, 1987), child-centred education encapsulates the idea that teachers should respond to children as unique individuals, and should avoid seeing them in collective terms. Some teachers at Greenhill and Millbridge found it quite confusing when asked to consider questions concerning the educational experience of girls and boys, and made comments such as:

> People are individuals. I don't even consciously think of male and female.
> (Mrs Lovell, head of house and teacher of English)

> I teach characters, not sexes.
> (Miss Maple, deputy head and teacher of maths)

Despite these utterances, classroom observation and other comments made by the same teachers showed that gender was a significant factor in their interaction with pupils. The ideology of child-centredness, however, discouraged them from recognising the salience of gender and acting on this awareness. This supports the findings of other commentators such as Kelly (1986) and Skelton and Hanson (1989). Kelly (1986) suggests that 'the strongly individualistic element in teachers' philosophy, with its emphasis on helping each child to fulfil her or his own potential, blinds them to their implications of their actions for groups.' Skelton's research on initial teacher training (Skelton and Hanson, 1989) suggests that the ideology of child-centred learning is particularly strong in the education of primary teachers, to the extent that even when teachers are aware of sex discrimination in their own lives, they abandon this knowledge when they assume their professional identity.

To summarise, then, in teachers' reluctance even to contemplate the implementation of anti-sexist measures, a number of educational ideologies seemed to be implicated. These were: their belief in the intractability of sex-role socialisation; an underlying and contradictory belief in biological determinism; and, finally, an adherence to child-centred ideology which insisted that pupils were capable of acting as autonomous agents in choosing subjects. This latter belief also discouraged teachers from looking at differences in outcomes for groups as opposed to individuals.

RESISTANCE TO GENDER-EQALITY POLICIES DERIVING FROM IDEOLOGIES OF FEMININITY

A very important influence on teachers' resistance to gender equality initiatives stemmed from their acceptance of traditional ideologies of femininity. These were revealed very clearly in the accounts which they gave of women's position within the school hierarchy. At both schools, women represented only a third of the teaching staff and very few occupied positions of responsibility, particularly on the academic side of the school. (The only female heads of department at both Greenhill and Millbridge were in French, home economics and secretarial studies.) At Greenhill, an HMI report produced in 1984 had commented on women's underrepresentation in positions of responsibility. At the end of the interviews I asked teachers for their view of why they thought this was the case.

At both schools, women's lack of power appeared to be so natural in many teachers' eyes as to be almost invisible. All the members of the hierarchy (heads, deputy heads and senior masters) said that promotion in teaching was purely on merit, and if there was any discrimination it was probably in favour of women. All the male teachers whom I interviewed accepted uncritically that since women elected voluntarily to have children, they thus make a clear statement about their lack of interest in a career. Mr Mottram, the head of physics at Millbridge, said:

> Women do break their service. They can hardly expect to pick up where they left off. Time's gone by and other people have taken their jobs . . . I wouldn't want my wife to go back to teaching when the children are 5 or 6 because I don't think she'd be able to do justice to both, being a mother and being a teacher . . . So in a sense I'd have thought that by having children my wife had compromised her teaching career, but I mean she's quite happy to do that.

This was a view repeated many times by male teachers, and reflects their belief that because women bear children it is obvious that they will be the ones to take full responsibility for their upbringing, and their position in the workforce must be regarded as of only secondary importance. Men's rightful position as breadwinners was similarly asserted. Mr Fison, a teacher of geography at Greenhill, had this to say:

> I have to send my wife out to work to survive. She brings up the child during the day and she has to work as a waitress in the evening. That hurts my sense of pride. Not that the work is belittling, but I should at the age of 31 with five years' industrial experience, a joint honours degree, be able to support a wife in a modest house and a child without being this close to the breadline.

Whilst complaints about teachers' low pay are obviously legitimate, Mr Fison justified his dissatisfaction by appealing to a belief in the family wage and the ideologies of masculinity and femininity which underpin it. The fact that this was a widely accepted view was illustrated by the case of Mrs Fleet, a PE teacher in her forties who had previously been head of department in a large London school. According to her, when she asked the headmaster for a scale point she had been promised for a job she was already doing, she had been told:

> What d'you want more money for? Your husband's got a perfectly good job. There are plenty of men with families to support who haven't got scale points.

A further aspect of teachers' ideology of femininity was revealed when male teachers discussed women who had been promoted. First of all, it was suggested that only single women could hope to be promoted:

> If you're a head of department, you've got to be prepared to work every evening of the week till about 9 or 10 o'clock in my area anyway. That means, as I read it, you've got to be a single woman.
> (Mr Straw, head of physics, Greenhill)

Having said this, the sexuality and essential femininity of such women was then called into question. Mr Lill at Greenhill, for instance, said that Joan Mitchem was a typical example of the sort of woman who got on in teaching. She was so totally committed to the job that 'The school's her husband.' Mr Mason, the deputy head, also said that the sort of women who got to the top in teaching were 'rather peculiar'. This was said in such a way as to imply that these women were probably lesbians. He also discussed in turn, in the middle of a tape-recorded interview, all the women who had been promoted, and claimed that in every case this was due to good fortune rather than ability. Cunnison (1985), in her study of a mixed-sex high school, similarly found that senior women were automatically assumed to be incompetent, and Woods (1979) describes the way in which both senior and younger women teachers were the constant butt of jokes about their appearance and mannerisms. As far as Mr Sluggett, a Greenhill history teacher, was concerned:

> women if they stay in teaching for a long time tend to become too wrapped up in it, too emotional and much too intense . . . I don't think they're necessarily as rounded as men.

From these comments of male teachers, it would appear that

women are caught up in a no-win situation. The only women who are fit to be promoted are non-mothers, who are by definition not proper women and who therefore should probably not be promoted anyway.

Young women teachers who sympathised with feminist ideas were highly critical of these sorts of assumptions. Miss Steiner, a probationary home economics teacher at Greenhill, was very angry that all women as potential mothers could be excluded from power:

> They say, 'What about a family?' and you have to say, 'No, I'm not interested at all.' You have to lie because otherwise they'll have somebody else. It makes me mad, it makes me really sick . . . It's just as likely that a man could have long-term absence from school.

Mrs Grayson, head of French at Greenhill, who had just come back from maternity leave, was also horrified at the attitudes of some male teachers:

> I mean quite unashamedly I've heard senior staff going through application forms saying, 'We need a man, we need a man, we need to balance this department for trips and excursions and that sort of thing.' And I've also seen them go through applications and say, 'This woman's been out of teaching for 6 years, she'll be very rusty.' I'm just horrified. Or else, 'This one's got young children, she's not very reliable, she'll be off every five minutes for chicken pox and all the rest of it, so she's not the sort of person we want,' which I think is terrible.

She herself said that she was struggling against the assumption that she would automatically give up work once she had children.

It was also very difficult for women teachers to organise support for themselves within the institution. Chris Grayson told me about the rapid rise and fall of the women's group at Greenhill, which had met once to discuss issues of common concern:

> It actually turned out to be a very constructive meeting and very interesting. We all talked about our own situations and the discrimination we were suffering in our own

situations and we learnt all sorts of things that we'd never dreamt of before, like allocation of scale points and the way people had been treated, and the headmaster was so furious about this insurrection in the ranks that he absolutely forbade anything like that ever to take place again. It was amazing. It was incredible, and the men on the staff were so upset about it. Yet really we weren't criticising them personally, we were just trying to assess our own situation. So it sort of petered out.

Ball (1987) quotes a similar incident in which a letter by female staff to the head of a mixed comprehensive school about the distribution of scale points was dismissed out of hand. In this case, the teachers were simply told that the right people had been given the jobs. It would appear that the micropolitics of schools make it very difficult for women successfully to challenge underlying ideologies of femininity.

Not all women, however, questioned the system of promotion and the notion of appropriate spheres of female activity which underlay it. Mrs Prior, a part-time teacher of physics at Greenhill, felt that there was no discrimination against women and they could get to the top just as easily as men if that was what they wanted. She saw her own decision to stop work with the birth of her children as entirely voluntary. Miss Bishop, head of secretarial studies, was adamant that women enjoyed full equality:

I certainly don't think there is any enforced keeping down of the female in this school. Far from it. I think that the women are encouraged to improve their own position and it's up to them if they take it up or not. I don't think they're kept down. In the final analysis they just haven't been as good.

It would seem, then, that women who perceive themselves as experiencing the effects of discrimination are most likely to question common assumptions about work and motherhood. Women who see themselves as having made a free choice to opt out of full-time teaching, or feel that they themselves have not been restricted as women, are more likely to endorse the view that promotion in teaching is purely on merit. These women were not against equal opportunities *per se*, but felt that no form of positive action was necessary to achieve this goal. The fact that women do not share a common perspective on male/female power relations clearly makes it difficult for them to unite in challenging their unequal position. In turn, the lack of a unified political stance makes it impossible for individual women to challenge injustice. Mrs Fleet said that when she was refused promotion on blatantly sexist grounds she had considered taking her case to the Equal Opportunities Commission (EOC), but the fact that it was upsetting her home life made her decide to drop it. Another woman, who had been promised a scale point which never materialised, said that she had decided not to push her case 'because it's important for the woman to be joyful in the home', but still wondered if she had made the right decision. Vera Chadwick's account (1989) of her protracted struggle to prove sex discrimination by Lancashire County Council suggests that these women might have been right in their judgement that the anguish of proceeding with the court action could outweigh the benefit of winning. Although Chadwick won her case, the effect on her personal and professional life was devastating and the damages she received were derisory.

To summarise, then, at both Millbridge and Greenhill schools the majority of male teachers and some women teachers subscribed to an ideology of femininity which represented all women as mothers or potential mothers, and therefore marginalised them as workers. The sexual status of women who somehow escaped these categories was called into question. This clearly compromised many teachers' commitment to anti-sexist measures. Even though they might pay lip-service to the notion of sexual equality, it was clear that their own position within the system of male/female power relations made them reluctant to question its underlying ideologies. To do so would cause them to examine critically their own relationships and family structures, and most were not prepared to do this. On the whole, it was more comfortable to believe that schools were value-free institutions and that any persistent inequalities might be laid at the door of parents, employers or the media. A minority of women recognised the existence of unequal power relations which affected not only themselves, but girls in the schools too. There are elements of my account of teachers' attitudes to gender equality which coincide with Connell's

(1986) analysis. He also recognises the fundamental split between teachers who nominally support equal opportunities and those who go further and endorse positive action. There is one marked difference between our findings, however. Whereas Connell 'came across some traces of those contradictory and almost comic figures, feminist men', (p. 187) these characters were notably lacking from the Westshire scene. Had the research been conducted a few years later, perhaps they might have arrived.

CONCLUSION

In this chapter I began by exploring the explanations offered by teachers for the production of a sex-stereotyped curriculum and the power which the school might have to challenge this outcome. Differences in teachers' response based on sex, age, position in the school hierarchy and subject taught were all explored. It was found that older teachers, who were all members of the hierarchy, believed in the overwhelming power of external socialising influences. According to them, the school was not at all involved in the channelling process and any attempt at positive discrimination to encourage girls into science and technology would be to undermine their freedom of choice. Younger teachers also emphasised the power of socialisation, but indicated that processes in the school were also involved, and a small number of feminist women teachers said that they thought the school could and should embark on a programme of positive action. There was some indication that teachers of maths and technology were less likely to favour active programmes to counter sex-stereotyping than teachers of arts and humanities.

In the second part of the chapter, the ideologies underpinning teachers' resistance to gender equality policies were further examined. These derived in part from the way in which teachers stressed socialisation rather than structural factors as the main cause of gender differentiation in school, and were willing to fall back on theories of biological determinism when positive action appeared to have failed. Child-centred ideologies which tend to discourage the examination of the position of particular groups further militated against the espousal of gender equality policies, as did a belief in the right of pupils to make free choices irrespective of context. Teachers' own position in the gender hierarchy was also implicated in their attitudes towards equal opportunities. As beneficiaries of male supremacy in the home and the school, there was little incentive for male teachers to reappraise their own attitudes. Only a few women recognised the structural nature of their subordinate status, making female solidarity very difficult to achieve. The instant suppression of women's attempts to establish a common understanding of their position indicated that this was seen as a serious threat to the institution.

Some commentators such as Connell (1986) have argued that whilst it has proved difficult for teachers to develop a unified stance, none the less 'feminism has had a significant impact on teachers' outlook; conversely, teachers have become an important vehicle for feminism' (p. 189). It would appear that feminist women teachers at Millbridge and Greenhill had encountered both opposition and apathy, although it might be argued that without their pressure the issue would not even have appeared on the agenda for discussion. What are the chances for more radical developments in the future? Where equal opportunities initiatives have been successful, this has often been due to concern at the grassroots among ordinary teachers rather than the fostering of equality policies from above (Weiner, 1986). If this is the case, then clearly work undertaken with beginning teachers to sensitise them to the issue is likely to be highly significant. Unfortunately, there is little research on initial teacher education and that which exists suggests that the current emphasis is not on the development of a critical social awareness, but on technical competence within the classroom (Skelton and Hanson, 1989; Menter, 1989). Menter argues that the guidelines produced by the Council for the Accreditation of Teacher Education (DES, 1984) serve to promote a 'fundamentally technicist view of teaching' in which teachers are certainly not encouraged to consider the implications of their actions for disadvantaged groups. Greater emphasis on students learning through school-based experience may also discourage the serious consideration of social justice issues, for if practising teachers consider these issues to be unimportant, there is every likelihood that student teachers will accept this view. Although initial teacher education may not have a marked effect on raising consciousness of gender issues, it would be wrong to be totally pessimistic. At both Millbridge and Greenhill, committed teachers, often spurred on by their own experience of discrimination, were struggling to keep the issue of gender equality alive. A point which emerges with great clarity from this research is that equal opportunities for girls cannot be tackled in isolation from power relations in the entire school. This was reflected most clearly in the position of women teachers. Unless the whole school ethos is one in which equality in its broadest sense flourishes, then piecemeal measures – such as displaying the occasional equal-opportunities poster – are unlikely to have any effect.

Part III

GIRLS, THEIR FAMILIES AND THE CONSTRUCTION OF FEMININITY

Part III suggested that the school organisation, whilst ostensibly supporting an equal-opportunities ethos, was instrumental in conveying highly traditional messages to pupils concerning appropriate curriculum territory for girls and boys. Teachers, who are of course the principal mediators of school ethos, displayed divergent approaches to issues of gender equality. Some male teachers were disparaging of feminism and the majority of both male and female teachers were lacking in commitment to equal-opportunities policies. A few women expressed enthusiastic support for anti-sexist measures. Part III explores the relationship between the gender codes of pupils, their parents and the school, questioning whether, contrary to teachers' expectations, positive attitudes to gender equality might be found in the culture of local families. I ask whether pupils and parents are implicated in perpetuating traditional gender divisions in the curriculum or whether their cultures may exert pressure for change against the more conservative influence of the school.

A theme which emerges strongly from the literature on pupils' culture is the changing nature of girls' construction of femininity. Until recently, most commentators have seen these sub-cultures as ultimately reproductive. Valli (1983), in her study of how American high-school students acquire their identity as future clerical workers, has suggested that there are three possible responses to the process of cultural transmission: acceptance, rejection and resistance. 'Acceptance of specific aspects of culture tends to occur when these messages are congruent with the past and the perceived future. Negotiation and resistance, both of which imply rejection of cultural messages and practices, occur when there is an element of incongruity, when the culture is experienced as imposed, when it does not fit with a sense of self.' Valli's young women were generally engaged in recreating their own subordinate culture, seeking protection from the demands of capital by refusing to define themselves as serious workers. This view of female sub-cultures in schools as both accommodating and resistant to certain aspects of male supremacy has also been advanced by writers such as McRobbie (1978) and Anyon (1983). However, as mentioned earlier, a rather different and challenging view has been put forward by Weis (1990). In her study of working-class American females in a former steel town with very high levels of male unemployment, she suggests that 'male and female identities are currently on a collision path: the boys envisioning male-dominant relations in the home and the girls exhibiting a challenge to these relations in some important ways' (p. 79). In her view, white working-class girls are now exhibiting a strong feminist consciousness and are resisting male attempts to control their lives in much the same way that young black women have asserted their autonomy. Connell (1986) also discusses the way in which changing patterns of gender relations are causing pupils to alter their relationships with teachers. When this is expressed as a greater commitment to academic study and pursuit of career, then this is highly acceptable to teachers. On the other hand, if girls' new self-confidence is expressed as rowdiness and sexual aggressive-ness, as it may well be by working-class girls, then this is clearly perceived as confusing and threatening (see Chapter 7 on patterns of classroom interaction).

It would appear, then, the girls' cultures are increasingly clashing with the more traditional gender codes of parents and teachers. The following chapters consider the extent to which girls and their families do indeed appear to support traditional gender divisions in the curriculum, or whether they are exhibiting a new critical consciousness. I explore their aware-ness of the ideas of the women's movement and the variety of responses to it which they make. The evidence suggests that the gender codes of girls and their families are characterised by both progressive and traditional elements with complex under-lying causes, including their personal biographies and class position. Overall, however, it is clear that women's and girls' understandings of femininity are increasingly critical and questioning, despite the fact that they may not as yet be taking action to bring about concrete changes in their lives.

5

PUPILS' UNDERSTANDINGS OF SCHOOL SUBJECTS

The recontextualisation of gender

INTRODUCTION

The analysis of the ideological messages conveyed by the school through its handling of option choice suggested that a process of selection was in operation. Although some parents felt the school played an unhelpful role in channelling pupils in particular directions, there was no evidence of pupils and parents challenging this position. The aim of this chapter is to consider pupils' accounts of why they made conventional subject choices, and the cultural meanings they attached to specific school subjects. The question which particularly concerned me was whether the tendency to make sex-stereotyped choices did in fact signal an uncritical acceptance of gender divisions in the wider society. In attempting to answer these questions, I draw on both quantitative and qualitative data.

PUPIL'S PERCEPTION OF THE GENDER APPROPRIATENESS OF PARTICULAR SUBJECTS

As I pointed out earlier, although the schools clearly suggested to pupils which courses might best suit their needs, they did not absolutely dictate their option choices. In order to examine pupils' perceptions of the gender appropriateness of particular subjects, an item on the questionnaire invited them to rate the subjects on the third-year curriculum with regard to their importance for girls and boys. Figures 5.1 and 5.2 reveal clear differences in the ratings of certain subjects for girls and boys, and, apart from a few details, closely similar patterns were seen in both schools. Subjects rated highly for both girls and boys were maths, careers and English. In other areas, large subject

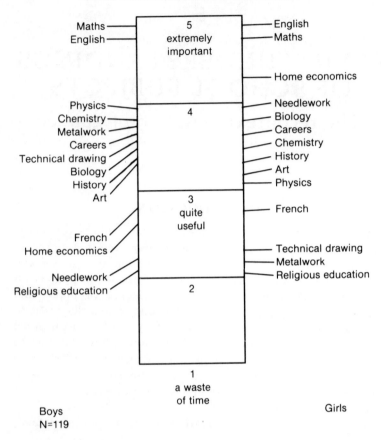

Figure 5.1 Millbridge pupils' mean ratings of subject importance for boys and girls

divisions emerged. Thus for boys, physics, chemistry, metalwork and technical drawing were rated highly. For girls, the surprising finding was that home economics and needlework were rated next in importance after English and maths. Biology was deemed the most important science subject for girls. Clearly, no ground had been gained at either school in establishing the gender neutrality of craft and technology subjects – metalwork and technical drawing were considered of least importance for girls and needlework was in a similar position for boys. Home economics was apparently considered safer territory for boys at Millbridge.

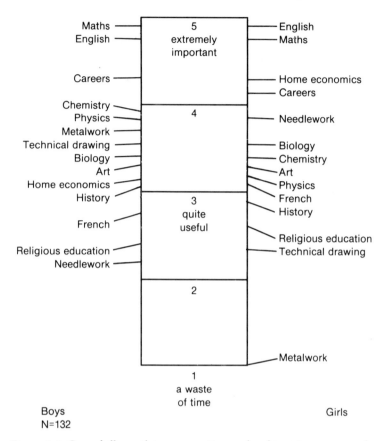

Figure 5.2 Greenhill pupils' mean ratings of subject importance for boys and girls

Statistical tests showed differences in the rating of craft and science subjects for boys and girls by all groups (boys, girls, working-class and middle-class pupils) were statistically significant (see Tables 5.1 and 5.2). Girls, then, were not inclined to view the curriculum in a less sex-stereotyped way than boys, nor working-class pupils than middle-class pupils. It is worth noting that pupils' assessment of the gender appropriateness of science subjects in particular was not simply a reflection of their perception of difficulty. For instance, boys appeared to enjoy physics more than girls (Tables 5.3 and 5.4) but the majority of both boys and girls named it as the most

Table 5.1 Wilcoxon test applied to Millbridge pupils' perception of subject importance for girls and boys

Subject assessed for boys and girls	Group doing the assessing					Sex for whom subject rated more important
	All pupils	Girls	Boys	Working class	Middle class	
French	ns	ns	ns	ns	ns	—
Physics	$z = -6.735$ $p < .001$	$z = -6.703$ $p < .001$	$z = -4.372$ $p < .001$	$z = -4.987$ $p < .001$	$z = -4.015$ $p < .001$	Boys
Chemistry	$z = -3.792$ $p < .001$	$z = -2.978$ $p < .01$	$z = -2.379$ $p < .05$	$z = -3.650$ $p < .001$	ns	Boys
Biology	$z = -1.913$ $p < .05$	ns	ns	ns	$z = -1.988$ $p < .05$	Girls
Technical drawing	$z = -7.253$ $p < .001$	$z = -5.336$ $p < .001$	$z = -4.937$ $p < .001$	$z = -5.561$ $p < .001$	$z = -4.703$ $p < .001$	Boys
Metalwork	$z = -7.722$ $p < .001$	$z = -5.777$ $p < .001$	$z = -5.159$ $p < .001$	$z = -5.968$ $p < .001$	$z = -4.937$ $p < .001$	Boys
Home economics	$z = -7.630$ $p < .001$	$z = -5.711$ $p < .001$	$z = -5.191$ $p < .001$	$z = -6.154$ $p < .001$	$z = -4.563$ $p < .001$	Girls
Needlework	$z = -7.541$ $p < .001$	$z = -5.579$ $p < .001$	$z = -5.220$ $p < .001$	$z = -6.108$ $p < .001$	$z = -4.453$ $p < .001$	Girls
Art	$z = -1.988$ $p < .05$	ns	ns	ns	ns	

Table 5.2 Wilcoxon test applied to Greenhill pupils' perception of subject importance for girls and boys

Subject assessed for boys and girls	Group doing the assessing					Sex for whom subject rated more important
	All pupils	Girls	Boys	Working class	Middle class	
French	z = -3.708 p < .001	ns	z = -3.421 p < .001	z = -3.163 p < .01	ns	Girls
Physics	z = -6.382 p < .001	z = -4.519 p < .001	z = -4.525 p < .001	z = -4.783 p < .001	z = -2.073 p < .05	Boys
Chemistry	z = -3.125 p < .01	ns	z = -2.874 p < .01	z = -2.485 p < .05	ns	Boys
Biology	ns	ns	ns	ns	ns	
Technical drawing	z = -7.448 p < .001	z = -5.160 p < .001	z = -5.373 p < .001	z = -5.220 p < .001	z = -3.180 p < .001	Boys
Metalwork	z = -8.284 p < .001	z = -6.031 p < .001	z = -5.711 p < .001	z = -5.777 p < .001	z = -3.621 p < .001	Boys
Home economics	z = -7.334 p < .001	z = -4.764 p < .001	z = -5.511 p < .001	z = -5.228 p < .001	z = -3.059 p < .01	Girls
Needlework	z = -7.689 p < .001	z = -4.955 p < .001	z = -5.841 p < .001	z = -5.099 p < .001	z = -3.724 p < .001	Girls
Art	ns	ns	ns	ns	ns	

Table 5.3 Percentages of girls, boys, working-class and middle-class pupils naming particular subjects as the ones they enjoyed most, and results of the chi-square test for Millbridge pupils

Subject	% Girls	% Boys	Results of chi-square test	% Working class	% Middle class	Results of chi-square test
English	24.6	11.1	ns	20.5	14.6	ns
Maths	7.7	24.1	$\chi^2 = 4.955$ df1 p < .05	17.9	9.8	ns
Physical science	6.2	22.2	$\chi^2 = 5.236$ df1 p < .05	7.7	24.4	$\chi^2 = 5.083$ df1 p < .05
Biology	10.8	13.0	ns	15.4	4.9	ns
Humanities	55.4	24.1	$\chi^2 = 10.680$ df1 p < .01	42.3	39.0	ns
Art	21.5	18.5	ns	23.1	14.6	ns
Technical crafts	4.6	35.2	$\chi^2 = 16.318$ df1 p < .001	16.7	22.0	ns
Domestic crafts	15.4	1.9	$\chi^2 = 4.926$ df1 p < .05	9.0	9.8	ns
Languages	12.3	3.7	ns	6.4	12.2	ns

Notes: Physical science = physics and chemistry; Humanities = history and geography; Technical crafts = technical drawing, metalwork and woodwork; Domestic crafts = home economics and needlework; Art = pottery and art; Languages = French and German

N = 119

Table 5.4 Percentages of girls, boys, working-class and middle-class pupils naming particular subjects as the ones they enjoyed most, and results of the chi-square test for Greenhill pupils

Subject	% Girls	% Boys	Results of chi-square test	% Working class	% Middle class	Results of chi-square test
English	29.7	13.2	$\chi^2 = 4.400$ df1 $p < .05$	16.7	33.3	ns
Maths	7.8	10.3	ns	9.1	7.4	ns
Physical science	9.4	38.2	$\chi^2 = 13.422$ df1 $p < .001$	19.7	33.3	ns
Biology	14.1	14.7	ns	9.1	25.9	ns
Humanities	34.4	19.1	ns	30.3	22.2	ns
Art	26.6	11.8	$\chi^2 = 3.788$ df1 $p < .05$	10.6	22.2	ns
Technical crafts	1.6	17.6	$\chi^2 = 7.880$ df1 $p < .01$	12.1	3.7	ns
Domestic crafts	25.0	2.9	$\chi^2 = 11.813$ df1 $p < .001$	15.2	18.5	ns
Languages	14.1	4.4	ns	7.6	11.1	ns

Notes: Physical science = physics and chemistry; Humanities = history and geography; Technical crafts = technical drawing, metalwork and woodwork; Domestic crafts = home economics and needlework; Art = pottery and art; Languages = French and German

N = 132

difficult subject (Table 5.5). This suggests that empathy with the culture of a subject is very important in convincing a pupil that the intellectual energy demanded represents a worthwhile investment.

A further interesting point to emerge from this analysis was the tendency of boys to emphasise the importance of stereotypically feminine subjects for girls and vice versa (Tables 5.6 and 5.7). For example, at Millbridge, physics for boys was rated significantly higher by girls than by boys. At both schools, home economics and needlework for girls were rated higher by. boys than girls. In these subject areas, then, it appeared that both girls and boys were anxious to maintain gender boundaries for the opposite sex.

Overall, despite the schools' claim that subject choice was a matter of pupils exercising free choice in a neutral environment, this was in reality far from the truth. Rather, many subjects appeared to carry powerful messages concerning their gender appropriateness. To investigate how and why these subjects became so closely associated with one sex or the other and whether Westshire girls entirely subscribed to the very traditional gender codes which their subject choice and assessment of subject importance indicated, I turned to data from interviews and observation.

THE CONSTRUCTION OF GENDER IDENTITY AND THE MAINTENANCE OF GENDER BOUNDARIES

Feminist writers on the subject of gender and the curriculum have drawn our attention to the way in which adolescent pupils are actively involved in the construction and maintenance of gender identities (Kelly, 1987; Measor, 1983). Arnot (1984) discusses the way in which pupils recontextualise externally received models of masculinity and femininity into more school-based forms, such as 'doing science' or playing football in the case of boys. One of the aims of the interviews was to consider whether such a process was at work, and if so why pupils should be engaged in such an enterprise. To gain access to this information, I asked pupils why they had chosen some subjects and rejected others. The pupils whom I quote here were from Greenhill.

One of the first points to emerge was the way in which girls' dislike of physics and technical subjects was rooted in a firm belief that there was something intrinsically masculine and therefore alien about these subjects. Physics was singled out for particular loathing by both working-class and middle-class girls who described it as boring and irrelevant. Bernadette Coles, whose father was a doctor, had this to say about it:

> It's a bit stupid really. You're not going to want to know how magnets [said with contempt] work. Unless you want to make something that works on magnets. In a factory, say, you're not going to need to know how electro-whatsits . . . er magnets . . . work. Circuits and all that. Boring.

'Boring' was a word used over and over again to express their

Table 5.5 Millbridge pupils' assessment of the most difficult and easiest subjects (broken down by sex and class of pupil)

| | Total | *Sex of pupil* | | *Class of pupil* | |
		Boys	*Girls*	*Working class*	*Middle class*
Subject rated most difficult					
Physics	50 (43.5)	17 (33.0)	33 (51.6)	34 (45.9)	16 (39.0)
Chemistry	27 (23.5)	8 (15.7)	19 (29.7)	18 (24.3)	9 (22.0)
Maths	18 (15.7)	12 (23.5)	6 (9.4)	11 (14.9)	7 (17.1)
History	9 (7.9)	7 (13.7)	2 (3.1)	6 (8.1)	3 (7.1)
English	8 (7.0)	5 (9.8)	3 (4.7)	4 (5.4)	4 (9.8)
Biology	3 (2.6)	2 (3.9)	1 (1.6)	1 (1.4)	2 (4.9)
Totals	115 (100)	51 (100)	64 (100)	74 (100)	41 (100)
Subjects rated easiest					
History	34 (29.6)	11 (21.6)	23 (35.9)	24 (32.4)	10 (24.4)
Biology	25 (21.7)	11 (21.6)	14 (21.9)	15 (20.3)	10 (24.4)
English	23 (20.0)	10 (19.6)	13 (20.3)	14 (18.9)	9 (22.0)
Maths	18 (15.7)	8 (15.7)	10 (15.6)	13 (17.6)	5 (12.2)
Physics	10 (8.7)	6 (11.8)	4 (6.3)	6 (8.1)	4 (9.8)
Chemistry	5 (4.3)	5 (9.1)	0 (0.0)	2 (2.7)	3 (7.3)
Totals	115 (100)	51 (100)	64 (100)	74 (100)	41 (100)

Note: Whole numbers are shown first, followed by percentages in parentheses

feelings about physics, and it held a wealth of meaning from disinterest to hostility and frustration. Of course there is the possibility that girls were exaggerating their loathing of physics to impress me or each other, although their mass exodus from the subject suggests that this was not the case. Even if an element of sensationalism had been involved, this would have been interesting in itself since boys generally expressed liking of the subject. This, too, might not have been a true reflection of their feelings in all cases, given the difficulty many admitted to experiencing.

Technical subjects were also often seen by the girls as irrelevant to their likely future. Jackie Alcott, whose father worked in a building society, was asked whether she thought it would be a good thing if more girls did technical subjects. She replied:

Table 5.6 Mann–Whitney U test applied to differences between Millbridge girls and boys and working-class and middle-class pupils in their assessment of the importance of a subject for a given sex

Groups whose assessment is compared (subject and sex)	Girls/boys	Working class/ middle class
French – boys	u = 970.0, z = −3.787, p < .001 G	ns
French – girls	u = 919.5, z = −3.524, p < .001 G	ns
Physics – boys	u = 1242.5, z = −2.006, p < .05 G	ns
Physics – girls	ns	ns
Chemistry – boys	ns	ns
Chemistry – girls	ns	u = 1023.0, z = −2.601, p < .01 M
Biology – boys	ns	ns
Biology – girls	ns	ns
TD – boys	ns	ns
TD – girls	ns	ns
Metalwork – boys	ns	ns
Metalwork – girls	ns	u − 1079.0, z = −1.979, p < .05 M
HE – boys	ns	ns
HE – girls	u = 1151.0, z = −2.243, p < .05 B	ns
Needlework – boys	ns	ns
Needlework – girls	u = 964.0, z = −3.366, p < .001 B	ns
History – boys	u = 1221.0, z = −2.297, p < .05 G	ns
History – girls	ns	ns
RE – boys	u = 1092.0, z = − 3.016, p < .01 G	ns
RE – girls	u = 1015.0, z = −2.994, p < .01 G	ns
Art – boys	u = 1184.0, z = −2.200, p < .05 G	ns
Art – girls	ns	ns

Notes: (1) G = subject for given sex assessed as more important by girls; B = subject for given sex assessed as more important by boys; M = subject for given sex assessed as more important by middle-class pupils; W = subject for given sex assessed as more important by working-class pupils. (2) TD = technical drawing; HE = home economics; RE = religious education

Table 5.7 Mann–Whitney U test applied to differences between Greenhill girls and boys and working-class and middle-class pupils in their assessment of the importance of a subject for a given sex

Groups whose assessment is compared (subject and sex)	Girls/boys	Working class/ middle class
French – boys	ns	u= 499.0, z = −2.561, p < .01 M
French – girls	ns	ns
Physics – boys	ns	ns
Physics – girls	u = 1367.5, z = −2.048, p <.05 B	u = 455.5, z = −3.060, p < .01 M
Chemistry – boys	ns	ns
Chemistry – girls	ns	u = 534.5, z = −2.135, p < .05 M
Biology – boys	ns	ns
Biology – girls	ns	ns
TD – boys	ns	u = 536.0, z = −1.987, p < .05 W
TD – girls	ns	ns
Metalwork – boys	ns	u = 528.5, z = −2.165, p < .05 W
Metalwork – girls	ns	ns
HE – boys	ns	ns
HE – girls	u = 1239.0, z = −2.729, p < .01 B	u = 421.5, z = −3.389, p < .01 W
Needlework – boys	u = 1349.0, z = −2.570, p < .01 G	ns
Needlework – girls	u = 1283.0, z = −2.105, p < .05 B	u = 473.5, z = −2.570, p < .01 W
History – boys	ns	ns
History – girls	ns	ns
RE – boys	ns	ns
RE – girls	ns	ns
Art – boys	u = 1427.0, z = −1.999, p < .05 G	ns
Art – girls	ns	ns

Notes: (1) G = subject for given sex assessed as more important by girls; B = subject for given sex assessed as more important by boys; M = subject for given sex assessed as more important by middle-class pupils; W = subject for given sex assessed as more important by working-class pupils. (2) TD = technical drawing; HE = home economics; RE = religious education

I don't know. It depends what you're going to be when you leave school. If you're just going to be a normal housewife or just do a normal job it's not worth it, is it?

Girls even expressed these views when their experience of the division of labour in their own homes might have led them to rethink. Yvonne Roundhay, a working-class girl, and Marie Painter, a middle-class girl, had this discussion of why boys got on better with physics than girls:

> *Yvonne*: Well, this electricity bit, the boys are more into it than what we are, like we were doing a plug weren't we, but we already know how to do it and put a fuse in if we really had to. I know my Dad can't do it. My Mum can but my Dad can't.
> *Marie*: Yes, my Mum usually does more stuff around the house than my Dad does.

Although Yvonne's and Marie's families did not maintain rigid gender boundaries in the division of household chores, they nevertheless designated physics a male subject because of its concern with subjects which they regarded as masculine, such as electricity. This suggests that designation of school subjects as male or female is not a simple reflection of parental beliefs and activities.

THE USE OF BOYS AS A NEGATIVE REFERENCE GROUP

The process of recontextualisation appeared to be linked with girls' use of boys as a negative reference group in the establishment of gender boundaries. Since physics and technical subjects were clearly taken by boys and were concerned with male interests, the assumption was made that moving into such an area posed a threat to female gender identity. Yvonne Roundhay felt that she would not want to take a technical craft subject because of the need to conform with male standards of behaviour that this would necessitate:

> *Yvonne*: Well if you are going to work with the boys, I think you have to act like boys as well a bit. You have got to go along with their stupid pranks.

Girls who ventured into male areas of the curriculum were seen by other girls to be risking contamination, and were described in a range of negative terms, one of which was 'brainy'. This conversation between Cathy Deare, Chloe Gover and Judith Bargate shows how a girl's attractiveness and sexuality might be called into question through her association with masculine areas of the curriculum:

> *Chloe*: My mum says [mimics mum's voice] 'You stick at it and you'll find out it's really interesting'. She's weird. Must be. Physics. Nobody likes physics.
> *Cathy*: There's this girl who likes physics and she's weird.
> *Judith*: Just because you don't like her.
> *Cathy*: No, she's weird because she likes physics. She even looks weird. Her brother's a weirdo as well.
> *Chloe*: If she likes physics she must be different. She enjoys doing things that hurt people doesn't she?

Of course, it may be that the girl in question is strange in some way, but liking physics is clearly seen as a central part of her deviance from the normal boundaries of femininity. Comments about boys in domestic craft subjects also suggested that by entering these areas their sexuality was likely to be called into question. According to the girls, a boy doing home economics would be regarded as 'a bit of a pufffter' by his peers. Generally, girls were keen at least in principle on the idea of boys doing home economics, but textiles was beyond the pale:

> *Pat Rennick*: I reckon it's all right doing cooking 'cos I know a boy who wants to be a chef and he's taking it. I don't know about textiles. I mean there is men designers but it's a bit puffy. It's all right with cooking 'cos they've got to learn how to cook when they leave home.

Boys' comments indicated that they were also active in maintaining the masculine identity of science. A few said that it would be a good thing if there were more girls in these areas of the curriculum, but the majority attributed girls' absence from physics and technical craft to their lack of mental ability or physical strength. One boy said that the only girls who would do metalwork or woodwork were the ones who did not care about their appearance, and another said that he could only tolerate girls in these areas if they did not think they were better than the boys.

It would appear, then, that in the same way as boys in co-educational schools may use girls as their negative reference groups (Shaw, 1980), girls may use boys in a similar manner. Kohlberg (1966) argues that 6-year-old children do not have the idea of gender constancy and believe that, for example, a boy may change sex by dressing like a girl. Later on, he says, children learn the difference between biological and social characteristics, and therefore become less anxious about gender deviance. Evidence presented here suggests that many of these pupils believed that by venturing into non-traditional areas of the curriculum, both boys and girls compromised their gender identity. It may well be that, at this particular point of their development, adolescents experience anxiety about their sexuality, and use option choice as a means of consolidating their sense of masculinity or femininity.

MAINTENANCE OF FEMALE SANCTUARIES WITHIN A MALE CULTURE

Girls' resistance to participation in masculine areas of the curriculum was not only to do with their definition of themselves in negative relationship to males. It was also to do with their positive identification with other girls and women. The atmosphere in physics lessons was described by many girls as uncomfortable and alienating. For Yvonne Roundhay, the physics teacher's form of humour seemed to exemplify a particularly male way of relating which she found childish and irritating:

> *Marie Painter*: He always tries to embarrass you, doesn't he?'
> *Yvonne Roundhay*: He said to me, 'You've got your left finger up your left nose and your right finger up your right nose' and I said, 'I've only got one nose.' He's really annoying, I don't like him. He mucks around and jokes around and then he blames it on us.

By way of contrast, lessons which were taken exclusively by girls were generally described enthusiastically. Here, it seemed, girls were able to establish a much more equal relationship with women teachers based on common interests. Pat Rennick, for instance, described how well she got on with her secretarial studies teacher:

> *Pat*: She's just like your mum . . . She talks to you as if you're her daughter or something.
>
> *S.R.*: Is there a nice atmosphere in that group?
>
> *Pat*: Yeah. She joins in all our conversations and it goes right off the subject on to boys and that. And her little boy. Then she says, 'Oh, we must get back on to the lesson'.

It was in subjects like this that girls were able to enjoy their friendships uninterrupted, which played a very important part in their lives:

> *Jackie Rivers*: It's important to have a good relationship with your friends. Being able to trust them – just being good friends.
>
> *Jan Ellis*: At least you can have a permanent friend then, because with boys you're always chopping and changing.

The need for girls to find a place for themselves in the school where they could enjoy each other's company away from the presence of boys was strongly illustrated by their description of the sexual harrassment which was an everyday part of school experience. Pat Rennick and Janet Fields described the sort of interaction which was quite common:

> *Pat*: They used to call me dog, and when I was going out with one of their mates called Sean they used to go on to me like mad. Kevin can be a right pig. He comes up to you and says things like, 'Are you a virgin?'. Really horrible. We were standing round in the snow and these boys walked by and called 'Ruff' like that, just like a dog. If we were to say the same to them they'd get mad.

Several girls made comments about the boys' emotional immaturity, such as:

> I don't think they've got much feelings at the moment.
>
> (Jackie Rivers)

I think really girls have got more feeling than boys.

(Debbie Dowland)

This sort of sexually derogatory name-calling is very much like that found by Cowie and Lees (1981) in a London comprehensive school, and from the accounts of girls themselves and classroom observation it appeared commonplace at Millbridge and Greenhill. (See Chapter 8 for further discussion of teachers' manipulation of gender codes in maintaining classroom control.) In explaining why they chose to reject some subjects, a number of girls made it clear that this had to do with an atmosphere of underlying sexuality which characterised the lessons of some male teachers. In view of this, girls felt attracted to areas of the curriculum where they were more likely to have female teachers. Susan Piper described one experience thus:

> We've got a bloke teaching us English at the moment and he's very peculiar. He says things to us like, 'Where d'you get your top from?' and 'I like your skirt.' He doesn't say it to any one else. It makes me feel yuck and every time he comes near my desk I get up and walk away.

It is interesting that Susan was one of the girls who sometimes deliberately adopted exaggerated forms of femininity to challenge teachers' authority in the classroom, including, on occasion, the use of sexual joking (see Chapter 7). Her behaviour might thus be regarded as confusing and contradictory, and a male teacher responding to her in a sexual way might well argue that he was merely reacting to messages coming from her in the first place. Kelly *et al.* (1985), writing about the GIST project, notes that 'many of the sex-differentiated interactions that we observed originated not with the teacher but with the pupil', and it was partly for this reason that 'teachers remained unwilling to see their own part in either the problem or the solution' (p. 140). This seems to me to be a very important point. Obviously, teachers bear the major responsibility for the nature of classroom interaction, and so it is important for them to ensure that the way in which they relate to girls in the class is not likely to be damaging to the pupil's intellectual development. To understand what is happening within the classroom clearly demands careful thought and analysis, and unless teachers are prepared to engage in this sort of discussion they may well continue to argue that sex differentiation in classroom interaction is nothing to do with them.

GIRLS' OPPOSITION TO OVERT DISCRIMINATION

Male culture, then, dominated not only the physical space of the school, but also the atmosphere of many lessons. As a reaction to this, girls tended to be attracted to all-female areas of the curriculum where they did not feel threatened. They also felt the need to distance themselves from boys' behaviour and the subject areas which they felt epitomised masculinity. If this were the total picture, we would be left with the rather depressing impression that Westshire girls were quite accepting of gender divisions in the curriculum and the wider society, but this would only be a partial picture. Although the process of gender construction involved the policing of gender boundaries, another very different theme could be detected in what the girls had to say about the school's more blatant attempts to enforce traditional gender divisions in the curriculum. This involved a highly critical awareness of the unfairness of gender divisions and a sense of outrage at how this injustice affected them on a personal level. Jan Ellis, for instance, said that in the interests of equality all craft subjects should be taken by both boys and girls :

> I think boys should learn to cook 'cos they seem to think, 'Oh, girls can do it, leave them to it'. They expect girls to do everything. And I think girls should be able to do woodwork and metalwork.

Despite believing this in principle, however, she had no intention of actually doing these subjects herself, thus illustrating the gap between supporting feminist principles in theory but shrinking from putting them into practice. Another example of this was an incident which had occurred at Greenhill Middle School and which was commented on by almost all the girls. They had apparently not been allowed to do metalwork at this school because it was taught at Wellington Army Camp which, according to Laura Sayers, was considered an unsuitable place for them to be:

> The army people were swearing and they said it was not a girls' language. So the girls weren't allowed to do it. It was a bit daft.

Yvonne Roundhay said that she had been very annoyed at this and had gone to the head of year to complain, because even though she did not want to do it, it was wrong for her to be excluded.

There was, then, a conflict here which for many of the girls remained unresolved. On the one hand, they disliked the personal experience of discrimination and protested about it, but on the other hand they felt that they had an interest in maintaining a distance between themselves and the boys. The experience of the occasional girl who did take a technical craft subject tended to discourage others from following her example. Sian Roberts commented that she had not at all enjoyed being the only girl in a class of boys. 'The more you have to work with them the less you like them' was her comment. It was interesting that even though most of the girls said that they were in favour of boys doing home economics, they complained about the disruptive influence of the two boys who were in their class, and said they thought it was a waste of time for them to be there. Had the process of crossing gender boundaries been easier, then perhaps more would have risked it.

GIRLS' SURVIVAL STRATEGIES IN MALE SUBJECT AREAS

One of the few girls at Greenhill who actually said she liked physics and thought she was good at it was Catherine Thomas, and it was clear that she was challenging the traditional construction of femininity in many areas of her life. Despite being small and rather round herself, she resented girls' exclusion from various sports and had taken up weightlifting:

> The first week at weighlifting I was told by the boys, 'You can't do that, girls aren't allowed to do that.' Rubbish . . . But you don't half get some posers going, they really do

think they're so strong and you look at them and you think, 'Oh God, I don't know what they see in theirselves' when you see them struggling to lift the bar. Boys really do think they're so strong. I'd rather challenge them, and they don't like that, girls especially challenging them to do something.

As we have seen, girls who crossed gender boundaries were likely to be treated with hostility by their peers, but Catherine had developed a number of strategies for dealing with this potential rejection. In lessons, she was always cheeky to teachers, and was regarded as something of an entertainment. She also helped other pupils with their work, and she made it very clear that her loyalties lay with other girls:

If there was a fight between a girl and a boy and I knew the boy and I liked him moderately and I hated the girl, I think I'd still side with the girl.

Susan Burton at Millbridge, who was hoping to take three sciences at 'A' level, had a similarly calculated strategy. She said she had been teased and called a fool by other girls for taking sciences and languages, but established her credentials as one of the girls by the way she dressed. For school, she said, her hair had to be 'sprayed solid', her skirt short and sometimes worn with fishnet tights, large dangly earrings and rather more make-up than was permitted. Mrs Burton told me how the physics teacher had at first regarded Susan as an empty-headed girl but had subsequently been forced to change his mind.

Mrs B: They look quite with it, don't they, and the teacher doesn't always realise that under that there is some intelligence. I'm sure that happens. You come in with funky hair and dangly earrings and they think you're really way out. You look fairly frivolous. It's only when they start to talk to you that they realise there's something there.

Susan clearly enjoyed playing on the contradictory messages she projected:

But that's their fault for taking your appearance so seriously. They're creeping round me something chronic now.

CONCLUSIONS

Both patterns of subject choice and pupils' views of the gender appropriateness of particular subjects suggested that to some extent they shared the conservative perspective of the schools with regard to gender codes. Talking to girls and observing them in classrooms provided clues as to why many appeared unwilling to challenge the status quo. It appeared that, in the process of establishing their own gender identity, girls were using subject boundaries to mark out female from male terrain. Subjects identified as masculine tended to be seen as unattractive, uninteresting and suitable only for those who could be labelled 'weird'. Curriculum content and the behaviour of boys and male teachers all served to encourage girls to encapsulate themselves within safe and known boundaries. However, it was not simply the case that girls were the victims of the kind of aggressive masculinity described by Mahony (1985). Many actively preferred single-sex classes and women teachers and chose subjects accordingly. It would also be incorrect to assume that girls were opposed to the principles of gender equality. Indeed, many were outraged when they felt the schools were actively discriminating against them in debarring them from certain curricular areas. This suggests that if schools were to work closely with girls in encouraging their desire for social justice, there might be considerable hope for success in altering the gender balance of the curriculum. As it was, the few brave souls who did make non-traditional subject choices were given little support in coming to terms with their gender identity in a hostile environment. It is a tribute to their creativity and resourcefulness that they managed to survive as well as they did.

6

PUPILS' EXPECTATIONS OF THE FUTURE

Radical and conservative visions

INTRODUCTION

The previous chapter attempted to shed some light on why many girls made sex-stereotyped option choices and regarded subjects in key areas of the curriculum as representing either male or female terrain. The reasons were complex, hinging on pupils' desire to establish their own gender identity as well as protecting themselves from an unsympathetic male culture. The strategies employed by some girls who did successfully survive in male areas of the curriculum were touched upon. An interesting finding was that whilst girls felt that they had the right to stake out the boundaries of their own learning experiences, they were deeply resentful when they felt that the school was unjustly excluding them, and, in general terms, were in favour of the principle of equal opportunities. This chapter further explores these conflicting aspects of girls' culture in the context of their expectations of their future lives in the public sphere of education and work and the private sphere of the home and family. Again, I discuss data of both a quantitative and qualitative nature in order to represent the picture in as much detail as possible.

EDUCATIONAL AND OCCUPATIONAL ASPIRATIONS

As noted in Chapter 4, a number of teachers communicated to pupils their belief that gender inequality in school and the wider society was essentially caused by girls' lack of ambition and ability. In order to assess whether there were measurable differences between girls and boys in these respects, items on the questionnaires distributed at Millbridge and Greenhill asked pupils when they expected to leave full-time education and the jobs they were hoping to do when they left school. There was no association between sex and expected length of pupil's full-time education nor between desired job and sex for either Millbridge or Greenhill pupils (see Tables 6.1 – 6.4). Girls were certainly not keen to leave school earlier than boys and they were as likely as boys to aspire to higher levels of employment. This suggests that a deficit model, which blames girls' lower status in the labour market on their lack of ambition, is inaccurate. However, what is noticeable is that the actual jobs aspired to by girls and boys were highly sex-segregated. Thus, in the area of professional work, girls said they would like to be teachers, nurses or social workers whilst boys saw themselves as scientists, computer programmers or pilots. Outside the professional sphere, many girls continued to aspire to office work, whereas boys saw themselves in the future in skilled trades such as an electrician or a plumber. The problem which needed to be explained, then, was not why girls were failing educationally nor why they were uninterested in the world of work. Rather, it was why so many continued to be drawn towards traditional areas of women's work character-ised by low pay, low status and lack of advancement. The following section explores some of the reasons given by work-ing-class girls for their decision to take up secretarial studies.

CONFUSION AND CONFORMITY – THE CASE OF SECRETARIAL STUDIES

In this section I explore the reasons given by girls for opting into secretarial studies, since these illustrate the profound ambiguities and contradictions underlying apparently con-formist decisions. One might expect girls opting into secretarial studies to have fairly traditional attitudes with regard to appropriate work and behaviour patterns for women and men. However, as the following discussion reveals, they were far from passively accepting a subordinate role and there was evidence of opposition to the dominant ideology of femininity. This mixture of accommodation and resistance also character-ised the young women training as clerical workers in Valli's (1986) study, discussed at the beginning of Part III.

116

Table 6.1 Expected level of full-time education of Millbridge pupils (by sex, class and achievement) and results of chi-square test

	Easter leavers	Leave with CSEs and 'O' levels	Technical college	Leave with 'A' levels	Higher education	Totals
Working class	18 (23.4)	26 (33.8)	16 (20.8)	11 (14.3)	6 (7.8)	77 (100)
Middle class	2 (5.1)	12 (30.8)	5 (12.8)	1 (2.6)	19 (48.7)	39 (100)
Total	20	38	21	12	25	116 (100)
Girls	9 (14.1)	19 (29.7)	11 (17.2)	8 (12.5)	17 (26.6)	64 (100)
Boys	11 (21.2)	19 (36.5)	10 (19.2)	4 (7.7)	8 (15.4)	52 (100)
Total	20	38	21	12	25	116 (100)
High achievement	3 (10.3)	8 (27.6)	4 (13.8)	2 (6.9)	12 (41.4)	29 (100)
Above average achievement	3 (9.4)	7 (21.9)	7 (21.9)	5 (15.6)	10 (31.2)	32 (100)
Below average achievement	7 (18.4)	16 (42.1)	8 (21.1)	4 (10.5)	3 (7.9)	38 (100)
Low achievement	7 (41.2)	7 (41.2)	2 (11.8)	1 (5.9)	0	17 (100)
Total	20	38	21	12	25	116 (100)

Variables	Groups	Results of chi-square test
Level of education by sex	All pupils	ns
Level of education by class	All pupils	$\chi^2 = 29.534$ df4 p < .0001
Level of education by achievement	All pupils	$\chi^2 = 26.675$ df12 p < .01
	Girls	ns
	boys	ns
	Working class	ns
	Middle class	$\chi^2 = 27.782$ df12 p < .01

Note: Whole numbers are shown first, followed by percentages in parentheses

Table 6.2 Expected level of full-time education of Greenhill pupils (by class, sex and achievement) and results of chi-square test

	Easter leavers	Leave with CSEs and 'O' levels	Technical college	Leave with 'A' levels	Higher education	Totals
Working class	7 (11.5)	40 (65.6)	3 (4.9)	10 (16.4)	1 (1.6)	70 (100)
Middle class	0	5 (19.2)	1 (3.8)	10 (38.5)	10 (38.5)	26 (100)
Total	7	45	4	20	11	96 (100)
Girls	5 (9.4)	30 (56.6)	4 (7.5)	6 (11.5)	8 (15)	53 (100)
Boys	5 (8.1)	29 (46.8)	2 (3.2)	15 (24.2)	11 (17.7)	62 (100)
Total	10	59	6	21	19	115 (100)
High achievement	0	1 (6.7)	0	7 (46.7)	7 (46.7)	15 (100)
Above average achievement	1 (2.0)	21 (41.2)	4 (7.8)	15 (29.4)	10 (19.6)	51 (100)
Below average achievement	5 (11.4)	27 (61.4)	2 (4.5)	8 (18.2)	2 (4.5)	44 (100)
Low achievement	4 (26.7)	10 (66.7)	0	1 (6.7)	0	15 (100)
Total	10	59	6	31	19	125 (100)

Variables	*Groups*	*Results of chi-square test*
Level of education by sex	All pupils	ns
Level of education by class	All pupils	$\chi^2 = 34.009$ df4 $p < .0001$
Level of education by achievement	All pupils	$\chi^2 = 43.883$ df12 $p < .0001$

Note: Whole numbers are shown first, followed by percentages in parentheses

Table 6.3 Desired job level of Millbridge pupils (by sex, class and achievement) and results of chi-square test

Groups	Professional	Semi-professional	Skilled trade	Unskilled/ semi-skilled	Vague/ other	Totals
All pupils	24 (21.6)	15 (13.5)	29 (26.1)	43 (38.7)	5 (4.3)	116 (100)
Girls	12 (20.0)	13 (21.7)	14 (23.3)	21 (35.0)	3 (4.7)	63 (100)
Boys	12 (23.5)	2 (3.9)	15 (29.4)	22 (43.1)	2 (3.7)	53 (100)
Working class	9 (12.2)	11 (14.9)	19 (25.7)	35 (47.3)	2 (2.6)	76 (100)
Middle class	15 (40.5)	4 (10.8)	10 (27.0)	8 (21.6)	3 (7.5)	40 (100)
High achievement	9 (34.6)	3 (11.5)	5 (19.2)	9 (34.6)	—	26 (100)
Above average achievement	11 (34.4)	10 (31.2)	6 (18.7)	5 (15.6)	—	32 (100)
Below average achievement	3 (7.9)	1 (2.6)	15 (39.5)	19 (50)	—	38 (100)
Low achievement	1 (6.7)	1 (6.7)	3 (30)	10 (66.7)	—	15 (100)
Total	24	15	29	43	—	111 (100)

Variables	Groups	Results of chi-square test
Desired job level by sex	All pupils	ns
Desired job level by class	All pupils	$\chi^2 = 13.702$ df3 p $<$ .01
	All pupils	$\chi^2 = 33.413$ df9 p $<$ .0001
	Girls	$\chi^2 = 20.072$ df9 p $<$ .01
	Boys	$\chi^2 = 18.727$ df9 p $<$ .05
Desired job level by achievement	Working class	ns
	Middle class	$\chi^2 = 13.157$ df9 p $<$ .001

Note: Whole numbers are shown first, followed by percentages in parentheses

Table 6.4 Desired job level of Greenhill pupils (by sex, class and achievement) and results of chi-square test

Groups	Professional	Semi-professional	Skilled trade	Unskilled/semi-skilled	Vague/other	Totals
All pupils	27 (22.7)	12 (10)	17 (14.3)	44 (37)	19 (16)	119 (100)
Girls	8 (13.6)	5 (8.5)	10 (16.9)	26 (44.1)	10 (16.9)	59 (100)
Boys	19 (31.7)	7 (11.7)	7 (11.7)	18 (30)	9 (15)	60 (100)
Working class	5 (8.9)	6 (10.7)	10 (17.9)	32 (57.1)	3 (5.4)	56 (100)
Middle class	11 (40.7)	2 (7.4)	3 (11.1)	4 (14.8)	7 (25.9)	27 (100)
High achievement	9 (56.2)	0	0	3 (18.7)	4 (25)	16 (100)
Above average achievement	10 (19.6)	7 (13.7)	10 (19.6)	17 (33.3)	7 (13.7)	51 (100)
Below average achievement	7 (17.5)	3 (7.5)	5 (12.5)	18 (45)	7 (17.5)	40 (100)
Low achievement	1 (8.3)	2 (16.7)	2 (16.7)	6 (50)	1 (8.3)	12 (100)
Total	27	12	17	44	19	119 (100)

Variables	Groups	Results of chi-square test
Desired job level by sex	All pupils	ns
Desired job level by class	All pupils	$\chi^2 = 24.221$ df4 p $< .0001$
Desired job level by achievement	All pupils	$\chi^2 = 20.562$ df12 p $< .05$

Note: Whole numbers are shown first, followed by percentages in parentheses

The effect of opting for secretarial studies was to exclude many other possibilities, since at both schools it took up at least a double slot on the timetable. Discussions with parents revealed that personal experience of the local labour market was a major factor in explaining why working-class parents encouraged their daughters to take up secretarial studies even when this was at variance with the girls' stated interests. I wanted to see to what extent girls taking commercial subjects justified their choice in similar highly rational terms. What I had not expected to find, which amazed me in the early stages of interviewing, was that almost every girl expressed a lack of interest in the subject and hostility to the idea of working as a secretary. Forms of denial, in particular pragmatism, fantasy, and defeatism were all involved in the process of coming to terms with an inevitable, if unwelcome, future.

For Susan Piper, her choice of secretarial studies was justified in terms of a fall-back position which she firmly hoped she would not have to rely upon:

> It's something to fall back on if you don't get the job you're looking for. 'Cos there's a lot of people looking for secretaries in garages and things like that. It's something just to fall back on really, isn't it?

Susan actually wanted to be a fashion designer, but she had little idea about how to set about achieving this objective and was gradually coming to see it as an unattainable dream. Most of the girls offered this 'fall-back position' as their main reason for choosing office-based subjects.

For some girls, it appeared that denial of the likely outcomes of their choices was centrally involved in the decision-making process and Jackie Rivers' ambivalence towards her future employment was typical:

> Jackie: It's my ambition to be a secretary . . . I think everyone wants to be a secretary at some point. With me it's just stuck.
> S.R.: What's your picture of what a secretary's life would actually be like?
> Jackie: I think it seems really dull. But I still want to be one. Just cooped up in an office all day. But it suits me.
> S.R.: Why's that then? Because when you said 'cooped up

all day' it didn't sound as if you thought it would be a very exciting job.

Jackie: No, secretaries in an office, it sounds sort of drab. But it carries some good moments with it as well, I suppose.

S.R.: What d'you think the good moments would be?

Jackie: More exciting work, you know, like you might get to go abroad and work. See the world. You might be lucky

Here Jackie is using the fantasy of secretarial work as high-powered and glamorous to offset a much bleaker reality. The metaphor of being cooped up, helpless and restricted, is very vivid and is expressed with more commitment than the image of excitement and high-living, which is a subsequent ration-alisation. Jackie's desire for independence is undoubtedly genuine, but she seems not to have a clear idea of how to set about achieving this in reality. In the absence of a pattern to follow, she plumps for subjects which are objectively very unlikely to give her the freedom she desires.

Another means of accepting a potentially dreary future was to use a form of denial, pretending that the future job would not really be secretarial work at all. For instance, some girls felt that working as a secretary in the police force or the army would be preferable, since it might hold out the hope of a bit more excitement:

Laura Sayers: I'd like to feel I was doing something for somebody instead of just sitting at a desk every day. I'd rather be outside than inside, doing something different.

S.R.: But if you're doing secretarial work won't that involve being stuck in an office?

Laura: It's different than just writing letters. You'd feel as if you're helping somebody because you're doing something important.

For these girls, opting for secretarial studies was accompanied by the hope that for them the job would somehow be different, not the servicing routine which they knew to be the reality of most office work, but exciting and active.

Many girls who were doing commercial subjects justified this on the grounds that they had already discovered their real goal was unattainable. Their replies expressed both anger and fatalism. Jackie Alcott, for instance, had wanted to go into the army but had been prevented by her Dad:

> He says all the women in there are slags. He says all the women go with all the army people. They're not very nice to know. So that was out.

Polly Loder was almost apologetic about her real ambition:

> Well I'd like to be a fashion designer, but everybody wants to do that, don't they? [Sounds a bit embarrassed] Everybody that likes design and that – it's a bit far-fetched.

Monica Sale, too, was doing secretarial studies because she had discovered how hard it was to be a mounted policewoman:

> It makes me really furious. They think we're really feeble just because men are a bit stronger. It's the same in the army. They won't let women fight. And at places like King's Park, the law enforcement academy, you're not allowed there either. All they do is like train the troops for the queen, nothing really hard. It's just a bit mucky and getting up early. I don't see why women can't do that either.

The majority of girls, then, had little interest in the subject, and were simply doing it because of their recognition of the unlikelihood of their getting any other job. Many would rather be engaged in more adventurous and creative work, but were already realising that the careers service was unlikely to be offering employment in these sorts of areas. By justifying their decisions in terms of pragmatism, fantasy or defeatism, they persuaded themselves that their actions were perfectly rational and their future might not be as unremittingly bleak as they imagined. Some of these strategies are very like those described by Prendergast and Prout (1980) as underpinning girls' acceptance of the inevitability of motherhood. In the following section there is further discussion of this issue.

However, it should be noted that there was a minority of working-class and middle-class girls who not only expressed a strong desire for autonomy and financial independence, but had also thought carefully about how to achieve these goals.

Catherine Thomas, the daughter of a dairyman and nursing auxiliary, wanted to be a doctor. She had no intention of bowing to the suggestion which had been made by the school that a nursing career might be more appropriate:

> I couldn't stand being a nurse and having to do the dirty work . . . I hate having orders given to me. Nurses might know something but they're not allowed to say it. Or if they do say it the doctors aren't very pleased . . . I like to voice my opinion and I could only do that if I was, say, a doctor or a matron.

Although most working-class girls, unlike Catherine, were resigned to the fact that they were very likely to end up in sex-stereotyped jobs, it was clear that most were determined to sort out their own lives, resenting advice and offers of help from parents and teachers. However, lacking a clear idea of how to secure financial autonomy in their future lives, their insistence on making independent choices was instrumental in locking them even more firmly into sex-segregated positions within the labour market. Jane Shelton typified the view expressed by many girls that by choosing secretarial studies and rejecting more academic options she was making rational choices about the future direction of her life.

> S.R.: Do your mum and dad agree with the options you've chosen?
>
> *Jane Shelton*: Well they wanted me to take a language but they didn't want to force me because it's my life. It's nothing to do with them really.

Helen Downes also said that she did not want any help from her mother, but at the same time felt that she was not very interested anyway:

> My mum said it was my choice, my future, it was up to me. She says she spends all her time doing things for my brother and me and it was about time we started doing things for ourselves.

These findings were reinforced by data from the questionnaires, which showed that at Greenhill, in particular, working-class pupils and girls were less likely to receive advice on option choice from parents and teachers than middle-class pupils and boys (see Tables 6.5 and 6.6). Data gathered from interviews with the mothers of Westshire girls also reinforced the view that working-class girls tended to resent suggestions from parents about possible directions and, in any case, very often their mothers did not feel sufficiently knowledgeable to help them. Mrs Murrell, for instance, a parent who worked in a small factory making head gaskets, said that when Sharon chose her subjects she was not influenced by her parents or anyone else for that matter:

> When she chose her subjects she said, 'These are my subjects', and that was that. She picked them all out what she wanted to do and we asked her why and she sat down and told us, and we said, 'All right, you've got to do them.' No, she picks subjects I never would have expected her to so she's got to cope with them.

Similar accounts were given by many parents of working-class girls. Mrs Rennick said Pat was certainly not influenced by her or her husband:

> I just told her to choose the subjects she liked best.

Mrs Field, too, said Janet's option choice was made quite independently:

> She just took the subjects that I think she liked doing and was good at. So she decided to take them. I mean we didn't say anything to her about what she should or shouldn't do. It was her choice.

By way of contrast, middle-class parents in general, whether they had sons or daughters, tended to be very involved in their children's option choice, frequently making contact with the school through both formal and informal channels. A number of the parents knew teachers out of school and felt able to have chats with them about option choice when they met socially. Most admitted to exerting some pressure on their children to make sure they were making sensible decisions, and a number revealingly referred to 'our' subjects and what 'we' were going to do in the future. As mentioned in Chapter 3, the preferred course for boys was the physical science route, whereas girls were encouraged to opt for languages and, even for the brightest pupils, home economics was considered important.

Table 6.5 Summary of which people gave Millbridge pupils most useful advice when choosing subject options

Group	Both parents	Father only	Mother only	Parent and teacher	Teacher	Nobody	Totals
All pupils	26 (41)	8 (13)	5 (8)	6 (10)	2 (3)	16 (25)	63 (100)
Girls	16 (41)	4 (10)	3 (8)	4 (10)	2 (5)	10 (26)	39 (100)
Boys	10 (42)	4 (17)	2 (8)	2 (8)	0	6 (25)	24 (100)
Working class	12 (32)	5 (14)	3 (8)	5 (14)	1 (3)	11 (29)	37 (100)
Middle class	14 (54)	3 (11)	2 (8)	1 (4)	1 (4)	5 (19)	26 (100)

Note: Whole numbers are shown first, followed by percentages in parentheses

Table 6.6 Summary of which people gave Greenhill pupils most useful advice when choosing subject options

Group	Both parents	Father only	Mother only	Parent and teacher	Teacher	Nobody	Totals
All pupils	24 (28)	6 (7)	9 (11)	7 (9)	0	39 (45)	85 (100)
Girls	9 (23)	5 (13)	3 (8)	3 (8)	0	19 (48)	39 (100)
Boys	15 (33)	1 (3)	6 (13)	4 (9)	0	20 (43)	46 (100)
Working class	10 (22)	3 (6)	3 (6)	3 (6)	0	27 (60)	46 (100)
Middle class	6 (38)	1 (6)	1 (6)	3 (19)	0	5 (31)	16 (100)

Note: Whole numbers are shown first, followed by percentages in parentheses

The parents of working-class boys, although they tended to be less involved in option choice than middle-class parents, often stressed that they had taken steps to make sure that the subjects that their son was taking would be adequate for the sort of work he was hoping to do. This sometimes involved making informal contact with prospective employers. Mrs Smith, for instance, whose son wanted to get an apprenticeship in the army, said they let him choose the subjects he wanted to, but her husband made two trips to the army information office to make sure these were the right ones.

Working-class girls, then, appeared to be distinctly different from other groups in terms of making decisions autonomously. This strong streak of independence is commented on by writers such as Coffield *et al.* (1986) and Wallace (1987), who have described working-class girls' transition to adulthood. Wallace, for instance, argues that the early commitment to motherhood and domesticity which working-class girls often make is not a random response, but a conscious decision to take control of their lives. In the context of subject choice, working-class girls' desire to act independently was important to their sense of self-esteem and autonomy. Unfortunately, their determination to make independent decisions based on the limited range of information available to them was probably one of the reasons why their option choices were markedly more sex-stereotyped than those of middle-class girls. Gaskell (1984), in her Canadian study of gender and course choice, points out that in later years the knowledge that they have voluntarily chosen a particular path may be particularly damaging for working class girls, since they may 'accept responsibility for the consequences of their choice – and blame themselves for the restrictions they face later' (p. 93).

Working class girls' decisions to opt for secretarial studies, then, was not indicative of a wholesale acceptance of traditional feminine ideology characterised by a belief in an essentially passive and subordinate role for women. On the contrary, they saw their actions as rational and responsible, and their rejection of parental advice was seen as evidence of the adult status for which they were striving. They did have some inkling that, once achieved, secretarial work might not offer a great deal of freedom, but this knowledge was generally suppressed.

Middle-class girls differed from their working-class sisters in that they were certainly not interested in opting into secretarial studies and were highly ambitious academically. At Millbridge, for instance, one of the girls' mothers told me that there was 'a little clique' who were all hoping to go to Oxbridge. However they were also considerably undecided about what they might do there or the area in which they might work afterwards. Susan Burton, for instance, said that she wanted to be 'a psychologist or one of those people who finds out the mysteries of the world'.

Middle-class boys often had a clearer idea of the subjects they were hoping to do at 'A' level and even the precise degree course for which they were aiming. Working-class boys had often been given detailed advice by their fathers about suitable jobs and essential qualifications.

With regard to their future working lives, then, many working-class girls expressed a degree of ambivalence about the type of jobs to which their choice of subjects was likely to lead. A significant minority, on the other hand, were making choices which were likely to open up wider possibilities for the future and were very much aware of the significance of these decisions. With regard to pupils' view of their future role in the private sphere of the home and the family, similar contrasting views emerged. Let us first look at what some of the questionnaire findings reveal about pupils' present domestic involvement and the roles they anticipated for themselves and their partner in the future.

PUPILS' VIEWS OF THE DOMESTIC DIVISION OF LABOUR: PRESENT AND FUTURE

Clearly, a key aspect of the culture of femininity is the nature of the domestic division of labour which is regarded as appropriate. A number of items on the questionnaire were designed to investigate whether there were any significant differences between girls and boys in their assessment of how this division of labour was currently being worked out in their own homes and what they considered desirable in their future families. A list of household tasks was given to Greenhill pupils and they were asked to say whether they regularly helped with these tasks or not. Table 6.7 shows that a number of jobs were done

Table 6.7 The percentage of girls and boys at Greenhill who regularly help with various household tasks at present

	% Girls	Level of significance measured by chi-square test	% Boys
Cleaning	70.5	p < .001	35.4
Cooking	72.1	p < .0001	27.7
Mending clothes	39.3	p < .01	15.4
Ironing	55.7	p < .0001	9.4
Gardening	32.2	p < 0.25	52.4
Taking out rubbish	37.7	p < .05	56.9
Washing car	19.7	p < .025	38.5
Minor household repairs	9.8	p < .001	36.9
Making own bed	95.1	p < .001	69.2
Shopping for food	49.2	—	35.4
Washing up	83.6	—	72.3
Tidying own room	83.6	—	80.0
Laying table	70.5	—	60.0

Note: N = 125

significantly more by either boys or girls. Boys tended to take rubbish out, do minor household repairs and gardening, whereas girls tended to clean, make their own beds, mend clothes and do the ironing. Shopping, washing up, room tidying and laying the table were done by both sexes. Clearly, these divisions are in accordance with traditional views of the boundary between routine, indoor and clean jobs for girls and occasional, mainly outdoor and dirty jobs for boys. It is important also to notice the area of overlap, with boys as well as girls assisting with food shopping and other standard domestic chores.

An impression of the potential for future change, however, emerged from Millbridge pupils' accounts of the division of labour which they expected to have in their own families in the future. They were given a list of jobs and were asked: 'When you have your own family, who do you think will do these jobs in the home?'. Their responses, showing whether they thought the job would be done by men, women or both partners, are summarised in Table 6.8. Mending fuses and doing repairs were identified as male jobs, whereas cleaning, cooking, washing clothes, mending clothes and ironing were identified as female jobs. However, doing the shopping, washing up, decorating, disciplining the children, visiting the children's school, looking after the children, paying bills and earning money were identified as jobs which would be done by both men and women. Differences in pupils' categorisation of the jobs was statistically highly significant in all cases. Although the majority of daily servicing tasks were still regarded as female and the majority of occasional technical jobs as male, a large number of jobs, including both childcare and wage earning, were seen as appropriate for both sexes. This clearly represents a sharp move away from the view that the primary responsibility of women is to manage domestic matters and the principle male role is that of breadwinner. At the same time, the boundaries between women's work and men's work have certainly not dissolved. Interestingly, more girls than boys said both partners should earn money (χ^2 = 4.063 df1 p $<$ .05) but this was the only significant difference between boys' and girls' responses.

Overall, then, it would appear that the division of household tasks in pupils' families is such that both boys and girls are allocated or voluntarily undertake sex-stereotyped jobs with their attendant symbolic messages. In the future, they envisage sharing certain key areas of responsibility particularly in the areas of wage earning and childcare but certain tasks are still regarded as uniquely masculine or feminine. Oakley, writing in 1974, suggested that the modern companionate marriage still involves distinct sexual divisions even if the boundaries between male and female roles have blurred a little. Westshire pupils' view of the sexual division of labour reveals aspects of both the changing nature and enduring quality of masculine and feminine gender codes.

FUTURE FAMILY LIVES – QUESTIONING THE IDEOLOGY OF FEMININITY?

Discussion with girls at both schools shed further light on their attitudes towards the domestic and familial dimension of their lives. Many girls, particularly those of working-class origin, envisaged balancing part-time work with child care

131

Table 6.8 Single sample chi-square test applied to Millbridge pupils' expectations of whether women, men or both will do particular household tasks in their future families

Household task	Number of pupils who say task will be done by:			Results of chi-square test
	Women	Men	Both	
Mending a fuse	0	98	20	$\chi^2 = 51.559$ df1 p < .001
Doing repairs	1	102	15	$\chi^2 = 152.254$ df2 p < .001
Cleaning house	67	3	47	$\chi^2 = 54.974$ df2 p < .001
Cooking	70	1	46	$\chi^2 = 62.923$ df2 p < .001
Mending clothes	98	1	17	$\chi^2 = 139.879$ df2 p < .001
Ironing	90	4	23	$\chi^2 = 104.667$ df2 p < .001
Decorating	4	46	67	$\chi^2 = 52.769$ df2 p < .001
Making sure there are clean clothes	99	2	16	$\chi^2 = 140.974$ df2 p < .001
Disciplining children	10	9	98	$\chi^2 = 133.897$ df2 p < .001
Shopping	45	3	68	$\chi^2 = 56.190$ df2 p < .001
Washing up	30	11	76	$\chi^2 = 57.282$ df2 p < .001
Paying bills	2	42	74	$\chi^2 = 66.169$ df2 p < .001
Visiting children's school	6	3	108	$\chi^2 = 183.231$ df2 p < .001
Earning money	0	34	84	$\chi^2 = 21.186$ df1 p < .001
Looking after children	19	2	93	$\chi^2 = 123.211$ df2 p < .001

rather than seeing their careers as the fulcrum of their future experience. But at the same time, just as the prospect of being a secretary filled the girls with little enthusiasm, their feelings about being housewives, mothers and part-time workers were equally ambivalent, and many spoke of the negative rather than the positive aspects of the domestic role they envisaged. Many girls' views of married life were very dreary, and at this point they were in no hurry to rush into it. Hazel Toms, for instance, commented:

> I wouldn't mind getting married, but I want to get on and enjoy life first.

This was her perception of what life was like for young married couples:

> They buy a house and stay in it and don't go out. They just watch the telly.

Children, although a central part of the projected future, were certainly not romanticised. A number of girls spoke of the violent feelings they could imagine themselves having towards children:

> *Nicky Thompson*: They're annoying. When you see them in the street and they're crying you just want to go and strangle them.

The wife, according to Hazel and Janet, got the worst part of the deal:

> *Janet Ellis*: The husband's probably at work.
> *Hazel Toms*: And you're left with the screaming kids if you've got any, doing the housework.

Despite this negative view, they still believed that after a brief fling this was their inescapable lot in life.

For many working class girls there seemed to be an irreconcilable gap between the work they would really like to do and their responsibilities as mothers, and here, too, they expressed conflicting views. Earlier in our interview, Sharon Murrell said she thought it was a good thing for women with children to carry on working because otherwise they got fat at home, buying sweets for the kids and eating them themselves. She wanted to do something different, and being a long-distance lorry driver was her life-long ambition. Later, however, she said she would like to get married and have children, but she did realise that the two were not easily compatible

> It wouldn't fit in with what I want to do 'cos you always have to think of the kids if you get called out for anything. You can't exactly dump them anywhere, can you?

However, this depressing vision of childcare did not stop many of the girls from supporting the ideology of full-time motherhood and, like their mothers, they were generally highly critical of women who wanted to have children and work while they were young:

> *Yvonne Roundhay:* No, I wouldn't want to leave them while they were really young like some mothers do. I think that's wrong.
>
> *S.R.:* Why d'you think that's wrong?
>
> *Yvonne Roundhay:* Well, say if they have babysitters to look after them during the day they get more attached to that person than actually to you, because they spend more time with them. I think a mother should be at home when they are growing up, but when they are our age and they know where their mother is then they can go out.

At the age of thirteen, Yvonne was already anticipating a long wait for freedom after the arrival of her children.

A far less typical view was expressed by Catherine Thomas, who had this to say about children:

> I wouldn't really want any. I'd make sure that I didn't have any. To me, they've got nothing to do with my life at all until I've finished [school], passed [my exams], but until then they don't count at all.

More commonly, girls supported traditional notions of the primacy of the private sphere in women's lives, whilst at the same time being highly sceptical of certain aspects of the ideology of femininity. Many were clear that they desired a fulfilling working life, but felt that the claims of the home would win. Some girls were able to articulate the nature of the contradiction, if not resolve it. Clare Smart, for instance, was well aware of the gap between the romantic vision of domestic bliss and the reality, and articulated the contradiction clearly:

> *S.R.*: Have you ever imagined what you'll be doing in ten years' time?
>
> *Clare*: Yeah, loads of times. Well, I want a house that's modern and nice modern couches and everything, all in white and red and everything, and you've got this man of your dreams and everything [exaggerated voice] and you sort of fly away to holidays and go to all these places and then you look at somebody in real life and you think 'Good heavens.' [Laughs] 'Cos this couple I know and they were a really perfect couple and the husband walked out on the wife a few weeks ago and I found that out yesterday and it changed my entire impression of everything because they seemed to me to be the perfect young couple. They'd got a little son and one on the way and he just left her.

Very often, this articulation of apparently insoluble contradictions was made in the context of discussing their perceptions of their mothers' lives. Sometimes a daughter's perception of her mother's frustrations made her determined to avoid a similar situation herself. At other times, the tendency was to express a feeling of resignation. For Lisa Parkes, a working-class girl, determination to avoid a similar fate was clearly the overriding concern:

> I just could never be a housewife. I wouldn't mind living with someone, but I'm not going to cook and clean for them. My mum's always complaining that she never goes out anywhere . . . she'd like a part-time job but my little brother won't let her . . . He says she's not brainy and all that. He says: 'You wouldn't be able to pick me up from school.' He says he wouldn't go to stay with anyone else.'

Susan Burton, whose mother was a dentist and a single parent, was similarly very clear about the conflict which might occur between the demands of the public and private spheres and the solution which held the strongest appeal for her. She felt that she had gained a great deal both from the perception of her mother's successful career and from having to play a part at an early age in looking after herself and helping to run the house. Her attitude towards working-class girls who found themselves prematurely drawn towards domesticity was partly one of pity and partly of contempt:

> Some girls in our group are getting married next birthday and I feel really sorry for them, especially the ones who are marrying soldiers. I can't really see it working out. I know some who've been pregnant or had abortions already and I think 'You stupid cow'. As far as I'm concerned, my job would come before my family – well, at least my husband, I'm not sure about my family.

So, although many working-class girls were aware of the inadequacies of their mothers' situations and considered their own futures in this context, the majority reluctantly accepted that their lives would be similar. A minority of middle-class and working-class girls sought much more radical change. Despite their general sense of resignation, working-class girls also conveyed a sense of their critical awareness of the injustice of existing power relations. This emerged very strongly from items on the questionnaire designed to measure general attitudes to gender equality.

PUPILS' ATTITUDES TO GENDER EQUALITY

In the final section of the questionnaire, pupils were given a range of statements which they were asked to rate in terms of agreement or disagreement. These statements were intended to examine pupils' attitudes to a number of issues, but particularly with regard to the issue of gender equality. They were similar in content to the statements presented to parents, but the wording was more direct and simple. Responses to each of these statements was analysed by sex and class of pupil for all pupils, (boys, girls, working-class and middle-class pupils) and the results are shown in Tables 6.9 and 6.10. At both Millbridge and Greenhill, boys tended to respond in a more sex-stereotyped way than girls. Significant differences were found between middle-class and working-class pupils at Greenhill, with working-class pupils responding in a more sexist way. For Millbridge pupils, however, the responses of working-class boys and girls were only significantly different on the question of whether girls were strong enough for farm work. These responses are similar to those of the parents, in that fathers tended to express more sex-stereotyped attitudes than mothers. Middle class girls had the least sex-stereotyped attitudes among the pupils.

Factor analysis was then used to construct a scale of attitudes to gender equality, referred to as the sexist scales. From the pupils' responses to the questionnaires, factor analysis was used to identify those statements which discriminated between pupils most effectively on their attitues to gender equality. For Millbridge pupils these were statements 2, 3, 6, 9, 13, 15 and 16 (see Table 6.9) and for Greenhill pupils statements 3, 4, 7, 12 and 15 (see Table 6.10). The sexist scales consisted of the sum of pupils' responses to each of these statements, with statement 16 on the Millbridge questionnaire recoded in SPSS so that (5) become the most sexist response. The sexist scales were analysed by pupil's sex, class and achievement (Tables 6.11–6.14). There was a significant relationship between pupil's sex and score on the sexist scales for both Millbridge and Greenhill pupils, but no association between class and score on the scales. Boys, regardless of class, generally expressed more sex-stereotyped views than girls. At Millbridge, there was no association between score on the sexist scale and pupils' achievement, but at Greenhill there was a significant difference between pupils of different achievements, with higher achieving pupils having lower sexist scores.

This scale seems to provide further evidence that Westshire girls, regardless of their class position, are questioning the received culture of femininity and seeking more radical alternatives. This chapter explored the pragmatic reasons underlying working-class girls' orientation towards stereotypically female areas of the labour market and their acceptance of a traditional division of labour in the home. However, as pupils' accounts make abundantly clear, their acquiescence does not necessarily imply total acceptance of a subordinate role. It will be interesting to see whether these critical attitudes will be accompanied by stronger challenges to the status quo in future years.

Table 6.9 Mann–Whitney U test applied to statements 2 to 16 (by sex and class of pupil) for all Millbridge pupils, girls, boys, working-class and middle-class pupils

Number of statement	Working/middle class			All pupils	Girls/boys Working class	Middle class	Most Sexist response
	All pupils	Girls	Boys				
2	ns	ns	ns	ns	ns	ns	
3	ns	ns	ns	ns	ns	u = 129.0 z = -2.163 p < .05	Boys
6	ns	ns	ns	u = 901.5 z = -4.694 p < .0001	u = 426.0 z = -3.324 p < .0001	u = 83.0 z = -3.472 p < .001	Boys
9	ns	ns	ns	u < 1229.0 z = -2.287 p < .05	ns	u = 99.0 z = -2.906 p < .01	Boys
13	ns	ns	ns	u = 1320.0 z = -2.110 p < .05	ns	u = 128.0 z = -1.972 p < .05	Boys
15	ns	ns	ns	ns	ns	ns	
16	ns	ns	ns	u = 1163.5 z = -3.1241 p < .001	ns	u = 109.0 z = -2.688 p < .01	Boys

Notes: Only analysis of pupils' responses to statements concerning gender roles are shown. (2) Statement 2 – boys are better at science than girls; statement 3 – men control classes better than women; statement 6 – girls are not strong enough for farmwork; statement 9 – when unemployment is high women shouldn't work; statement 13 – it is more important for a girl to be good-looking than clever; statement 15 – a boy who wanted to be a woman's hairdresser would be a bit of a softy; statement 18 – women would make as good engineers as men

Table 6.10 Mann–Whitney U test applied to statements 2 to 15 (by sex and class of pupil) for all Greenhill pupils, girls, boys, working-class and middle-class pupils

Number of statement	Working/middle class			Girls/boys			Most sexist response
	All pupils	Girls	Boys	All pupils	Working class	Middle class	
3	u = 604.0 z = 2.339 p < .05	ns	ns	u = 1282.0 z = 3.682 p < .001	u = 326.0 z = -2.234 p < .05	u = 58.0 z = -2.001 p < .05	Working class boys
4	ns	ns	ns	u = 1361.0 z = -3.010 p < .001	ns	ns	Boys
7	u = 597.0 z = -2.97 p < .05	ns	ns	u = 970.5 z = -5.042 p < .0001	u = 225.5 z = -3.645 p < .001	u = 44.0 z = -2.325 p < .05	Working class boys
12	u = 566.0 z = -2.290 p < .05	ns	ns	u = 1075.0 z = -4.587 p < .0001	u = 309.0 z = -2.255 p < .05	ns	Working class boys
15	ns	ns	ns	u = 1102.5 z = -3.842 p < .0001	u = 293.0 z = -2.219 p < .05	u = 38.5 z = -1.942 p < .05	Working class boys

Notes: (1) Only analysis of pupils' responses to statements concerning gender roles is shown. (2) Statement 3 – boys are better at science than girls; statement 4 – men control classes better than women; statement 7 – girls are not strong enough for farm work; statement 12 – when unemployment is high women shouldnt work; statement 15 – a boy who wanted to be a woman's hairdresser would be a bit of a softy

Table 6.11 Mann–Whitney U test to analyse sexist scale by sex and class of pupil (for Millbridge pupils)

Variables	Results of Mann–Whitney U test	Comment
Sexist by sex	u = 1131.5 z = −3.332 p < .001	Boys more sexist
Sexist by class	ns	than girls

Table 6.12 Chi-square test used to analyse sexist scale by pupils' achievement level (for Millbridge pupils)

Variables	Results of chi-square test
Sexist by achievement	ns

Table 6.13 Mann–Whitney U test used to analyse sexist scale by sex and class of pupil (for Greenhill pupils)

Variables	Results of Mann–Whitney U test	Comment
Sexist by sex	u = 975.0 z = −5.492 p < .0001	Boys more sexist
Sexist by class	ns	than girls

Table 6.14 Chi-square test used to analyse sexist scale by pupils' achievement level (for Greenhill pupils)

Variables	Results of chi-square test	Comment
Sexist by achievement	χ^2 = 27.639 (df12) p < .01	Lower -achieving pupils more sexist

CONCLUSION

In this chapter I have drawn together data from the interviews and the questionnaires to shed light on girls' anticipated role in the home and the workplace. Again, we have evidence of contrasting constructions of femininity, with working-class girls expressing ambivalence towards the future limitations of their lives, which they anticipated in terms of a struggle to balance the demands of domestic responsibility and potentially unfulfilling work. They were generally not unaware of the frustrations and limitations of their prospective futures, since they could see clearly the conditions of their own mothers' lives. Very often, however, they chose to ignore this evidence.

Prendergast and Prout (1980) discuss similar disjunctions between the normative construction of motherhood as the ultimate in feminine fulfilment and teenage girls' perceptions of their mothers' depressing circumstances. In the light of this clash between their own perceptions and the received wisdom, the girls rejected their private knowledge as illegitimate. Further, the authors suggest that girls reconcile legitimate and illegitimate knowledge by using a number of strategies or 'let-out clauses', such as promising themselves that they would postpone the experience until they had had a good time. The data presented here certainly confirm that girls experience a degree of dissonance between received ideology and private knowledge. Prendergast and Prout argue that if girls are to be able to use this 'proto-knowledge' to make choices about their future, they must be offered a framework of interpretation and given time to discuss the significance of their experience. Possibilities which they might wish to consider are 'non-dependent sexual relationships, economic systems which recognise the existence of motherhood and patterns of living which do not assume the predominance of female domestic labour'. Schools are the obvious places for such discussion to take place but at neither school in this study was any serious attempt made to discuss equal opportunities issues. As the national curriculum is introduced into secondary schools, the chance to discuss and develop common understandings of the operation of patriarchal relations are unlikely to be more forthcoming, since time for social and political studies is likely to become increasingly scarce.

A smaller number of girls, some, but not all of whom were middle class, expressed a very different view of femininity, whereby family commitment was not necessarily rejected, but was envisaged as representing only a partial component of a life in which work would also play a very major part.

7

COMPETING GENDER CODES IN THE CLASSROOM

INTRODUCTION

In earlier chapters, we have seen the way in which many girls appeared to endorse traditional gender divisions in the curriculum whilst at the same time supporting the general principle of equal opportunities. This apparently contradictory position appeared to be related to conflict between normative definitions of acceptable femininity and their own observations of the reality of women's lives at work and in the home, often based on their perceptions of their mothers' lot in life. A minority of working-class and middle-class girls had developed more radical notions of femininity and were rejecting traditional curricular, vocational and domestic paths. This chapter uses the long periods which I spent observing and chatting in classrooms to analyse how these widely differing notions of femininity manifested themselves in pupils' everyday behaviour.

A number of writers have seen the classroom in terms of a power struggle between pupils and teachers. For instance, Davies (1984) focuses on gender-specific aspects of the struggle and Connell et al. (1982) and Connell (1986) explore the problem of discipline in working-class schools. They argue that because teachers are committed to the academic curriculum and the educational mobility of a minority of working-class pupils, this automatically necessitates the use of controlling strategies on the majority. Corrigan (1979) explores the pupils' perspective and suggests that, for many, education is experienced as a form of repression. Even for pupils who are well motivated, there is competition to capture the maximum amount of teacher time. For some writers, the concept of deviance has been replaced by the concept of resistance. Willis (1977) and Anyon (1983) have described pupils' disruptive behaviour in terms of their rebellion against social injustice. Hargreaves (1982), on the other hand, has suggested that 'resistance' may be used as a catch-all phrase to describe any behaviour that is not positively pro-school, and as such it has lost its utility. In this chapter, I consider the utility of the term in making sense of some of the behaviour which I observed.

The following account suggests that conflict in the classroom was often manifested in the manipulation of traditional gender codes and struggles over competing gender codes. This happens in two ways. First, teachers base their coping strategies and sanctions on their typifications of male and female pupils. These are, of course, based on normative concepts of masculinity and femininity. Second, pupils base their opposition to schooling on the exploitation of the contradictions and inconsistencies of traditional gender codes, and sometimes challenge them outright. I will argue that both teachers' attempts to maintain their authority in the classroom and pupils' opposition to this power generally reinforce rather than undermine traditional gender codes. Some girls, however, do engage in activity which fundamentally challenges traditional constructions of masculinity and femininity, and I will also consider these. Paradoxically, the behaviour of these girls tends to be less overtly disruptive and more conformist than those girls who assume traditionally masculine modes of behaviour in their opposition to schooling. In the light of data presented in this chapter, the term 'resistance' is discussed. First, I will briefly describe the typifications of girls and boys which underlie teachers' coping strategies.

TEACHERS' TYPIFICATIONS OF GIRLS AND BOYS

Clarricoates (1980) found that many teachers, when they were asked whether there were any differences in the behaviour and attitudes of boys and girls in their class, said that it was possible to identify distinctive characteristics. Data presented here support her view. Usually, girls were described as more mature, neater and more conscientious than boys, and data from Millbridge teachers emphasised these themes.

All the teachers I spoke to commented on the maturity of the girls relative to the boys. Mrs Marshwood, an English teacher, had this to say:

> Boys are much much more aggressive and immature. I find the girls quite amenable, you can talk to them on quite a normal level, whereas I find the boys, and I always have, very silly and childish, and that tends to carry on until the beginning of the fourth year.

The 'maturity' of the girls, which generally seemed to mean that they were better behaved and quieter, was often attributed to their more rapid physical development. For instance, Mr Jones, the head of biology, told me:

> When you look at the girls most of them have been or are going through their growth spurt. Half the boys in the class are still little boys – some of them in mentality are still two years behind.

Many teachers, it seemed, were attributing girls' maturity not to any qualities they had worked hard to achieve, but rather to some quirk of biological development. Often 'maturity' was immediately linked with some other negative quality:

> the girls are more sensible but perhaps more petty – well, girls tend to be like that for another year or two – 'she's not speaking to me' sort of thing.
> (Mrs Lovell, head of house at Millbridge)

It is also interesting to note that girls' supposed maturity was used to excuse boys' poorer academic performance. At one of the options interviews I attended, Mr Mottram, the head of physics at Millbridge, who was interested in girls' under-achievement in science, had this to say to a boy whose science grades were rather low to be considering taking all three subjects:

> Your grades are a bit low now, but research shows that boys tend to be a bit behind at this stage and then catch up later, so you should be all right.

Two other qualities which both male and female teachers frequently attributed to girls were their neatness and con-scientiousness. In biology and geography, for instance, the

144

teachers felt that the girls' neatness accounted for their success. Mr Douglas, a geography teacher at Millbridge, said:

A bright girl will not only produce work that's correct but a map, say, will always be meticulously neat. They seem to be capable of doing this, whereas very few boys will spend the time necessary to produce a very neat map.

This neatness, however, was perhaps not an unqualified advantage for the girls' academic progress. Mr Tiller, a Millbridge maths teacher, told me that one girl presented her work so beautifully that he never liked to put any marks on it. In fact, far from being seen in positive terms, girls' neatness and hard work were seen as evidence of their intellectual inferiority:

I think some of the boys have got behind the girls lower down through lack of discipline probably and the girls have been naturally hard-working and have tended to get ahead. And in maths, as long as you've got a modicum of intelligence you can get a very long way . . . But when it comes to seeing through a problem, where a bit of flair is needed, then I think the boys have an edge. When it's just a routine approach – you know, you do one on the board and they do the others with just a few small variations – then the girls, by virtue of following carefully what you've done, and taking it down neatly and reading about it and so on, they do better. I think the boys, if you wanted to devise another way of doing the problem, other than the one you've shown them, I think I would plump for a boy finding that.

(Mr Ginger, Millbridge deputy head)

Walden and Walkerdine (1982, 1985), in their study of discontinuity in girls' performance in maths between primary and secondary school, encountered a similar phenomenon. Girls were believed to be 'naturally' good at the more routine approaches to mathematics, but less skilled in higher level problem solving and lacking in 'flair'. They describe this as a 'Catch 22' situation:

If they fail at mathematics they lack true intellect but are

145

truly female. If they succeed they are only able to do so by following rules and if they conquer that hurdle then they become somehow less than female.

The qualities attributed to girls, then, of neatness, hard work and maturity were decidedly double-edged and they also coincided with prevailing cultural definitions of femininity. It would be easy to argue, as some researchers such as Clarricoates (1980) have done, that teachers impose their gender codes on passively receptive pupils, but I would suggest a further process is at work. Girls were certainly quieter in class, and in this respect my data support the findings of other researchers such as Kelly (1986). However, teachers' explanation of the reasons for this, in terms of biological development and inherent intellectual qualities, suggests that they were interpreting objective reality within a cultural framework which did not take account of the circumstances in the classroom producing this response. In the following sections, I will argue that gender construction in the classroom was an essentially two-way process. Teachers based their coping strategies (see Hargreaves, 1978) for further discussion of this concept) on their typifications of male and female pupils, and in this way transmitted traditional conceptions of masculinity and femininity. Pupils responded either by conforming, or by resisting teachers' authority through the parody and contradiction of these gender codes. Much of this resistance, however, was ultimately destined to reinforce rather than undermine the status quo.

TEACHERS' COPING STRATEGIES

I will now consider exactly how teachers' coping strategies are based on their typifications of male and female pupils and reinforce traditional gender codes. Specifically, I will examine how teachers attempt to win the consent of boys to their authority by allowing them to control the physical space of the classroom, the attention of the teacher and the content of lessons. I will also look at how male camaraderie is established in the classroom through the use of humour and the verbal denigration of women. The control of girls through teachers' use of traditional notions of femininity will be examined, and the establishment of female solidarity in certain areas of the curriculum will also be discussed.

Teacher authority, noisy boys and quiet girls

Although most teachers said they thought that they spent an equal amount of time with girls and boys in the classroom, observation of many lessons showed that they were forced to spend the majority of their time with boys simply to preserve some semblance of order. Middle-class and working-class boys tended to employ similar strategies to bring about this particular outcome. I will describe an art lesson given by Lois Roughton at Greenhill School to show how boys manage to maximise their share of teacher attention, and the strategies which the teacher is forced to adopt to deal with their behaviour. The purpose of the lesson is to paint an ordinary object such as a Mars bar wrapper in a subtly different form. Boys and girls sit at different tables and early on a group of boys attract the teacher's attention by making racist comments in a deliberately confrontational manner which she does not challenge directly. Instead of giving in to their demands for attention, she tells them to get on with their work. Ben Hayter, a middle-class boy, gives a lengthy monologue about a brilliant idea which he had for his homework. It eventually transpires that it was too complicated for him to actually carry out. Later on, when Miss Roughton is talking to me, he calls, 'Miss, Miss,' across the classroom in a voice which is almost a whine, rather like a small child. She breaks off the conversation immediately and goes across to him. Shortly afterwards, she becomes annoyed with Ben and Justin who have been wandering round the classroom making loud comments on other pupils' work, and shouts at them. Ben insists on having the last word in this exchange: 'Oh Miss, we were just having an intellectual discussion.'

The lesson continues with the teacher responding rapidly to the boys' demands, which often seem to reflect the belief that as a woman she is there to service their needs and receive their complaints: 'The paint runs', 'The sink's not working'. 'I don't like painting, Miss'. Ben gives the teacher advice on how to deal with his friends: 'I'd keep the packet of crisps Miss.' Another boy walks round the class with a pencil stuck through his jumper pretending it is a nipple, and is told to sit down. At the end of the lesson, a group of boys get up, and start to walk out in the middle of the teacher's explanation of homework, and Justin is kept behind at the end for an individual telling-off. By way of contrast, the girls have almost no disciplinary contact with the teacher, even though many are not doing much work either. At one point Miss Roughton walks over to a table where a group of girls are quietly chatting about a teacher at the Middle School who is splitting up from his wife. She says: 'This sounds more like a mothers' meeting than an art lesson.' And to me: 'This is where I get all my inside information from.'

Later, Miss Roughton tells me that the boys in the group are able but immature, whereas the girls can be relied on to work quietly by themselves. This lesson provides a clear example of how the boys' behaviour, and the teacher's interpretation of it, has forced her to adopt a particular coping strategy. She rewards their demands for attention with her time, and allows the girls to chat quietly rather than get on with their work simply because she does not have enough time and energy to insist that they do this. Were she to focus more attention on the girls, the boys threaten that their behaviour might get completely out of hand. Her actions are understandable in view of the enormous pressures on teachers to keep classes quiet at all costs (Denscombe, 1980). However, it is also important to recognise that the way in which she justifies this division of time, in terms of fulfilling the boys' needs, prevents her from examining her actions critically. In this example, we can see how the gender codes which girls and boys bring to the classroom shape their behaviour and initiate a particular response from the teacher, which is then justified by her conception of natural male and female behaviour.

Lesson content

At both schools, it was apparent that the content of lessons was often shaped to hold the attention of potentially disruptive boys. A history teacher at Millbridge, for instance, was giving a talk on twentieth-century history and spent the entire lesson describing in graphic detail the sort of deaths which men experienced in the trenches during the First World War. He read one account of a man's head being blown off while his body continued to run forward, and when one girl complained that she did not want to hear any more of this, she was told that she must listen because this was how history was created. Boys, on the other hand, made a great show of enjoying these accounts. In English lessons, almost all the books which were used featured boys as the main characters, often dealing with the problems of the male adolescent. When I discussed this with one particular English teacher she said that this had never occurred to her before, but it was clearly not fair:

> We certainly wouldn't expect boys to put up with listening to stories about girls all the time, but we do expect girls to do it.

When teachers did make an attempt to appeal to girls, this sometimes also reinforced sexist stereotypes. An extreme example of this was provided by Mr Sluggett's history lessons at Greenhill. Queen Mary I's persecution of Protestants, he told them, was due to the fact that she had had a very unfulfilled life because she had not been allowed to marry for political reasons. The girls in the class were asked to imagine her situation:

> When you leave school you may have a career and you may want to return to it afterwards, but still at the heart of your lives will be getting married and having children. It's the most natural thing in the world despite what some feminists might like to say.

Another blatant example of the reinforcement of traditional gender codes through lesson content was provided in a physics lesson at Greenhill. The physics teacher, Mr Lill, was explaining electricity by asking the class to imagine that positive charges were girls and negative charges were boys. They all knew, he said, that girls tended to run after boys, but were nasty to other girls, and of course boys did not like each other unless they were queer. This analogy was used for several weeks, interspersed with comments about queers and fruitie boys, and was even extended to the description of an ammeter as a dirty old man standing on the street corner counting girls going by. Mr Lill explained his strategy thus:

> I always try to get rid of the abstract terms in physics. That's why I talk about girls and sex. I say it's the girls

149

who do most of the running round and the boys are interested but quite lazy.

Quite apart from the fact that his explanation was rather inappropriate given the fact that most girls and boys preferred single-sex friendship groups, it did not occur to him that this explanation might be less than helpful in undermining the masculine image of science.

The examples which have been used here are of a rather extreme nature, and the content of the majority of lessons which I observed was more neutral than this. In many lessons, the masculine bias was fairly subtle: for instance, science lessons would often draw on examples from boys' experience, and deal with subjects with which boys were likely to be familiar – such as electricity and magnetism. There were also many lessons which could not be said to be aimed specifically at either boys or girls. A small minority of lessons actually challenged traditional gender codes: for instance, one drama lesson involved an entire class acting out a space fantasy where they landed on a planet on which gender roles were reversed. This idea was conveyed to pupils in a very interesting way. The teacher, who was also in role, demanded to be taken to the group's leader, and became very angry when a boy was picked for this part, saying that the space travellers were clearly joking. It took some time for the class to realise that a girl had to be picked as leader, and the boys were clearly reluctant to relinquish their leadership role. Overall, however, a significant number of lessons with all groups I observed were based on very traditional conceptions of girls' and boys' interests, and it was apparent that at times the teacher was deliberately appealing to the supposed attraction of violence for boys to hold the attention of a group of potentially disruptive male pupils.

Humour and the derogation of women

Some male teachers dealt with the threat of boys' potentially disruptive behaviour by attempting to establish an atmosphere of male camaraderie based on sexual joking. I asked Mr Broughton, a woodwork teacher at Millbridge, who was also Head of House, whether it made any difference having girls in the classes he taught, and he described how he used the supposed universal appeal of the dirty joke in all boys' groups, which was not possible if girls were present:

> All boys enjoy a dirty joke – I do myself as long as it's clever as well. And if it's all boys you can get them to remember things with it. For instance, you see those pipes over there, well the joints you call male or female for obvious reasons and we have a bit of a laugh over that. That's the nice thing about having all boys – if you've got girls there you can't really do that and you've got to watch your language.

Some of the male teachers' joking specifically involved the derogation of women: for example, at the end of a metalwork lesson boys were told that if they forgot their aprons again they would be issued with frilly pinafores and bras and panties. Cunnison (1989) also talks about the use of gender joking in the staffroom, sometimes as a means of asserting male superiority over women who might overtake them in the promotion race. She makes the point that it may not always be appropriate to use the term 'sexual harassment' to describe this joking, since women may sometimes play along with it or use it for their own ends. Although some of the girls were quite capable of using sexual innuendo themselves, many expressed uneasiness with this type of joking. Girls often objected to the vulgarity of male repartee: for instance, one physics teacher's references to nose-picking were the source of a number of complaints.

Humour, lesson content and allocation of teacher time, then, were all ways in which teachers created an ethos of masculinity in the classroom, which formed an essential part of their strategy for the containment of boys.

The establishment of female solidarity

Just as male teachers appealed to shared notions of masculinity as a central part of their classroom coping strategies, so women teachers in female areas of the curriculum drew on a culture of femininity to win girls' co-operation in the classroom. In art/textiles at Greenhill, for instance, Lois Roughton mingled with the girls as they engaged in a whole range of activities such as dyeing clothes which they brought in from home, screen-printing large covers for floor cushions and making clothes from newspaper patterns. The atmosphere of this lesson, as girls tried on clothes and talked about boys, parents, friends and teachers, was more like a cosy chat in a bedroom than a school lesson. Working-class girls like Susan Piper and Helen Downes, who were often very disruptive, were always co-operative in this particular class. Clearly, these lessons were a welcome escape from the confrontational atmosphere of much of the school day, but also represented a strange contradiction. In some ways, they challenged male power through the estab-lishment of female solidarity which underlies feminist con-sciousness. In other ways, however, these lessons were reinforcing the idea of the appropriateness of domesticity for women. Writers such as Holly (1987) and Wolpe (1988) have begun to draw attention to the importance of young women's developing sexuality in affecting their attitudes towards educa-tion. Early experiences of menstruation, for instance, may be extremely difficult for girls to cope with, particularly in an environment where this is regarded as something shameful. Prendergast (1987) suggests that many girls may use up an immense amount of energy concealing the fact that they have a period, trekking home at luchtime to wash because the toilets are dirty at school and they will be jeered at by boys if sanitary towels are discovered in their bags. Clearly, schools which are concerned about gender differentiation in the curriculum must do some serious thinking about the general ethos both inside and outside the classroom. It is clearly their responsibility to ensure that where girls and boys are together there is a comfortable and relaxed atmosphere in which all pupils can learn effectively. Until this happens, girls will continue to seek out their own space, no matter what the educational cost.

Gender and coercive sanctions

When attempts to win the consent of boys to teachers' auth-ority failed, then male teachers would use physical violence as a sanction, drawing on notions of the acceptability of male aggression as a means of control. Mr Broughton said that it was because of the availability of this sanction that he found boys easier to control:

The boy thinks he might get a smack either round the ear

or up the backside or whatever, whereas the girl knows you won't do it. I think there is this built in thing that boys can be beaten into submission at home or at school. It's historical more than at present.

This teacher was not typical of male teachers at Millbridge, but since he was head of house he had considerable influence, being responsible for the discipline of a quarter of the children in the school. The symbolic power of the cane as the ultimate sanction against male pupils was clearly demonstrated at Greenhill. Shortly after the start of the autumn term, three boys who had been involved in feuding between the different middle schools were caned, and Mr Flanders, the head of year, held an assembly for the boys in which he displayed the cane and said that the boys who had been punished in this way were really cowards. Many teachers said they supported this show of toughness because it showed the power of those in authority in the school.

Sanctions used by male teachers in the control of boys, then, reinforced traditional notions of the legitimacy of male control through the use of violence. Similarly, traditional meanings of femininity were drawn upon in the control of female pupils. For some teachers, this was a consciously formulated strategy: for instance, Mr Jones, the head of biology at Millbridge said:

> I certainly use sex in the way I teach. I tease girls much more than boys – with quiet girls it's the only way to get them to say anything. It's one of my teaching weapons.

Cunnison (1984) describes female teachers who also used their power as sexually mature women in order to control boys. However, I found this was a much more common strategy among men as a means of controlling girls. Only one woman at Greenhill said that she found older boys easier to deal with than younger ones, because as boys matured it was easier to appeal to them on a semi-serious level of flirtation. Many male teachers referred to girls as 'love' or 'dear', and allowed 'the ladies' to leave the class before the boys. Cajoling or humouring was often used by male teachers as ways of avoiding confrontation with girls. Pat Rennick, a Greenhill pupil, was sent out of RE for shouting at a teacher, and this is her account of what happened:

He says, 'Get out, I'm not having you shouting like this in my lesson. Come back when you're better behaved.' And then when he comes out he turns it into a joke. He's laughing and says, 'There's no need to get like that.' And I says, 'It's my Dad and that . . . I'm so used to my Dad keeping on to me, you know he teases me, I just crack up in the end, I can't help it.'

Pat is able to escape responsibility for her rudeness by drawing on the teacher's sympathy for her emotional state. Buswell (1984) describes similar incidents where male teachers control girls by appealing to their emotionality. Ultimately, she says, this is against girls' interests because they are learning how to survive through the use of manipulative strategies in relationships with men which are fundamentally unequal. Girls' exploitation of traditional gender codes as a form of contestation will be returned to later in this chapter.

So far, then, it has been argued that both male and female teachers appealed to traditional notions of masculinity and femininity in controlling girls and boys in the classroom. Pupils were able to contest teachers' power by adopting modes of behaviour which apparently reflected, but in reality parodied, these gender codes. They also brought their own conceptions of masculinity and femininity with them to the classroom, which did not necessarily conform to those of teachers, and the contradictions between competing gender codes could be used by pupils in their opposition to education. I will now consider exactly what form this contestation took, and whether it represented effective challenging to broader gender and class divisions, or whether it was simply a manifestation of individual anger without radical implications.

BOYS' MANIPULATION OF TRADITIONAL GENDER CODES AS A MEANS OF CONTESTATION

Boys and the culture of masculinity

In the previous section it has been argued that male teachers appealed to a shared culture of masculinity – based on acceptance of violence, sexual bravado, and derogation of women – in their attempts to win the consent of boys to their authority in the classroom. Some boys accepted this definition of masculinity, but far from seeing it as a legitimation of teacher authority, used it to challenge this very authority. It is interesting that this was most apparent at both schools in metalwork lessons, where traditional masculinity was presented in its crudest form in order to contain the most disaffected working-class pupils.

A description of one particular metalwork lesson at Greenhill will perhaps give some idea of the general atmosphere. In many ways the workshop felt like a factory, with very high noise levels caused partly by the work and partly by pupils kicking bits of metal around and shouting to each other above the din. Boys showed a great deal of physical aggression to each other, and sometimes hammered each other's work destructively. Sexual imagery was used in a less than subtle way. One boy walked round with a bit of metal tubing between his lags pretending that he had an erection. Confrontation with the teacher was almost continuous, who shouted at them several times that this was 'a man's workshop, not a little kid's workshop'. The atmosphere between the teacher and one particular boy, Desmond Rawlinson, was almost electric. Desmond crashed around the room muttering: 'I hope he punches me and then I'll punch him back.' Ultimately, the head of year was sent for, causing great excitement and anticipation: 'I bet he gets caned.'

Although not popular with the other boys, who regarded him as a bit of a bighead, Desmond was also looked on with a certain amount of admiration: 'He's a nutter, he doesn't care what he says to anyone.' This particular pupil was clearly challenging the teacher's claim to a monopoly on the use of violence and aggression, and other boys followed his example in a less extreme form. Appeals to Desmond to behave like a man were clearly wasted, since his behaviour was a logical extension of the code of masculinity which operated in this classroom. The sanctioning of macho behaviour was a particular problem for women teachers who were not able to use the threat of violence as a means of control. Carol Jenkins, a woman RE teacher at Millbridge talked about this:

The boys can ride their motorbikes through the social area and it really does not matter. I think that makes life very difficult for women teachers because the law of the jungle starts to apply. The men who can actually assert themselves physically and be menacing are just fine, and the individuals who can't do that not only suffer because some individuals can do that but because you can't do it yourself. You fall back on methods of discipline that I don't approve of, and I wouldn't want to implement even if I could, which I can't.

Encouragement of a code of masculinity based on the legitimacy of male aggression was particularly prevalent in classes where working-class pupils predominated. It was, however, a dangerous strategy, in that it could be used to undermine as well as uphold teachers' authority. It also had the potential to undermine the authority of women teachers who had to base their discipline on what Cunnison (1984) has termed moral rather than macho authority. It is interesting to note that a pervading theme of recent literature (Connell, 1986; Weis, 1990; Crump, 1990) is the tendency for masculine culture to remain relatively unchanged whilst girls increasingly seek out new understandings of femininity.

Sexual harrassment of women teachers

Another way in which boys could exploit accepted notions of masculinity was through their aggressive behaviour towards women teachers. Walkerdine (1981) has observed that liberal educational philosophy legitimises any expression of male aggression as natural and normal, and this allows boys to contest the authority of women teachers. Although this was not the normal pattern of behaviour at either school, I observed clear instances of sexual harassment at both. At Greenhill, for instance, three boys in a Main Group 5 class persistently abused their home economics teacher. In one lesson, she was called a wanker and told to fuck off by one of the boys, but instead of rebuking him for these comments, he was told to make less noise. On another occasion, James made a piece of dough into a penis and followed the teacher round the room with this. Again, the sexual implications of his behaviour were ignored, and he was told to get on with his work. Perhaps these boys felt that their gender identity was compromised by their presence in a female area of the curriculum, and therefore felt the need to assert their masculinity in this exaggerated form. Boys, then, challenged teachers' authority by assuming an exaggerated form of masculine behaviour which was legitimised by the established gender code of the classroom. I will now consider how girls, too, manipulated traditional gender codes in order to challenge teacher power.

GIRLS' MANIPULATION OF TRADITIONAL GENDER CODES AS A MEANS OF CONTESTATION

The exploitation of the code of femininity

Just as some boys manipulated traditional constructions of masculinity to oppose teachers' authority, so girls parodied the accepted code of femininity in their contestation of schooling. Almost all girls were involved in this to a greater or lesser extent. For instance, uniform would be subverted by accompanying it with red lacy fingerless gloves or many dangly earrings. A continuum seemed to exist, with some girls abiding completely by the rules of uniform, some diverging slightly, and others using dress and make-up in an obviously rebellious fashion. The latter group were predominantly, but not exclusively, working-class. At Greenhill, a little make-up was allowed to be worn by girls because this was considered to be attractively feminine, but some girls would wear a large amount of punk style make-up, clearly exploiting the fact that it was impossible to draw a clear line between the conventional and subversive forms of feminine style. In almost every lesson, girls could be seen doing their hair, and in some cases this was taken to the limits of absurdity. During one maths lesson, Helen Downes produced a large make-up kit, with a mirror which illuminated when the lid was open. She proceeded to spread out the cosmetics on the desk-top as if it were a dressing table, and apply the make-up, asking for comments from the girls nearby. Amazingly, the male teacher completely ignored what was going on. For most girls, the styles they adopted did not seem to represent a conscious challenging of the school's notion of acceptable forms of femininity. However, there were some exceptions. Susan Burton, a high-achieving girl at

157

Millbridge, for instance, talked about the way in which she deliberately wore make-up and short skirts because she resented the way in which teachers immediately assumed you were stupid if you dressed stylishly. For her, there was a certain amount of satisfaction in confounding their expectations.

Other examples of girls' exploitation of the code of femininity was their use of male teachers' reluctance to confront (see earlier description of this particular coping strategy). This conversation with Susan Piper provides a vivid illustration.

> S.R.: D'you think girls can get away with more with male teachers?
>
> Susan: Yes. Like Mr Fison said to me the other day, 'cos I didn't hand my homework in and he gave the boys that didn't a mouthful and he says to me he goes, 'You hand it in to me on Monday morning.' He goes, 'You bat your eyelids and it melts my heart.' So we put on our sweet and innocent look.

Particularly in masculine areas of the curriculum such as physics, girls exploited the assumption of helplessness by withdrawing and doing very little work at all. A few male teachers at both schools said they were aware of this strategy, but were unsure of how to deal with it:

> I know one or two girls say things like, 'Oh, it's probably me. I seem to get most things wrong' . . . Sort of like, 'Oh women, they're the weaker sex. They don't get things right, they get things wrong. Therefore I've got this thing wrong. Therefore don't be cross with me. It's wrong. If you'd helped me . . .'. That's the kind of inference. And I'm sure some of them turn on a bit of charm or whatever to take the edge off things.
>
> (Mr Douglas, geography teacher at Millbridge)

Girls, then, were able to use the assumption that females were quiet, helpless, emotional and very conscious of their appearance to avoid aspects of school that they found boring or difficult.

Girls' expropriation of male characteristics

A further way in which girls were able to contest the teachers' authority was by directly challenging the prevailing code of femininity with their own cultural understandings. As we have already noted, the naturalness of girls' maturity, seen as synonymous with quietness and good behaviour, was assumed by most teachers. In both schools, recognisable groups of girls totally confounded these expectations. At Millbridge, for instance, one group of girls would exasperate the teacher by talking in just audible voices, making funny noises, pulling each other's hair, reading magazines under the table and always being on the wrong page. Julie explained their behaviour like this:

> We really hate Mr Pinkerton because he won't explain anything to us. But the lessons are quite good fun because we really wind him up. He really lost his temper with me once and hit me. He looked ever so funny.

Far from gaining status in the girls' eyes, this teacher lost credibility even further by resorting to physical violence, a sanction which transgressed the accepted code of femininity. The teacher himself felt confused about the way in which the behaviour of these girls deviated from his idea of approporiate feminine behaviour. He expressed this by referring to them as 'that posse of girls' and calling them by their surnames like the boys.

As we have already seen, sexual joking and allusions were taken to be perfectly normal for boys but unacceptable for girls. During one physics lesson, Helen Downes and Susan Piper openly challenged this norm. A diagram on the board showing a hand holding a metal bar elicited the following comment from Susan: 'Cor, I can think of something better to have your hand round.' Later, when the girls were told to hurry up with their work, Helen reminded Mr Savage of the accepted code of femininity: 'You've got to be gentle with us sir.' When the class were gathered round the front bench listening to the teacher's explanation of an experiment, Susan repeated in a clearly audible voice: 'Undo your trousers. Undo your trousers.' Mr Savage was clearly embarrassed and ignored her for several minutes. Finally he told her to go and stand in a corner without telling her why. When she demanded an explanation, he said: 'Because you keep on saying "Undo your trousers".' To which Susan replied: 'It's only a joke.'

This incident is very similar to the behaviour of the boys in the home economics lesson described earlier. However, whereas such behaviour was quite common among boys, it was very rare among girls, and clearly caused the teacher a great deal of consternation. Part of the shock value of Susan's behaviour was that it confounded expectations of female sexual passivity and ignorance, and might thus be described as 'breaking role' (Cunnison, 1985). On several other occasions, these girls used similar oppositional strategies: for instance performing an elaborate striptease when asked to take off a coat in an RE lesson.

But even though Susan and Helen's behaviour might be seen as a challenge to the traditional code of femininity, this was undermined by their other actions. They described female teachers, even those who were generally sympathetic to the girls' perspective, as 'bitchy' and used sexually derogatory language such as 'dog' and 'slag' against other girls. Cowie and Lees (1981), reporting work they carried out in a London comprehensive school, describe similar examples of boys using sexually derogatory language against girls, and girls themselves using it against each other. Even though Susan and Helen expressed a great deal of loyalty to each other, they clearly felt no solidarity towards other women and girls, and were taking on an aggressive role in attacking them. As mentioned in Chapter 4, Connell (1986) notes the problems of women teachers in relating to the feminism of working-class girls, which is very different from that of the intellectuals. According to Connell, working-class feminism 'is often manifested in schools as uncontrollable behaviour by girls, sexual aggressiveness, hostility to the authority of teachers; things that define the pupil as a trouble maker, not an ally' (p. 191). He asserts that one of the effects of teachers' middle-class feminism is to split off a small group of working-class girls in an attempt to attach them to 'the teachers' mode of career-orientated feminism' (p 191). At both schools, it was indeed possible to detect a small group of working-class girls who were less likely to challenge teachers' authority in the classroom and were determined to change the pattern of established gender relations. Catherine Thomas, for instance, a working-class Greenhill pupil, wanted to gain access to areas of work and leisure restricted to boys, and was actively critical of traditional female spheres of activity. Although she said she loved 'making havoc in a class where the teacher was really pathetic', she also believed in 'work time and playing-in time'. Disrupting lessons through the challenging of gender codes would not have assisted her in her ambition to become a doctor, and she was dismissive of girls who wasted time in physics and metalwork. Her behaviour was very like that of the black girls described by Fuller (1983), who had to tread a difficult path between working for the academic qualifications they needed to secure their independence, whilst at the same time not appearing to condone the school's authority. Middle-class girls like Susan Burton were also involved in challenging gender relations in ways which were acceptable to teachers, in her case by negotiating the right to be both sexually attractive and intellectual. There is clearly substantial evidence here to support Connell's contention that a number of versions of femininity are evident in the classroom, which both the school as a whole and individual teachers either reward or reject. A moot point which remains, however, is whether the gender code of working-class girls like Susan Piper is genuinely productive of radical change, as Connell argues, or whether it is more likely to result in the reconstitution of women's subordinate status.

CONCLUSION

Recent work in the sociology of education, reacting to over-deterministic functionalist and Marxist accounts of schooling, has tended to stress the problematic nature of social reproduction, and has highlighted pupils' resistance to many elements of compulsory schooling. A number of writers – for instance, Willis (1977) and Anyon (1983) – have argued that resistance to schooling may ultimately reinforce rather than undermine traditional class and gender codes. Anyon has pointed out that resistance to the ideology of femininity:

> is often a defensive action (no matter how creative) that is aimed not at transforming patriarchal or other social structures, but at gaining a measure of protection within these.
>
> (Anyon, 1983, p.000)

Hargreaves (1982) has discussed the problem of discriminating between actions which challenge social relations, and those which merely represent a negative response to education. Aggleton and Whitty (1985), in an interesting discussion of middle-class children's 'resistance' to schooling, maintain that a distinction must be made between individualised contestation and effective resistance to prevailing patterns of class and gender relations. One of the problems of making such a distinction is that it is impossible to know the long-term effects of pupils' resistances, nor to have complete access to their intentions. However, despite these problems of interpretation, it was apparent that much of the parodying and contradiction of traditional gender codes supported rather than undermined patriarchal relations. In their exaggerated displays of masculinity and femininity, pupils were locking themselves firmly into restricted gender roles. Even the few girls who deliberately rejected the conventional notion of femininity in their opposition to schooling were, in my view, strengthening gender divisions by uncritically adopting male modes of behaviour, and sometimes oppressing other women. On this point, Connell would disagree with me. By way of contrast, girls who endorsed at least some of the school's aims, but were challenging male domination of particular areas of activity within the school, were probably offering more effective resistance to traditional gender ideology. Black (1987) has argued that disruptive classroom behaviour has occupied too much of the attention of educational sociologists, who have ignored the analysis of conformist patterns of behaviour adopted by the majority of pupils and especially by girls. Here, I have tried to explore the significance of both confrontational and conformist behaviour, and have suggested that we should not exaggerate the potential of contestational behaviour per se to bring about radical change in school.

In this chapter, I have analysed particular incidents in the classroom to illustrate the way in which male social dominance was achieved. Teacher coping strategies, based on their typifications of male and female pupils, were identified as a central means by which traditional constructions of masculinity and femininity were conveyed to pupils. Pupils' opposition to schooling was often based on the manipulation of these gender codes, either by adopting them in an exaggerated form or, in the case of some girls, by assuming modes of behaviour normally associated with boys. Far from weakening existing gender divisions, contestation of this sort possibly streng-thened them. Girls who were not totally rejecting schooling, but attempting to use it for their own ends, were perhaps more likely to be successful in subverting the traditional code of femininity. The contradictions embedded in many girls' view of the world, conveyed so powerfully in the interviews, are also apparent in the nature of their interactions with other pupils and teachers in the classroom. My overwhelming impression was of the girls' lack of access to any sort of analysis which would help them to make sense of the different strands of their experience. The seeds of discontent which may form the basis of radical change were present, but without discussion or analysis, all that most girls could do was to work out their own personal survival strategy.

8

PARENTS AND THE
CULTURE OF FEMININITY

INTRODUCTION

Analysis of pupils' construction of gender codes suggested that
although they were continuing to make traditional subject
choices and in general terms felt that some subjects were more
suitable for one sex or the other, in some respects they were
beginning to envisage change in their adult roles. A minority of
middle- and working-class girls were anticipating joint
responsibility with their partner for work and childcare. In
their general attitudes towards gender equality, girls exhibited
a greater capacity than boys to critique traditional gender
codes. Interviews and observation highlighted some reasons for
their decision to stick to female areas of the curriculum rather
than venturing into masculine territory. Working-class girls
often saw no alternative to routine office work and accepted,
albeit unwillingly, the restrictions motherhood would inevitably place on their lives. A minority of girls were envisaging
far more major structural changes in the division of domestic
labour to enable them to fulfil a greater role in the world of paid
employment. This chapter shifts the focus to parents' constructions of masculinity and femininity and questions whether they
are likely to exert a progressive or a conservative influence
with regard to girls' developing construction of femininity.

This discussion is particularly relevant in the light of teachers' view that parents' attitudes represented the most
significant obstacle to breaking down gender divisions in the
curriculum. The school as an institution, on the other hand,
was seen as a neutral or benign influence, trying to help each
pupil to fulfil his or her potential, and both child-centred

ideology and the ideology of free choice were used as justifica-
tions of this position. The effect of this belief was, of course, to
absolve the schools and individual teachers from responsibility
for taking any action to dissuade pupils from making sex-
stereotyped option choices. One of the aims of exploring
parents' gender codes was to investigate whether teachers
were right to make these assumptions.

I was also interested in exploring the validity of some of the
theoretical ideas which have been put forward with regard to
patterns of gender socialisation at home and at school. David
(1981), for example, has argued that the family and the school
are two key institutions which work in a mutually supportive
way to reproduce traditional gender relations. Arnot (1982) has
suggested that there may be a degree of dissonance between
the official gender code of the school and that received from
children from different social backgrounds, and discipline problems in the classroom may occur when such a clash occurs (see
Chapter 6 for further discussion of this point). Little work has
been carried out to test these ideas empirically, although the
research of Kelly (1982) is a notable exception. One of my
objectives, therefore, in carrying out detailed research with
parents was to attempt to understand how their views on
gender relations articulated with those of the school.

PARENTS' PERCEPTIONS OF THE GENDER
APPROPRIATENESS OF PARTICULAR SUBJECTS

As an indicator of their general attitudes towards gender
divisions within the curriculum, parents were asked, like the
pupils, to rate the importance of each subject on the third-year
curriculum for girls and boys on a five-point scale. Mean
ratings of subjects for girls and boys are shown in Figures 8.1
and 8.2. The pattern at both schools was broadly the same, with
physics and chemistry rated higher for boys than girls and craft
subjects also strongly sex-stereotyped. It is interesting to note
that in the case of boys, academic subjects had higher mean
ratings than technical subjects, whereas for girls, at both
schools home economics was rated after English, maths and
careers in front of all other academic subjects. The fact that
home economics for boys at both schools was rated higher than
needlework and at about the same level as French, indicates

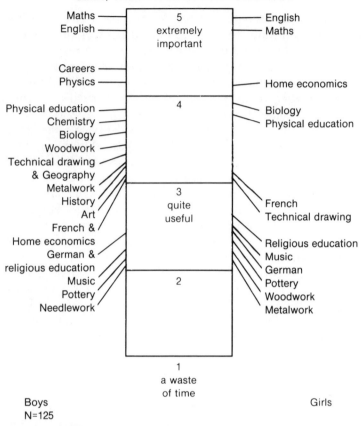

Figure 8.1 Millbridge parents' mean ratings of subject importance for boys and girls

that parents might be more sympathetic to boys crossing gender boundaries here than in needlework, for example.

Tables 8.1 and 8.2 reveal which of these differences in ratings were statistically significant for Millbridge and Greenhill parents respectively. At both schools, the differences in parents' ratings of physics, chemistry and craft subjects for boys and girls were found to be very significant. Women's ratings of these subjects were just as sex-stereotyped as men's and there were also no significant differences between working-class and middle-class parents, although middle-class parents made slightly less distinction between the importance of chemistry for boys and girls than did other groups.

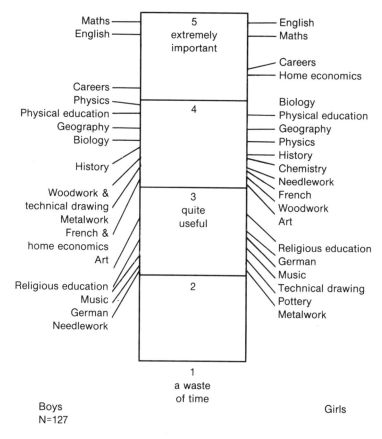

Figure 8.2 Greenhill parents' mean ratings of subject importance for boys and girls

The ratings of a particular subject for a single sex by women and men and working-class and middle-class parents were also compared (Tables 8.3 and 8.4). No significant differences were found for science, although a more detailed analysis showed that middle-class mothers at Greenhill rated physics for girls higher than working-class mothers. At both schools, there were far fewer differences in the ratings of subjects by women and men than by working-class and middle-class parents. Technical drawing, metalwork and woodwork for boys, however, were rated higher by working-class parents than middle-class parents at both schools. Similarly, at both schools, home

Table 8.1 Wilcoxon test applied to Millbridge parents' perceived importance of subjects for girls and boys

Subject assessed for boys and girls	Group doing the assessing					Sex for whom subject rated more important
	All parents	Women	Men	Working class	Middle class	
Physics	z = -6.093 p < .001	z = -4.541 p < .001	z = -4.107 p < .001	z = -5.303 p < .001	z = -3.059 p < .01	Boys
Chemistry	z = -4.317 p < .001	z = -2.741 p < .01	z = -3.375 p < .001	z = -3.735 p < .001	z = -2.201 p < .05	Boys
Technical drawing	z = -6.955 p < .001	z = -5.303 p < .001	z = -4.541 p < .001	z = -5.905 p < .001	z = -3.724 p < .001	Boys
Metalwork	z = -7.898 p < .001	z = -5.905 p < .001	z = -5.313 p < .001	z = -6.618 p < .001	z = -4.372 p < .001	Boys
Woodwork	z = -7.826 p < .001	z = -5.905 p < .001	z = -5.188 p < .001	z = -6.420 p < .001	z = -4.541 p < .001	Boys
Home economics	z = -6.630 p < .001	z = -4.469 p < .001	z = -4.563 p < .001	z = -5.711 p < .001	z = -3.007 p < .01	Girls
Needlework	z = -8.136 p < .001	z = -6.031 p < .001	z = -5.502 p < .001	z = -6.629 p < .001	z = -4.782 p < .001	Girls
Geography	z = -2.310 p < .05	z = -2.023 p < .05	ns	z = -2.028 p < .05	ns	Boys
Music	z = -2.023 p < .05	ns	ns	ns	ns	Girls

Note: Only those subjects have been included for which significant differences were found in ratings for boys and girls.

Table 8.2 Wilcoxon test applied to Greenhill parents' perceived importance of subjects for girls and boys

| Subject assessed for boys and girls | All parents | Group doing the assessing | | | | Sex for whom subject rated more important |
		Women	Men	Working class	Middle class	
Physics	z = -5.012 p < .001	z = -3.724 p < .001	z = -3.408 p < .001	z = -4.015 p < .001	z = -2.521 p < .01	Boys
Chemistry	z = -3.920 p < .001	z = -3.059 p < .001	z = -2.521 p < .01	z = -2.934 p < .01	z = -2.023 p < .05	Boys
Technical drawing	z = -6.567 p < .001	z = -5.232 p < .001	z = -4.015 p < .001	z = -5.159 p < .001	z = -2.666 p < .01	Boys
Metalwork	z = -7.525 p < .001	z = -5.905 p < .001	z = -4.703 p < .001	z = -5.777 p < .001	z = -3.920 p < .001	Boys
Woodwork	z = -7.138 p < .001	z = -5.352 p < .001	z = -4.782 p < .001	z = -5.579 p < .001	z = -3.621 p < .001	Boys
Home economics	z = -6.636 p < .001	z = -5.159 p < .001	z = -4.184 p < .001	z = -4.806 p < .001	z = -3.296 p < .001	Girls
Needlework	z = -6.550 p < .001	z = -4.975 p < .001	z = -4.286 p < .001	z = -4.992 p < .001	z = -3.059 p < .001	Girls
Geography	z = -2.023 p < .05	ns	ns	ns	ns	Boys
Maths	z = -2.521 p < .01	ns	z = -2.023 p < .05	z = -2.023 p < .05	ns	Boys
French	z = -2.030 p < .05	ns	ns	z = -2.366 p < .05	ns	Girls
German	z = -2.030 p < .05	ns	ns	z = -2.030 p < .05	ns	Girls
Pottery	z = -2.201 p < .05	ns	ns	ns	ns	Girls
Careers	z = -2.023 p < .05	ns	ns	ns	ns	Boys

Note: Only those subjects have been included for which significant differences were found in ratings for girls and boys.

Table 8.3 Mann–Whitney U test applied to differences between women and men and working-class and middle-class parents at Millbridge in their assessment of the importance of a subject for a given sex

Groups whose assessment is compared		Women/men	Working-class/middle-class parents
French {	Boys	u = 1335.5, z = -2.774, $p < .01$, Mo	u = 1342.9, z = -2.2231, $p < .05$, Mi
	Girls	u = 1376.0, z = -2.705, $p < .01$, Mo	u = 1308.0, z = -2.681, $p < .01$, Mi
Technical drawing {	Boys	ns	u = 993.0, z = -3.746, $p < .001$, W
	Girls	ns	ns
Metalwork {	Boys	ns	u = 1063.5, z = -3.3516, $p < .001$, W
	Girls	ns	ns
Woodwork {	Boys	ns	u = 1190.0, z = -2.614, $p < .01$, W
	Girls	ns	ns
Home economics {	Boys	u = 1398.5, z = -1.959, $p < .05$, Mo	u = 1140.0, z = -3.377, $p < .001$, W
	Girls	ns	ns
Needlework {	Boys	ns	u = 1208.5, z = -2.927, $p < .001$, W
	Girls	ns	ns
PE {	Boys	ns	ns
	Girls	u = 1391.0, z = -2.2873, $p < .05$, F	ns

Notes: (1) Mo = subject rated more important by mothers; F = subject rated more important by fathers; W = subject rated more important by working-class parents; Mi = subject rated more important by middle-class parents. (2) Only those subjects have been included for which significant differences were found between the ratings of different groups.

Table 8.4 Mann–Whitney U test applied to differences between women and men and working-class and middle-class parents at Greenhill in their assessment of the importance of a student for a given sex

Groups whose assessment is compared		Women/men	Working-class/middle-class parents
French	Boys	ns	u = 652.5, z = −4.122, p < .0001, Mi
	Girls	ns	u = 823.0, z = −3.124, p < .01, Mi
German	Boys	ns	u = 791.5, z = −2.950, p < .01, Mi
	Girls	ns	u = 884.0, z = −2.469, p < .01, Mi
Maths	Boys	u = 1656.0, z = 2.592, p < .01, Mo	ns
	Girls	u = 1620.5, z = 2.399, p < .05, Mo	ns
Technical Drawing	Boys	ns	u = 724.5, z = −3.4767, p < .001, W
	Girls	ns	ns
Metalwork	Boys	ns	u = 725.5, z = −3.531, p < .001, W
	Girls	ns	ns
Woodwork	Boys	ns	u = 647.0, z = −4.002, p < .0001, W
	Girls	ns	ns
Home economics	Boys	ns	u = 806.5, z = −2.688, p < .01, W
	Girls	ns	u = 566.5, z = −4.987, p < .0001, W
Needlework	Boys	ns	u = 687.0, z = −3.999, p < .0001, W
	Girls	ns	ns
Music	Boys	ns	u = 780.5, z = −3.089, p < .001, Mi
	Girls	ns	u = 857.0, z = −2.858, p < .001, Mi
PE	Boys	ns	ns
	Girls	ns	ns
Careers	Boys	ns	u = 718.5, z = −3.238, p < .001, W
	Girls	ns	u = 808.0, z = −2.676, p < .01, W
Religious education	Boys	ns	u = 843.5, z = −2.036, p < .05, Mi
	Girls	ns	u = 900.0, z = −2.083, p < .05, Mi

Notes: (1) Mo = subject rated more important by mothers; F = subject rated more important by fathers; W = subject rated more important by working-class parents; Mi = subject rated more important by middle-class parents. (2) Only those subjects have been included for which significant differences were found between the ratings of different groups.

economics and needlework were rated higher by working-class parents than middle-class parents, but again, only for girls. So although middle-class parents made significant differences in the importance of craft subjects for boys and girls, they generally attached less importance to these subjects than working-class parents. This is certainly reflected in the sex and class of pupils who opt into these subject areas and may also explain the craft teachers' frequent lament that their subjects occupied very low status in the school. It is also interesting to note that languages for both sexes were rated higher by middle-class than working-class parents and working-class parents apparently placed more importance on careers than did middle-class parents. So it would appear that class, as well as sex of parent and sex of child, was an important factor in affecting parents' perception of subject importance.

An interesting comparison can be made here with the findings of Kelly *et al.* (1982). In this study, parents of third-year pupils in a Manchester comprehensive school were asked to rate the importance of subjects on the third-year curriculum for their particular child rather than for girls and boys in general. Few sex differences in the importance ratings of subjects for boys and girls were found, the only exceptions being woodwork and metalwork which were rated higher for boys, and home economics and needlework, which were rated higher for girls. Fewer class differences were also found, with home economics and needlework for girls being rated higher by working-class than middle-class parents, and physics for boys and languages for girls rated higher by middle-class parents than working-class parents. So, although the broad pattern between the Westshire and Manchester parents was similar, it would appear that there were more differences between Westshire working-class and middle-class parents. It is possible that some of these differences could be accounted for by the form in which the question was put, since Kelly asked about the importance of the subject for the parent's particular child whereas Millbridge and Greenhill parents were asked about the importance of subjects for boys and girls generally. However it is also possible that the findings represent real differences between parents in different geographical areas, with sex-typing of subjects being stronger among rural and small-town parents. Class differences would also appear to be more marked among Westshire parents, with working-class parents sex-typing certain areas of the curriculum particularly strongly. Variations in local labour markets, with narrower employment opportunities in rural areas might possibly account for some of these trends. A further factor which might have some influence is the attitude of the school itself. At Tall Trees School, where Kelly carried out her research, the female head and deputy head were both committed to the aims of the GIST project and the school operated a craft circus in the first two years so that all pupils did all craft subjects. At Greenhill and Millbridge, there was no similar positive endorsement of gender equality and the schools' reluctance to take this issue seriously may well have been apparent to parents. This might be an example of the way in which the school does not simply respond to parental attitudes, but actually plays a part in shaping them.

Like their sons and daughters, Millbridge and Greenhill parents were clear in their view of the gender-specific nature of particular curricular areas. Overall, physical science and craft subjects were the main areas where differences were found in the ratings of subject importance for girls and boys by all groups. There were also differences in these areas in the ratings of a particular subject for a given sex between working-class and middle-class parents and men and women. These areas have been identified as being of crucial educational importance, since they are necessary qualifications for the highest paid jobs in both professional and manual work. They also carry important symbolic messages concerning the appropriate behaviour, values and interests of men and women both in the work place and the home. Given these views, it is not surprising that most parents were on the whole accepting of the school's role in the process of option choice.

PARENTS' VIEWS OF WHY GIRLS AND BOYS CHOSE DIFFERENTLY

Despite the fact that many parents clearly endorsed gender divisions within the curriculum, most whom I interviewed said that they were in favour of the principle of equal opportunities and were not opposed to girls and boys entering non-traditional areas of the curriculum. When it came to the moment of subject option choice, however, many felt very worried about their own children deviating from the norm. As we saw in Chapter 4, teachers blamed individual pupils, their peer groups and their families for the reproduction of traditional social divisions within the curriculum. When parents were asked why they thought option choice resulted in the remaking of these divisions, they located the source of sex-stereotyping outside rather than within the family. It is worth considering parents' views on this matter in some detail, since this helps to explain why most parents were apparently acquiescent in the system of option choice.

A minority of parents felt that pupils' decisions resulted from given pre-dispositions within their genetic make-up and hence there was no effective action which the school could take to alter the situation. Mrs Brewster, for instance, felt that the school had no right to encourage girls to take up science:

> No, I don't think it should be encouraged. If they're science minded, they're going to take up science anyway, aren't they?

Most parents, however, like the teachers, subscribed to some degree of environmental determinism, blaming, amongst other things, peer group pressure, the media and the nature of toys given to children. Mr Smith, a long-distance lorry driver, suggested that boys' view of masculinity was instrumental in preventing more from taking up home economics:

> D'you think part of it is the boys think they might get hassle from other lads? I'm sure this is to do with it some time at school. Perhaps other lads have told them it's cissy . . . You do get a lot of this sort of bullying at school . . . I'm sure this must influence kids. And girls can be very catty and bitchy with one another.

Some parents felt that within their own families they had gone to great lengths to discourage sex-differentiated attitudes and saw it as evidence of the strength of peer group pressure when their children continued to be attracted to male or female areas of the curriculum.

Like the teachers, parents' perception of the overwhelming power of the forces of social conditioning led them to doubt the feasibility of innovations to bring about change. The views of

Mrs Drew, a teacher, were typical of those of many parents. The reason for girls and boys doing different subjects was, she said:

> Purely habit handed down over the generations – the boys doing technical things and the girls don't. Some people say it's inborn that girls play with dolls and boys play with cars. But it's the toys you buy them and how they're brought up, isn't it? It follows on – as they go to school.

Despite the fact that Mrs Drew was quite prepared to talk in general terms about sex-role stereotyping in the family, she was still reluctant to apply this to her own particular family, insisting that it was purely chance that Angela did not enjoy playing with the computer, whereas Mr Drew and his son spent hours working out new programs. It would appear that environmental determinism has a marked impact not only on teachers, but also on parents' view of what can be achieved by the education system. Similarly, parents were very quick to blame what was happening 'out there', but not to analyse critically what was happening within their own families.

It should be noted that there was a group of parents, many of whom were middle-class professionals, who felt that the attitudes of the school and the teachers themselves were strongly involved in this channelling process. Mr Roper, a technical college lecturer, said:

> It's a combination of obviously well-ingrained social pressures which have persisted for a long time and will continue to persist. I suspect that the same pressures affect teachers, who again, I suspect, probably do tend to unconsciously reflect these pressures in their attitudes to the different subjects for the different sexes. I don't know about Millbridge, but I know that some schools are blatantly sexist in the way they direct children to certain subjects. I know some schools where girls aren't allowed to do metalwork because there are only enough places in the workshop for boys, that sort of thing.

However, whilst many parents felt that social processes both inside and outside the school were responsible for channelling their children into narrow areas of the curriculum, there was considerable opposition to the school actually taking positive action to challenge this outcome. Some parents were suspicious of the idea that politically-motivated teachers might be attempting to influence their child's future and undermine their freedom of choice. Mr Fuller, for instance, a manager in a scientific instrument firm, was concerned about the implications of what he considered to be social engineering:

> I think that depends on how it's done. I could say yes absolutely and mean with the right kind of teacher in the right kind of way, then it could be a wonderful thing because it would help to change our society into a better thing. I could pick a teacher like Mr Robin and I'm sure he tests children by saying, 'Why don't you do this, why don't you do that?' And that's good. But there are some teachers who would do it to provoke a change in society rather than a healthy thinking attitude from the children, and I think that's a problem.

Mr Robinson, a technical college lecturer, who felt that teachers channelled children into sex-stereotyped areas of the curriculum, was sceptical about their ability to take positive action to change this:

> Well if I thought they could do it competently I'd agree, but I have little faith in the primary and secondary teaching profession in understanding the realities of life outside the teaching profession. I think there are very few who are qualified to advise children about what subjects they ought to be doing.

These fathers exemplified the limitations of a narrowly defined equal-opportunities stance. They were aware of the social pressures on individuals to conform to traditional gender codes but were opposed to attempts to challenge and change existing power relations. In this, they closely resembled members of the senior management team in the two schools, who were similarly hostile.

A minority of mothers had far more radical views on the role of the school both in creating gender divisions and in bringing about change. Mrs Brickell, a nurse educator, felt that a combination of factors was responsible for producing particular educational outcomes:

I think the boys are probably thinking more technically than the girls, and I still think very much that's the way society keeps them. I still don't think that in a lot of places people are ready for girls to be technicians and boys to be cooks, it's just not done, and I think there's a bias from teachers to do the same. Although they've been fairly positive in her reports about whether she should do the sciences or not, I wonder if perhaps more time is given to boys in the classroom than is given to the girls.

She felt that it was important for teachers to take action to change the out-dated view of femininity which characterised many of their actions.

Parents' accounts of why girls and boys opted for different routes reveal fundamentally different and opposing perspectives which emerge throughout the following account. First, there were parents who supported the existence of traditional gender divisions and saw these as inevitable. Second, there were the majority of parents who recognised the inequality of gender relations but were not in favour of a major restructuring of power. Finally, there was the small group, consisting almost exclusively of women, who saw gender inequality as a major social problem for which the school should take partial responsibility and should also play an important role in remedying by pursuing anti-sexist policies.

FAMILIES AND THE DOMESTIC DIVISION OF LABOUR

In order to investigate the gender codes which were evident in the everyday lives of families, parents were asked about the domestic chores which their children undertook regularly. Tables 8.5 and 8.8 report which jobs were generally done by girls, which by boys and which by both sexes. There were only four jobs at either school which were done by more than 50 per cent of children, so clearly these young people were adept in making themselves scarce when there was work to be done! In line with pupils' reporting of the domestic chores which they undertook, boys tended to engage in occasional outdoor tasks such as washing the car and gardening and girls were more likely to be involved in daily servicing jobs indoors such as

177

Table 8.5 Chi-square test applied to household jobs done by Millbridge girls and boys according to their parents

Household jobs	Number and % of girls doing job	Number and % of boys doing job	Results of Chi-square test	Which sex is more likely to do job
Cleaning	38 (55.1)	9 (18)	χ^2 = 15.159 df1 p < .0001	
Making own bed	62 (89.9)	34 (66.7)	χ^2 = 8.459 df1 p < .01	Jobs done mainly by girls
Cooking	42 (60.9)	16 (31.4)	χ^2 = 9.070 df1 p < .01	
Washing up	50 (72.5)	24 (47.1)	χ^2 = 6.968 df1 p < .01	
Laying table	43 (62.3)	18 (35.3)	χ^2 = 7.522 df1 p < .01	
Ironing	25 (36.2)	7 (13.7)	χ^2 = 6.489 df1 p < .01	
Taking out rubbish	14 (20.3)	29 (56.9)	χ^2 = 15.506 df1 p < .0001	Jobs done mainly by boys
Gardening	11 (15.9)	25 (49)	χ^2 = 13.744 df1 p < .0001	
Minor household repairs	3 (4.3)	21 (41.2)	χ^2 = 22.611 df1 p < .0001	
Shopping	27 (39.1)	19 (37.3)	ns	Jobs done equally by boys and girls
Washing car	9 (13)	14 (27.5)	ns	
Mending clothes	11 (15.9)	6 (11.8)	ns	
Tidying own room	56 (81.2)	38 (74.5)	ns	

Note: Whole numbers are shown first, followed by percentages in parentheses

Table 8.6 Time per week spent by Millbridge pupils on household jobs according to their parents

	Less than 1 hour	1–3 hours	More than 3 hours
All pupils	32 (28)	55 (52)	21 (20)
Girls	14 (23)	33 (54.1)	14 (23)
Boys	18 (38.3)	22 (46.8)	7 (14.9)
Working class	21 (31.3)	35 (52.2)	11 (16.4)
Middle class	11 (26.8)	20 (48.8)	10 (24.4)

Note: Whole numbers are shown first, followed by percentages in parentheses

Table 8.7 Results of chi-square test applied to Millbridge parents' account of time per week spend on household jobs by their children (by sex of child)

Variables	All parents	Working-class parents	Middle-class parents
Time spend on household jobs by of sex child	ns	$\chi^2 = 6.886$ df2 $p < .05$	ns

cooking and ironing. Shopping was one of the few areas where both sexes appeared to participate fairly frequently and to an equal extent. The amount of time spent by pupils at the two schools on household chores was also very similar (see Tables 8.6 and 8.9) and there were no overall significant differences between working-class and middle-class children. However, further analysis showed that at Millbridge working-class girls spent significantly more time on household jobs than working-class boys, whilst at Greenhill there was an overall significant difference between boys and girls, with girls doing more work than boys. At neither school was there a significant difference between time spent on household jobs by girls and boys in middle-class families.

Household tasks appear to be assigned in a strongly sex-

Table 8.8 Chi-square test applied to household jobs done by Greenhill girls and boys according to their parents

Household job	Number and % of girls doing job	Number and % of boys doing job	Results of chi-square test	Which sex is more likely to do job
Cleaning	29 (49.2)	16 (24.6)	$\chi^2 = 7.027$ dfl p < .01	
Making own bed	54 (91.5)	34 (52.3)	$\chi^2 = 21.223$ dfl p < .0001	
Cooking	38 (64.4)	15 (23.1)	$\chi^2 = 19.931$ dfl p < .0001	Jobs done mainly by girls
Mending clothes	18 (30.5)	4 (6.2)	$\chi^2 = 10.956$ dfl p < .0001	
Tidying own room	54 (91.5)	39 (60)	$\chi^2 = 14.755$ dfl p < .0001	
Ironing	24 (40.7)	3 (4.6)	$\chi^2 = 21.544$ dfl p < .0001	
Washing car	11 (18.6)	25 (38.5)	$\chi^2 = 4.973$ dfl p < .05	
Gardening	15 (25.4)	29 (44.6)	$\chi^2 = 4.173$ dfl p < .05	Jobs done mainly by boys
Minor household repairs	4 (6.8)	16 (24.6)	$\chi^2 = 6.014$ dfl p < .01	
Shopping	25 (42.4)	29 (44.6)	ns	
Taking out rubbish	14 (23.7)	20 (30.8)	ns	Jobs done equally by boys and girls
Laying table	38 (74.6)	38 (58.5)	ns	
Washing up	44 (74.6)	38 (58.5) ·	ns	

Note: Whole numbers are shown first, followed by percentages in parentheses

stereotyped way, with girls – particularly in the working class – spending more time on them than boys. In this respect, they were similar to the rural girls described by Mason (1987) and the girls living in a more urban area whose family lives are discussed by Kelly *et al.* (1982). Clearly, the pattern of participation in daily domestic chores is significant, since it represents a

Table 8.9 Time per week spent by Greenhill pupils on household jobs according to their parents

	Less than 1 hour	*1–3 hours*	*More than 3 hours*
All pupils	20 (32.8)	33 (54.1)	8 (13.1)
Girls	5 (16.7)	18 (60)	7 (23.5)
Boys	15 (48.4)	15 (48.4)	1 (3.2)
Working class	10 (58.8)	7 (41.2)	0
Middle class	5 (26.3)	12 (63.2)	2 (10.5)

Note: Whole numbers are shown first, followed by percentages in parentheses

Table 8.10 Results of chi-square test applied to Greenhill parents' account of time per week spent on household jobs by their children (by sex of child)

Variables	*All parents*	*Working-class parents*	*Middle-class parents*
Time spent on household jobs by sex of child	$\chi^2 = 14.035$ df2 $p < .001$	$\chi^2 = 9.759$ df2 $p < .01$	ns

crucial part of the backcloth of everday life. taken for granted and experienced by children from birth onwards. In the case of the children living in these particular Westshire families, it appeared that the messages they were receiving were likely to reinforce a traditional view of appropriate gender roles. To illustrate further the parents' attitudes to the domestic division of labour, I draw now on interviews which were carried out with mothers and fathers in their homes.

A marked difference emerged between those parents who strongly defended the traditional divisions operating within their own families and others who were questioning the status quo or who had already succeeded in bringing about changes in the domestic balance of power. A number of men stated very firmly their belief in the maintenance of strong gender boundaries within the family which should be reflected in the school curriculum. Mr Alcott, for instance, who had previously been in the army and now worked for an insurance firm, stated this view very firmly:

Girls should concentrate more on the women's things. I'm a bit old-fashioned in that sense. There's jobs for women and there's jobs for men. I think she [indicating his wife] should have done more sewing and knitting at school.

When asked what he meant by 'men's jobs' and 'women's jobs' he went on:

Well, the women should do things like knitting and sewing and crocheting and things like that, the women's side of things in the family, and the men's side is mending the door locks and looking after the greenhouse and looking after the garden and painting, things like that, that's the way we work it.

However the fact that real life did not fit in quite so neatly with this idealised world view was indicated in their final comments:

Mr Alcott: Except she doesn't do any knitting and crocheting, etc.
Mrs Alcott: And he don't do a lot of painting. [Both laugh.]

It is interesting that there were no examples of professional middle-class men making such overtly reactionary statements concerning the role of women and men. However, whereas many women were willing to challenge the sexual division of labour, men were much less likely to do this, suggesting that their commitment to equality was rather superficial.

Whereas some men were concerned to define housework as essentially women's work, women who held a conservative view of gender roles in the home often based their beliefs on a strong endorsement of an ideology of full-time motherhood. It was noticeable that working-class women were often very critical of mothers who had gone back to work when the children were young. Mrs Rennick, the wife of a heavy-plant operator who was herself unemployed, commented:

I know a friend of mine, this lady's mother looks after her baby several days a week, which I don't really agree with. 'Cos I mean, why have a child? She should have a child and bring it up and then go back to work afterwards. I don't really agree with that. The baby was only three months old and she was back working three or four days a week. But apparently her mother did it for her daughter as well and so she agreed to do it for her own daughter. I suppose if they're happy with that that's fair enough, but it doesn't seem right to me somehow. I don't see why not if your children are older.

This suspicion of women who 'abandoned' their children to return to work was shared by many working-class women despite their recognition that they themselves had been damaged by the narrow focus of their life. Interestingly, working-class women tended to be more tolerant of middle-class women returning to work with young children than they were of women like themselves doing so. Mrs Killick, a mother who was a Millbridge cleaner, said:

Some women can [continue to work while they have young children]. I couldn't. I can't even run this [indicating the house] properly. I think if you're that way inclined then why shouldn't you? You go through your pregnancy six months, then rest for three months, then have the children and get the nannies and that in. And then if you're clever enough a lot of women work from home. I don't mean stupid things like glove-making and this sort of thing but proper work.

Mrs Rennick also felt that it was all right for career women to combine work and family, but this was not a practical option for ordinary women like herself. She said she admired 'good career women, women who are managing directors and that sort of thing', but in her view the problem was how girls at the age of 16 were meant to know that that was what they were cut out to be. Although men tended to be less strongly opposed to women returning to work because of the dangers of child neglect, the majority felt that the best arrangement was for women to return to work after their children were older in order to supplement family income rather than for personal fulfilment.

Despite the fact that both women and men supported the traditional sexual division of labour in the family, there were a number of working-class and middle-class women who challenged this, insisting that women could combine work and motherhood, but that a redistribution of domestic labour was essential. Mrs Brickell, a Greenhill mother who was a former nurse, now hoping to enter the field of nurse education, was very much of this view.

S.R.: D'you think it's possible for a woman to combine having a career and a family as well?

Mrs Brickell: Yes, very much so, very much so. I think if the family's prepared to work with her and she's prepared to meet the other things both ways. I mean I have had to work very hard at both and it has been hard work at times when you're not sure which way to go but I have got a very supportive family and I think that is important. I gave up a lot to have the family and when I decided everyone was old enough I went back to work.

Mrs Thomas, an auxiliary nurse and wife of a coach driver, was again very adamant that work and family were not mutually exclusive options for women, but also stressed the need for a change in men's attitudes to domestic responsibilities:

Your father can go out to work and he can think about work and he doesn't have to think about anything else until he comes home and actually has to do it. But . . . there's no point in me coming home at 6 o'clock and all we've got is deep-frozen chops down there in the freezer and we've got no microwave to defrost the damn things, or I haven't been out and bought the milk. . . . A man concentrates on one thing at a time, a woman's always got more than one thing going on . . . It's not a question of whether I'd like to see it change because we're trying to equalise women's opportunities in employment, which means her role in employment is going to be the same as the man's and therefore we've got to bring the man in so they're not only sharing the job, they're also sharing the home.

Both Mrs Brickell and Mrs Thomas were determined that their daughters were not going to end up in dead-end jobs and were also critical of the school's failure to be sufficiently positive in tackling the problem of sex-stereotyping in the curriculum.

Overall, then, it would appear that although some women were questioning the sexual division of labour in the family, the majority of both women and men were reluctant to mount a direct challenge. Although women did not uphold the view that domestic chores were intrinsically women's work, many did support the ideology of full-time motherhood and working-class women were particularly strongly opposed to the idea that a woman with a young child should participate in the labour market. This may be linked with the type of survival strategy described by Valli as characterising the actions of working-class girls training as office workers. According to Valli, the recognition of the double burden imposed on working-class women by the combination of work and childcare with inadequate backup facilities led to their insistence on the primacy of their domestic role. In the case of the Westshire families, an attachment to traditional gender codes within the family seemed to play a significant part in shaping parental attitudes to children's option choices. Teachers were not altogether mistaken in their view that parents might represent a barrier to equal-opportunities policies. Their explanations, however, tended to be too simple, failing to take into account important differences in the attitudes of women and men and working-class and middle-class parents. Neither did they recognise that there was a group of parents, most of whom were women, who were strongly advocating change.

PARENTS' VIEWS OF WORK AND GENDER INEQUALITY

Parents' vision of the future role of their children in the public sphere of work was a further measure of their construction of masculinity and femininity. To access these views, I again used both quantitative and qualitative methods. A number of items on the questionnaire investigated parents' educational and occupational aspirations for their children. Whereas the questions about subject importance were asked for girls and boys in general, these questions were asked in relation to the parents' particular child. Tables 8.11–8.16 summarise findings with regard to educational aspirations and show that parents were just as educationally ambitious for their daughters as their sons. Indeed, at Millbridge, parents of girls had significantly higher expectations than parents of boys. This is an interesting finding in view of the popular belief, reflected by many of the teachers at the two schools, that parents had very low academic expectations of their daughters – certainly among the parents who completed the questionnaire this was far from the case.

Table 8.11 Millbridge parents' expectation of child's level of full-time education (for working-class and middle-class parents and parents of third-year girls and boys)

	Easter leaver	Leave with CSEs and O levels	Technical college	Leave with A levels	Higher education	Totals
All parents	5 (4.5)	42 (38.2)	9 (8.2)	23 (20.9)	31 (28.2)	110 (100)
Working class	6 (8)	37 (49.3)	3 (4)	17 (22.7)	12 (16)	75 (100)
Middle class	0	10 (23.3)	6 (14)	7 (16.3)	20 (46.5)	43 (100)
Parents of third year girls	3 (4.41)	21 (42)	6 (12)	1 (28)	24 (48)	68 (100)
Parents of third year boys	3 (6)	26 (52)	3 (6)	10 (20)	8 (16)	50 (100)

Note: Whole numbers are shown first, followed by percentages in parentheses

Table 8.12 Results of Mann-Whitney U test applied to Millbridge parents' expectations of child's level of full-time education (by class of family and sex of child)

Variables	Group	Result of Mann-Whitney U test		
Expected level of child's full-time education by class	All parents	u = 951.5	z = −3.879	p < .0001
Expected level of child's full-time education by sex of child	All parents	u = 1254.5	z = −2.546	p < .01

Kelly *et al.* (1982) also found that parents of girls in both working and middle classes had slightly higher educational aspirations than parents of boys. Again, in terms of the level of work aspired to, there were no significant differences between expectations for girls and boys. (Tables 8.17 and 8.19). It should

Table 8.13 Results of chi-square test applied to Millbridge parents' expectation of child's level of full-time education (by child's achievement level)

Variables	Group	Results of chi-square test
Expected level of child's full-time education by child's achievement	All parents	$\chi^2 = 35.555$ df 12 $p < .001$

be noted that class was a salient factor here, with working-class parents tending to have lower expectations. Further analysis, however, did reveal that although there were no differences in the level of work considered suitable for girls and boys, there were differences in the type of work.

Parents were asked to rate the suitability of specified jobs for their particular child on a scale from 1 to 5. Mean rating of job suitability and comparisons of group responses with regard to sex of child and class of family are given in Tables 8.21 and 8.23 for Millbridge and Greenhill parents. Ratings were generally quite low (less than 3.0) which suggests that parents were indeed thinking about the suitability of the job for their particular child, rather than its desirability in more general terms. The judgements of both sets of parents appeared largely to coincide with traditional sex segregation of the labour market. Stereotypically female jobs such as nurse, secretary and hairdresser were regarded as more suitable for girls, and engineer, draughtsman and electrician more suitable for boys. At Millbridge, it appeared that professional jobs were less likely to be sex-stereotyped than manual jobs. Thus, doctor, manager, social worker, teacher and computer operator were regarded as equally suitable for boys and girls. Greenhill parents were more traditional in this respect, with manager, teacher, shop worker and factory worker seen as equally suitable for both boys and girls, and all other jobs viewed as more appropriate for either boys or girls. No differences were found in the responses of men and women at either school. At Millbridge, there were no class differences either but at Greenhill, manager, teacher, social worker and doctor were given higher ratings by middle-class parents and hairdresser

Table 8.14 Greenhill parents' expectations of child's level of full-time education (for working-class and middle-class parents and parents of third-year girls and boys)

	Easter leaver	Leave with CSEs and O levels	Technical college	Leave with A levels	Higher education	Totals
All parents	4 (3.3)	35 (29.2)	29 (24.2)	18 (15)	34 (28.3)	120 (100)
Working-class	4 (6.7)	28 (46.7)	16 (26.7)	11 (18.3)	1 (1.7)	60 (100)
Middle-class	—	—	10 (25.6)	2 (5.1)	27 (69.2)	39 (100)
Parents of third-year girls	3 (5.3)	14 (24.6)	16 (28.1)	5 (8.8)	19 (33.3)	57 (100)
Parents of third-year boys	1 (1.6)	21 (33.3)	13 (20.6)	13 (20.6)	15 (24)	63 (100)

Note: Whole numbers are shown first, followed by percentages in parentheses

Table 8.15 Results of Mann–Whitney U test applied to Greenhill parents' expectations of child's level of full-time education (by class of family and sex of child)

Variables	Group	Result of Mann–Whitney U test
Expected level of child's full-time education by class	All parents	u = 226.5 z = −6.989 p < .0001
Expected level of child's full-time education by sex of child	All parents	ns

Table 8.16 Results of chi-square test applied to Greenhill parents' expectations of child's level of full-time education (by child's achievement level)

Variables	Group	Result of chi-square test
Expected level of child's full-time education by child's achievement level	All parents	χ^2 = 87.371 df12 p < .0001

and factory worker by working-class parents.

In the Manchester study, Kelly also found that manual jobs were particularly likely to be sex-typed, whereas some professional jobs currently dominated by men, such as manager and doctor, were likely to be regarded as equally suitable for girls and boys. She suggests that females entering male territory may be more acceptable in areas of work where they do not get their hands dirty. It is important to note that there are now approximately equal numbers of women and men entering such professions as law and medicine and in future years it will be interesting to see how the career profile of women develops in these areas.

It would appear, then, that even though parents are not

Table 8.17 Level of job desired by Millbridge parents for their child (for all parents, working class, middle class, and parents of third-year girls and boys)

	Top professional	Professional/ semi-professional	Skilled trade	Unskilled/ semi-skilled	Vague/other	Total
All parents	19 (16.5)	13 (11.3)	29 (25.2)	24 (20.9)	26 (22.6)	111 (100)
Working class	6 (8.3)	12 (16.7)	17 (23.6)	17 (23.6)	16 (22.2)	68 (100)
Middle class	13 (30.2)	1 (2.3)	12 (27.9)	7 (16.3)	10 (23.3)	43 (100)
Parents of third-year girls	8 (11.9)	8 (11.9)	19 (28.4)	14 (20.9)	17 (25.4)	66 (100)
Parents of third-year boys	11 (22.9)	5 (10.4)	10 (20.8)	10 (20.8)	9 (18.7)	45 (100)

Note: Whole numbers are shown first, followed by percentages in perentheses

Table 8.18 Results of chi-square test applied to level of job desired by Millbridge parents for their child (by class of family, sex of child and achievement level of child)

Variables	Group	Results of chi-square test
Level of job desired for child by class of family	All parents	$\chi^2 = 16.005$ df7 p < .05
Level of job desired for child by sex of child	All parents	ns
Level of job desired for child by achievement level of child	All parents	$\chi^2 = 48.243$ df12 p < .001

opposed to their daughters striving for success in the education system and the labour market, they do not expect them to challenge existing gender divisions. Interview data provided further insight into the reasons underlying these attitudes and also revealed considerable tension between women and men in their view of the justice of these divisions. These tensions emerged at a number of points during the interviews but were particularly apparent when parents were asked whether they felt women and men had equal chances of promotion at work. Amongst a number of middle-class couples, men seemed to feel that women did have full equality at work, whilst their wives disagreed. Dr and Mrs Baker, for instance, expressed very different views:

> S.R.: D'you think that women have equal opportu-
> nities at work nowadays?
> Dr Baker: It depends on the job I suppose. In some jobs
> they have a better opportunity.
> Mrs Baker: If you believe what you hear on the radio
> women have to be twice as good to get half as
> far. I mean I think in certain areas of business
> competition is so high and prejudice is still
> pretty deep. You'd have to be a very deter-
> mined young lady to force your way forward.
> Dr Baker: My own experience is that it's very hard to find
> a woman who's very keen to have a career and
> can't find an outlet because they're a woman.

Table 8.19 Level of job desired by Greenhill parents for their child (for all parents, working class, middle class, and parents of third-year girls and boys)

	Professional	Semi-professional	Skilled trade	unskilled/ semi-skilled	Vague/other	Total
All parents	24 (22.9)	9 (8.6)	17 (16.2)	22 (21)	33 (31.4)	105 (100)
Working class	4 (7.5)	4 (7.5)	11 (20.8)	20 (37.7)	14 (26.4)	53 (100)
Middle class	12 (32.4)	3 (8.1)	4 (10.8)	1 (2.7)	17 (45.9)	37 (100)
Parents of third-year girls	9 (18)	5 (10)	7 (14)	12 (24)	17 (34)	50 (100)
Parents of third-year boys	15 (27.3)	4 (7.3)	10 (18.2)	10 (18.2)	16 (29.1)	55 (100)

Note: Whole numbers are shown first, followed by percentages in parentheses

Table 8.20 Results of chi-square test applied to level of job desired by Greenhill parents for their child (by class of family, sex of child and achievement level of child)

Variables	Group	Results of chi-square test
Level of job desired for child by class of family	All parents	χ^2 = 22.765 df4 p < .0001
Level of job desired for child by sex of child	All parents	ns
Level of job desired for child by achievement level of child	All parents	ns

Table 8.21 Greenhill parents' mean ratings of job suitability for their particular child

Job	Mean for all parents
Computer programmer	3.124
Computer operator	3.100
Manager	2.915
Draughtsman	2.700
Engineer	2.642
Electrician	2.592
Teacher	2.583
Social worker	2.388
Secretary	2.308
Shop worker	2.174
Nurse	2.017
Hairdresser	2.016
Doctor	1.950
Factory worker	1.783

Dr Baker at this point appeared to be totally unaware that his wife was making a very different point, and also did not appear to feel that perhaps her views on this matter might be more relevant than his. The following exchange between Colin and

Table 8.22 Results of chi-square test used to compare Greenhill parents' suitability ratings of jobs (by parents of third-year girls and boys and working-class and middle-class parents)

Job	χ^2	df	Probability	Which sex job rated higher for	χ^2	df	Probability	Which class job rated higher for
Nurse	17.385	4	$p < .001$	Girls			ns	
Social worker	10.267	4	$p < .05$	Girls	9.714	4	$p < .05$	Middle class
Secretary	44.584	4	$p < .0001$	Girls			ns	
Hair-dresser	40.164	4	$p < .0001$	Girls	10.295	4	$p < .05$	Working class
Computer programmer	12.217	4	$p < .01$	Boys			ns	
Computer operator	10.676	4	$p < .05$	Boys			ns	
Draughtsman	17.988	4	$p < .001$	Boys			ns	
Engineer	44.423	4	$p < .0001$	Boys			ns	
Electrician	29.454	4	$p < .0001$	Boys			ns	
Doctor	9.542	4	$p < .05$	Boys	14.247	4	$p < .01$	Middle class
Manager			ns		11.112	4	$p < .05$	Middle class
Shop worker			ns				ns	
Factory worker			ns		15.144	4	$p < .01$	Working class
Teacher			ns		37.465	4	$p < .0001$	Middle class

Table 8.23 Millbridge parents' mean ratings of job suitability for their particular child and results of chi-square test used to compare suitability ratings of jobs by parents of third-year girls and boys

Job	Mean for all parents	χ^2	df	Probability level	Which sex job rated higher for
Computer operator	2.862			ns	
Manager	2.840			ns	
Secretary	2.719	56.961	4	p < .0001	Girls
Social worker	2.628			ns	
Teacher	2.579			ns	
Draughtsman	2.421	32.045	4	p < .0001	Boys
Engineer	2.400	35.183	4	p < .0001	Boys
Shopworker	2.333	27.074	4	p < .0001	Girls
Nurse	2.322	30.330	4	p < .0001	Girls
Electrician	2.298	60.322	4	p < .0001	Boys
Hairdresser	2.182	42.786	4	p < .0001	Girls
Doctor	1.950			ns	
Factory worker	1.752			ns	

Notes: When the chi-square test was used to compare the ratings of working-class and middle-class parents, no significant differences were found

Maureen York also shows how the husband's perception of the position of women in the labour market differs radically from his wife's view of the situation. I have quoted at some length because I think the dynamics of this conversation are particularly interesting:

> S.R.: When Sally starts work d'you think she'll have equal opportunities with the men she'll be working with?
>
> Mrs York: I don't think she will.
>
> Mr York: I think she probably will. [said at the same time]
>
> Mrs York: No, there's still . . .
>
> Mr York: I think by the time she's in a work situation . . . I've seen attitudes change quite substantially in

the last four or five years. Really, I mean that
sincerely. There's a lot more acceptance of
women in what have been traditionally men's
jobs. I see it much more than you would in a
school situation . . . you're in a fairly cloistered
environment. But out in the commercial world I
see a lot more acceptance and I think by the time
Sally is working it'll be even more so. And by
the time Zoe, in ten years, there won't be any
differences. I really believe that.

S.R.: D'you think that? [to Mrs York]

Mrs York: I'd like to think it, but I still think that women
are put down.

Mr York: I think nowadays the only women who are put
down are the ones who allow themselves to be
put down.

Mrs York: No . . .

Mr York: No. Let me finish. And the women who are
prepared to allow themselves to be put down
are decreasing all the time. And as they
decrease, and the majority of women are prepared to assert themselves more . . . you see
men as a species won't want to find themselves
in a confrontation situation with women where
they can't win, so they'll tend to back off rather
than get involved.

S.R.: D'you feel the differences are disappearing?

Mrs York: Well I'd like to think they would. Not working in
the outside world, perhaps I'm not up to date
with it all. I'm only going by what I hear and
other people tell me. I'd like to think she'd have
an equal opportunity. I think she should, but I
still think it's up to the individual, and if they
think they're better than a male opponent.

Within Mr York's terms, women's lack of power in the labour
market is essentially an individual problem. A number of
middle-class fathers expressed similar views and it was clear
that although they hoped that their daughters would have
successful careers, they were unaware of any structural
barriers which might stand in their way. Mr Roberts, for

instance, believed that his daughter would make opportunities for herself if these did not already exist, describing her as the sort of girl who 'sails through things and tramples over obstacles'.

Middle-class parents who believed that equal opportunities had already been achieved were in fact in the minority. The majority of parents felt that women did not have equal chances of promotion, but there were interesting differences in their explanations of this situation. Some men felt that male dominance of the workplace was due to their natural superiority, and they were quite happy for things to remain like this. Mr Alcott, for instance, who was quoted earlier, expressed this view quite categorically:

> S.R.: D'you think that men and women have equal opportunities at work nowadays?
>
> *Mr Alcott*: No.
>
> S.R.: Why's that?
>
> *Mr Alcott*: I mentioned it previously. I think men's got the whole thing sewn up for themselves.
>
> S.R.: And would you like to see that change?
>
> *Mr Alcott*: No, I wouldn't like a woman boss. I think a woman responds better to being told what to do by a man than what a man does being told what to do by a woman. That's nature.
>
> *Mrs Alcott*: [very quietly in background] I don't agree with that.
>
> *Mr Alcott*: It'll take hundreds of years for a woman to be able to monopolise a man in the same way as a man can monopolise a woman. It doesn't matter what qualifications they've got. You see it at work . . . you see it all the time. We haven't got any women bosses in our place whatsoever. There's one in Public Relations, and she's for the heave soon – I haven't told you which firm I work for, have I? The person I'm on about is just no bloody good. Whether it be male or female it wouldn't make much difference.

Similarly Mr Gordon, a self-employed builder, did not think that women had equal opportunities, but was not over-anxious

Table 8.24 Mann–Whitney U test applied to Millbridge parents' responses to statements 20, 24, 25 and 28 (by sex and class of parent) for all parents, women, men, working-class and middle-class parents

	Women/men			Working class/Middle class		
	All parents	Working class	Middle class	All parents	Women	Men
Statement 20	u = 1370.5 z = −2.517 p < .01 M	u = 523.5 z = −2.358 p < .05 M	ns	ns	ns	ns
Statement 24	u = 1350.0 z = −2.444 p < .01 M	u = 536.0 z = −2.157 p < .05 M	ns	ns	ns	ns
Statement 25	ns	u = 560.5 z = −2.135 p < .05	ns	ns	ns	ns
Statement 28	u = 1495.5 z = −2.223 p < .05 M	u = 557.5 z = −2.408 p < .05 M	ns	ns	u − 422.0 z = −2.066 p < .05 Mi	ns

Notes: (1) Only those statements have been included for which significant differences were found. (2) Statement 20 = women do most jobs as well as men; Statement 24 = nursing is a good job for a boy; Statement 25 = academic qualifications are more important for boys than girls; Statement 28 = men are more successful at work because they are naturally more aggressive. (3) M = mens' response more sexist than womens'; Mi = middle-class parents' response more sexist than working-class parents' response

Table 8.25 Mann–Whitney U test applied to Greenhill parents' responses to statements 15, 17 and 19 (by sex and class of parent) for all parents, women, men, working-class and middle-class parents

	Women/men			Working class/middle class		
	All parents	Working class	Middle class	All parents	Women	Men
Statement 15	ns	ns	ns	u = 920.0 z = -1.947 p < .05 WoC	ns	ns
Statement 17	ns	ns	u = 89.5 z = -2.809 p < .01 M	ns	u = 236.5 z = -2.384 p < .05 WoC	ns
Statement 19	u = 1442.0 z = -2.197 p < .05 M	u = 369.5 z = -1.972 p < .05 M	ns	ns	ns	ns

Notes: (1) Only those statements have been included for which significant differences were found. (2) Statement 15 = the man should be the main breadwinner in a family; Statement 17 = boys understand maths and physics better than girls; Statement 19 = women do most jobs as well as men. (3) M = mens' response more sexist than womens' response; WoC = working-class parents' responses more sexist than middle-class parents' responses

for change. Officially women were supposed to have equal opportunities but the reason they did not was deeply rooted in tradition:

> *Mr Gordon*: Employers prefer to employ men. They wouldn't say so in so many words, but that's still what happens.
> *S.R.*: Would you like to see that change?
> *Mr Gordon*: Pass on that one I think [laughs]. Don't know really. It's difficult in some industries to have women. No. Things seem to be all right as they are. I don't think there's any reason for change.

Some parents also attributed women's lack of equality at work to the fact that they were just not physically capable of doing certain jobs. Mr Woolbridge, a worker on a dairy farm, commented:

> If you get the odd girls who wants to do shall we say the more masculine tasks then she isn't going to be given the same opportunity because she just isn't physically able to do it so therefore they're going to say, 'Oh, don't do that, let some one else do it.' And although that might annoy the girl at the time, from the employer's point of view it's the obvious thing to do.

As far as he was concerned, girls should simply look at the situation in an unblinkered way and not attempt to do what didn't come naturally.

Many of the men quoted above, then, seemed complacent about the sexual division of the labour market, whereas women were much more likely to view these divisions critically.

To summarise, a minority of parents, mainly middle-class men, thought that there were no longer barriers to women's equality in the labour market, and it was the responsibility of individual women to take up the opportunities which were freely available. In couples where the man made this point, the woman often disagreed with him, drawing on her own experience as evidence. The majority of parents recognised the existence of gender divisions within the labour market and felt that women's opportunities were still limited. Working-class men in particular often defended the status quo, justifying inequality on the grounds of men's natural superiority and women's physical weakness. These men felt there was no point in girls making non-traditional option choices, since they would be unable to get jobs in these areas anyway. Working-class women, as we noted in Chapter 5, often envisaged very few possibilities for their daughters and tended to take the pessimistic view that since office work was the most likely prospect, it was prudent to gain qualifications in this area to fall back on as a last resort. Unfortunately, by restricting their curricular choices in this way, the chances that this would be a first rather than a last resort were increased.

The divergence between women's and men's gender codes was further illustrated by items on the questionnaire designed to investigate attitudes to gender equality. Responses are summarised in Tables 8.24 – 8.29. Factor analysis was used to identify those statements which discriminated between parents most effectively on their attitudes to gender equality. These were statements 20, 24 25 and 28 for Millbridge parents and statements 15, 17 and 19 for Greenhill parents. Recoding several statements so that the sexist response was always 5, scales were then constructed for Millbridge and Greenhill parents which represented the sum of their responses to each of these statements. Further details of scale construction are provided in Appendix 1. Broadly speaking, women emerged as more supportive of the general principle of equal power relations than men. This supports the view emerging from the interview data that men generally support more traditional constructions of femininity than women.

CONCLUSION

As we saw in Chapter 4, teachers believed that parents were largely responsible for the gender-divided curriculum by conveying extremely sex-stereotyped ideas to their children about the value of different subjects in their future lives. This chapter reveals that some parents did indeed support traditional divisions and oppose change. Whereas men often wished to protect their privileged position in the home and the workplace, women based their opposition to change on support for the ideology of motherhood. At the same time, a number of contradictory and opposing elements in mothers' and fathers'

Table 8.26 Mann–Whitney U test applied to sexist scale (by sex of parent, class of family and age of parent) for all Millbridge parents, women, men, working-class and middle-class parents

Variables	Groups	Results of Mann–Whitney U test
Sexist by sex of parent	All parents	u = 1496.0 z = −1.988 p < .05
	Working class	u = 542.5 z = −2.207 p < .05
	Middle class	ns
Sexist by class of family	All parents	ns
	Women	ns
	Men	ns
Sexist by age of parent	All parents	ns

Table 8.27 Kruskall–Wallis test applied to sexist scale (by parents' expectation of level of child's full-time education) for all Millbridge parents

Variables	Group	Results of Kruskall–Wallis test
Sexist by expected level of child's full-time education	All parents	$\chi^2 = 16.480$ p < .01

attitudes were also revealed, suggesting that teachers' view of parents as a homogeneous and uniformly conservative force is over-simplified.

Parents' attitudes to the division of labour in their own family appeared to have an impact on their views of appropriate curricula for girls and boys. Questionnaire data suggested that everyday tasks were still characterised by persistent gender divisions and interview data provided evidence of men strongly defending these divisions. Women's defence of traditional gender divisions within the family appeared to be underpinned by their attachment to the ideology of full time motherhood. In this way, mothers' attitudes were often shot through with contradictions and, as we saw in Chapter 5, daughters were

Table 8.28 Mann–Whitney U test applied to sexist scale (by sex of parent, class of family and age of parent) for all Greenhill parents, women, men, working-class and middle-class parents

Variables	Groups	Results of Mann–Whitney U test		
Sexist by sex of parent	All parents	ns		
	Working class	ns		
	Middle class	ns		
Sexist by class of family	All parents	ns		
	Women	ns		
	Men	ns		
Sexist by age of parent	All parents	u = 1457.0	z = −2.319	p < .05
	Working class	u = 337.0	z = −1.989	p < .05
	Middle class	ns		
	Women	ns		
	Men	u = 234.5	z = −2.345	p < .05

Table 8.29 Krushkall–Wallis test applied to sexist scale (by parents' expectation of level of child's full-time education) for all Greenhill parents

Variables	Group	Results of Kruskall–Wallis test
Sexist by expected level of child's full-time education	All parents	ns

well aware of these confusing messages. Again, often because of their own experience of managing a dual role in the home and the labour market, a minority of women were fundamentally challenging power relations in the family, and this was reflected in the encouragement they gave their daughters to consider alternatives to the traditional paths.

Whilst hoping that their daughters would achieve success at school and attain successful employment, most parents recognised the continued existence of gender divisions in the labour market. They varied, however, in the extent to which they saw this as a problem and in the solutions which they suggested. Middle-class men favoured individualistic strategies for their daughters, believing that if they were good enough they would be able to reach the top of their chosen profession. These men were clearly unlikely to offer very much to their daughters in the way of support or in consolation in the face of failure. Middle-class mothers, on the other hand, were generally far more aware of structural barriers to equality. Working-class men tended to see traditional divisions as natural and unchangeable and working-class women resented the restricted opportunities which were available both to themselves and their daughters, but again saw little hope of change. Where mothers and fathers were interviewed together, explicit disagreements on the issue of gender divisions and social justice often surfaced. Weis (1990) has discussed the way in which the cultures of Freeway girls and boys are currently set on a 'collision path'. These discussions suggest that the gender codes of parents, too, may diverge, with mothers increasingly attracted to new visions of women's developing role in the public sphere. Many men, on the other hand, appeared reluctant to challenge the known boundaries of male and female territory.

To some extent, then, teachers are right to recognise that parents may not initially be wholehearted in their support of equal-opportunities policies. However, the answer is not to abdicate all responsibility for change, but to think very carefully about how change may be implemented most successfully. If parents' support is to be won for equal-opportunities policies in school, then thoughtful communication of the school's goals is clearly essential, since, like teachers, parents have the power to sabotage educational reform through active or passive resistance.

Part IV

THE IMPACT OF THE NATIONAL CURRICULUM ON THE CONSTRUCTION OF GENDER DIVISIONS

In Chapter 1 of this book, I indicated that there was an ongoing argument concerning the power of individual schools to affect both the culture of pupils and the nature of educational outcomes. Whereas neo-marxists in the 1970s saw schools and teachers as relatively powerless in the face of the massive force of capitalism, more recent commentators have argued on empirical grounds that schools do make a difference to the progress of individual pupils. The curriculum has been singled out by writers such as Connell (1986) as a highly significant aspect of a school's culture. He states: 'It is clear . . . that relations of class and gender are embedded in the curriculum; it follows that reform of the curriculum is itself, in some measure, a recontextualisation of these structures' (p. 4).

Part II of this book corroborates this view, demonstrating how the organisation of option choice, the framing of particular subjects and the culture of teachers conveyed powerful messages to pupils with regard to the gender appropriateness of particular curricular areas. This is not to suggest that pupils and their families were passive in the process – indeed Part III provides much evidence on how pupils and parents received and responded to the schools' gender codes.

If we are to accept that the schools were strongly implicated in the production of gender divisions, then, as Connell suggests, change in curriculum structure should be capable of producing change in pupils' culture. Many grand claims have been made on behalf of the national curriculum which has recently been introduced into schools in England and Wales. For instance, an official statement on the aims of the national curriculum claims that its goal is to ensure that 'all pupils, regardless of sex, ethnic origin, and geographic location, have access to broadly the same good and relevant curriculum' (DES, 1987). Part IV examines this claim critically, considering whether the national curriculum represents a breakthrough for equal opportunities, a retrograde step or simply more of the same.

9

THE NATIONAL CURRICULUM
Solution or blind alley?

INTRODUCTION

Up to this point, I have considered the way in which Millbridge and Greenhill schools used the system of option choice to convey traditional and restricted gender codes to pupils. I have also considered the nature of the interaction between the gender codes of pupils, parents and teachers and the ways in which these impacted on each other. At the time when the research was conducted, it appeared that the more conservative constructions of femininity were still in the ascendancy and were reflected in pupils' option choices. None the less, a minority of radical pupils, parents and teachers were actively questioning received notions of femininity and were crafting new gender codes. A minority of mothers and daughters (some middle-class and some working-class) and female teachers were emphasising the centrality of career as well as family in women's lives. Working-class girls were notably emphasising autonomy, which often included rebellion against the discipline of school life. I have argued that the option choice system at Millbridge and Greenhill tended to encourage traditional outcomes and offered little support to those who were seeking to redefine the culture of femininity.

In view of these major criticisms of the option choice system, the introduction of a national curriculum in England and Wales under the terms of the Education Reform Act 1988 might be seen as possibly undermining the perpetuation of gender diivisions within the curriculum. In the following chapter, I first provide a brief overview of the background to the national curriculum. I then consider the debate which has been waged for many years concerning the potential power of a common curriculum to alter the established pattern of diverging curricular paths for girls and boys during the later years of secondary schooling. Having outlined the various possible outcomes of the national curriculum, I finally question what might represent a helpful balance between entirely free choice and a uniformly imposed, subject-based curriculum in terms of undermining differentiation in the curriculum for girls and boys and working-class and middle-class pupils.

BACKGROUND TO THE NATIONAL CURRICULUM

The 1980s have witnessed a flurry of wide-ranging legislation, which has generally been speeded through the statutory process with unceremonious haste. Consultation with professional groups has tended to be minimal. For example, discussion documents on the national curriculum were sent out to the education community just before the 1987 summer vacation, with responses demanded by early autumn. One of the most significant aspects of the Education Reform Act 1988 is undoubtedly the prescription of a national curriculum, since previous British governments have been very cautious about intervening in this area. Deem (1988) argues that political caution is one of the reasons why governments have feared to tread in this area, recognising that it was unlikely that they would remain in power for ever:

> If the machinery exists for one party to capture the content and organisation of schooling and lead it in a particular direction, then it is capable of being used by other groups and to lead in other directions. This is perhaps something which the Cabinet and the Secretary of State have given insufficient attention, or, alternatively, perhaps the present administration cannot imagine ever being removed from power.
>
> (Deem, 1988, p. 91)

It is also interesting to note the point made by Rendal (1985) that the provisions of the Sex Discrimination Act relating to education were deliberately not extended to the curriculum:

> It would have been impossible to deal with sex-typing in

school curricula and textbooks, both because of the ministerial opposition it would have aroused and because the content of education was not at that time open to direct ministerial intervention.

(Rendal, 1985, p. 91)

Recent legislation on the curriculum, then, raises interesting possibilities with regard to what a subsequent Labour government might choose to do, no longer constrained by the idea that the curriculum was sacrosanct from political intervention.

What, then, has been the intention of the government in introducing legislation to impose a national curriculum? As I noted in Chapter 1, different rationalisations have been offered on different occasions, but the most frequently stated argument has been the desire to raise standards of education to improve Britain's economic position. A clear effect of the national curriculum, related to its hidden agenda, is a further curtailment of the powers of teachers and local education authorities, envisaged as the 'producers' of education. In some respects there appears to be a measure of inconsistency between this part of the government's legislative portfolio and other aspects, for it is clear that the national curriculum is centralising power in the hands of the Secretary of State for Education rather than leaving more to market forces and the power of consumers. Indeed, if the government's ideal of consumer power were to be realised in schools, one would expect pupils to have even more freedom of choice than they do at the moment. Deem (1989), however, points out that although pupils might logically be seen as prime consumers of education, throughout recent legislation they are characterised as appendages of parents, who, along with local business, are conceived of as the real consumers. Much philosophical inconsistency pervades legislation on the national curriculum which lies uneasily alongside other measures. Maw (1988), commenting on the Education Reform Bill, suggests that it 'is the outcome of ideological conflict, not *between* politicians, HMI and DES bureaucrats, but ideological conflict *within* the political Right in general and the Conservative Party in particular'. In her view, 'the tensions between control and devolution, nationalisation and privatisation, uniformity and differentiation are inexplicable without such a concept' (p. 61). I return to a consideration of the overall meaning and impact of the national curriculum, specifically in relation to the education of girls, later on in this chapter. First, however, let us look in more detail at the content and changing format of the national curriculum.

THE NATIONAL CURRICULUM - A MOVING TARGET

For the last two years of compulsory secondary education (Key Stage 4) the national curriculum for England and Wales comprises English, mathematics and science as core subjects and history, geography, design and technology, modern foreign language, music, art and physical education as foundation subjects. Scotland has to date escaped the imposition of a national curriculum, on the grounds that a core curriculum is already in place for the 14-16 age group. National testing, however, is now mandatory north as well as south of the border. Welsh is an additional core subject in schools where this is the medium of instruction and a foundation subject in the remainder of schools in Wales. The subjects specified in the national curriculum are to be taken by all pupils of compulsory school age in maintained schools, and attainment targets, programmes of study and assessment arrangements are to be specified by the Secretary of State.

It was originally envisaged that in Years 4 and 5 of secondary school, the national curriculum would take up 80-90 per cent of a pupil's timetable, with the core subjects taking up 30-40 per cent of total time. However, it appears that Kenneth Baker was forced to abandon this idea at an early stage. Launching the Education Reform Bill in 1987, he said:

> We don't intend to lay down either in this Bill or in secondary legislation, a precise percentage of subjects. It was never the original intention. It will be up to schools, heads and local authorities to deliver the national curriculum and bring children up to the level of national attainment targets
>
> (Reported in *The Guardian*, 21st November 1987)

Clearly, Mr Baker may have been influenced by the fact that, had he insisted in setting time allocations for the different subjects, he would have been giving the teachers a very powerful weapon in salary negotiation, given the current levels of teacher shortages in key subject areas. This is only the first of many revisions which contribute to make the national curriculum substantially different from its original conception, and at the time of writing it is unclear what its final format will be. I will now consider the debate concerning whether a common curriculum may be seen as a means of achieving greater gender equality.

ARGUMENTS FOR A COMMON CURRICULUM AS A STEP TOWARDS GENDER EQUALITY

Interestingly, many women who have campaigned long and hard for educational equality have seen a national curriculum as representing an essential part of this programme. Byrne argues a strong case for teaching *the same* subjects in the same way to girls and boys:

> In common with most of my European Colleagues, I believe unreservedly that *equal means the same* – that is to say, the same across sex, race, rural and urban children of similar abilities and aptitudes. It does not mean uniformity across the full ability range, or across genuinely different interests and personalities. But it does mean uniformity for boys and girls in all that relates to the common core of knowledge, skills and attitudes and experiences without which no one will survive in happy and fulfilled, efficient and adaptable adulthood. And that means that this country has got to cease its evasion of that difficult but not uncomfortable task of defining the common core – a task that even the Third World countries, leave aside our continental colleagues, have not been afraid to face.
>
> (Byrne, 1985, p. 100)

Byrne's argument is essentially that girls and boys will have no chance of achieving equality in practice until both curriculum and its resourcing in mixed and single-sex schools are equalised. As mentioned earlier, it was a source of regret to many women that the curriculum was not included in the educational provisions of the Sex Discrimination Act. As I and others (Whyte, 1986) have argued, aspects of the subject choice system have tended to contribute to gender differentiation within the curriculum and to unequal educational outcomes more generally. Kelly (1988) has described the individualised curriculum as 'one of the great false turns of progressive education' (p. 168). She provides a strong defence of the potential of the national curriculum to provide a better deal for girls, arguing that 'despite eight years of Thatcherism, science education is currently moving in a democratic direction'. She sees among teachers a far greater awareness of gender and multi-cultural concerns, and recognises the space for radicals to exploit the shifting demographic pattern to argue for the interests of marginalised groups. However, even among those whoi support a common curriculum, there is considerable disagreement concerning its content, particularly with regard to science.

DEBATES CONCERNING THE NATURE OF SCIENCE EDUCATION WITHIN A COMMON CURRICULUM

Some equal-opportunities campaigns, such as Women into Science and Engineering (WISE), have operated on the rather simplistic expectation that all that needs to be done to achieve equality is to enlist females in traditionally male areas of the curriculum and the labour market without altering subject content or occupational structure and ethos. Other initiatives have taken a rather more thought-out approach to the problem, arguing that it is not simply up to girls to fit into a male-orientated curriculum. Rather, it is essential for the content and presentation of the curriculum to take account of girls' legitimate interests and needs.

Bentley and Watts (1987) distinguish three different approaches to the provision of a science curriculum which sympathetically reflects girls' interests. These are termed girl-friendly science, feminine science and feminist science, and they all involve a recognition of science as a socially constructed process closely tied up with the values of those who practise it. Girl-friendly science involves starting with the interests of girls, which are likely to centre on human concerns before moving on to abstract principles. Thus the study of an abstract concept such as heat or electricity might begin with consideration of an aspect of the human body or the social world, and move through various stages towards an understanding of the underlying principle. Feminine science focuses on altering the nature of classroom interaction, replacing competitive and aggressive behaviour with a caring and co-operative ethos. It also focuses on a more holistic view, encouraging the examination of social, moral and ethical questions. Feminist science, although incorporating some of the features of the two earlier categories, demands far more radical changes. Drawing on the work of writers such as Rich (1972), it involves a fundamental rethinking of what constitutes scientific method and knowledge. Those who advocate feminist science call for a revaluing of subjective understanding and intuition. Thus Bentley and Watts argue that:

> in a feminist school, science, feelings, reactions, values and intuitions become important starting points for the development of principles and theories. Evidence can be unique, anecdotal, partial and partisan, and seen to be so . . . to us this methodological and epistemological approach challenges the masculine heart of science, and brings to it the positive virtues of a feminist view of scientific enquiry.
>
> (Bentley and Watts, 1987, p. 96)

Feminist science has been criticised on the grounds that it assumes that women have always been excluded from the realms of scientific enquiry and that there is something intrinsic to science which makes it incompatible with women's way of viewing the world. Kelly (1988) comments:

> this view of feminist science tends to exaggerate the differences between males and females in a way that can easily slip over into biological essentialism and lead to reification of the very distinctions that feminists traditionally want to eliminate.
>
> (Kelly, 1988, p. 159)

ARGUMENTS AGAINST A COMMON CURRICULUM AS A STEP TOWARDS GENDER EQUALITY

Feminist opposition to the idea of a common curriculum has again often focused on the status of science. The feeling that much equal-opportunities literature imposes a simplistic deficit

214

model on girls has prompted some feminists to question the whole idea of a common curriculum for girls and boys as a solution to the problem, particularly in the area of science and technology . Elliott and Powell (1987), for instance, argue that the educational case for encouraging girls into these areas needs to be more carefully examined. Since almost all of women's work has suffered from de-skilling, and since women occupy the lowliest positions in all areas of work, they do not accept that doing more science would necessarily improve women's status. In support of this point, they compare the position of women in Malaysia with that of women in Britain. Although in Malaysia a higher proportion of women do advanced engineering courses and study science than in Britain, this is not reflected in their social status, where a strongly Islamic state ensures that they remain subordinate. Thus, Elliott and Powell argue, the study of science and technology is not a sufficient condition for achieving equality. Indeed, the high status of science may be part of the problem, for this reflects a mechanistic and essentially macho world view, where the natural world is simply seen as something to be dominated. By encouraging girls to abandon cutural and aesthetic areas of the curriculum, feminists are reinforcing a deficit model of female achievement. Creating girl-friendly science is unlikely to be very useful, since this might create yet another female ghetto.

Writing from a psychological perspective, Harding and Sutoris (1987) see girls' rejection of science and technology as resulting from structures of parenting in western society. They refer to Chodorow's (1978) use of object relations theory, which sees gender inequality as stemming from the fact that it is women rather than men who act as mothers. As boys grow up, this causes them to suffer from separation anxiety, since they are forced to reject the mother in establishing their separate masculine identity. For girls, the experience of being cared for by someone of their own sex results in merger anxiety, which manifests itself as an inability to act autonomously and a shaky sense of their own boundaries. Boys thus prefer the pseudo-objectivity of the world of science where they do not have to engage emotionally, whereas girls are attracted to aesthetic and affective areas of the curriculum. These patterns will not be significantly changed until parenting customs are altered. 'We may succeed in attracting more women into science but women will not succeed in science (or any other sphere) in greater numbers unless we provide girls with greater opportunities to devlop autonomy' (Chodorow, 1978, p. 34).

Clearly, these writers see girls' absence from science and technology as a manifestation of a much wider social problem to which a common curriculum does not offer a simple solution. Indeed, Elliott and Powell would oppose such a measure as reinforcing rather than undermining the superiority of masculine areas of knowledge.

Other criticisms of the national curriculum stem from a belief that the government has no real commitment to gender equality, and is simply hoping to train more young people of either sex in scientific and technological skills to meet the needs of the economy. This point has been made by a number of writers including Arnot (1989a and 1989b), Miles and Middleton (1990), Burton and Weiner (1990) and Myers (1989). Myers points to the danger of using women as a reserve army of labour in that they can be dispensed with as soon as the crisis abates. She draws parallels with the situation which American women faced at the end of the Second World War as depicted in the film *Rosie the Riveter*. When the women were needed to work in heavy industry:

creches flourished, easy-wear clothes became fashionable, recipes in women's magazines became short and simple. When the market forces changed and the men that survived the war returned, women's place was once against in the home, creches closed, skirts became tight, heels became higher and recipes became complicated.

(Myers, 1989, p. 559)

Quite apart from the criticism that the national curriculum reflects a response to market forces rather than a concern for social justice, there is the possibility that the real problems of sexism in the curriculum will simply be ignored. Arnot (1989a) sees it as a means of forcing girls into a male-defined curriculum which pays no heed to their legitimate interests and needs. She foresees the perpetuation of 'a national hidden curriculum in which traditional assumptions and discriminating practices still happily co-exist' (p. 9). If a national hidden curriculum were to be rigorously enforced, then girls' failure to perform well might be explained in terms of the genetic inadequacies of the pupils themselves rather than being legitimated through child-centred ideologies or beliefs in the legitimacy of free choice.

RESERVATIONS ON THE NATURE OF THE NATIONAL CURRICULUM

The Equal Opportunities Commission, which recommended the principle of a common curriculum to the government in 1985, made clear that it opposed certain features of the proposed national curriculum on pragmatic grounds (EOC, 1987). In its submission to the government on the proposals for the national curriculum, the Commission stressed that 'Arrangements for a national curriculum should ensure that girls and boys have *equal access* to the *same* curricular opportunities.' According to the EOC, the government would need to ensure that single-sex schools have access to the same curriculum as co-educational schools, which of course would entail large-scale expenditure to ensure that girls' schools are properly equipped with technology facilities. The Commission also expressed concern that home economics did not qualify as a foundation subject, suggesting that both boys and girls could benfit from lessons in personal independence which this subject could provide, with some re-orientation of its syllabus towards skills for living. If home economics was merely offered as a GCSE option in Year 4, the EOC pointed to the danger that 'girls flock into this examination option simply as a result of a general perception that girls should study home economics at some time during their school career'. Other reservations which the EOC expressed concern the need for a major reappraisal of the *content* of science and technology courses, to which insufficient attention was being paid. The Commission also emphasised the importance of careers advice incorporating a critical awareness of male and female received social roles, and recommended systematic equal-opportunities training in connection with the national curriculum for teachers.

Opposition to the national curriculum, then, has ranged from outright rejection of science and technology as a valid area of study for girls, to concern about the ability of the government to deliver what it has promised because of resource limitations.

Further doubts concern its underlying rationale and the danger that the real problem of unequal power relations between males and females within the education system will be glossed over rather than solved.

THE FUTURE IMPACT OF THE NATIONAL CURRICULUM ON GIRLS' EDUCATION

Feminist responses to the national curriculum, then, have varied from enthusiastic acceptance through suspicion to outright rejection and, clearly, since it is still only in the early stages of implementation, it is impossible to be sure which of these assessments is right. Critics note that it might well have some unintended beneficial consequences for girls and women teachers. Arnot (1989a), for instance, notes that teachers will have to collaborate to moderate assessment procedures, and that gender issues might emerge in these groups. Similarly, with the ground being prepared for the greater involvement of parents at various stages of the educational process, possibilities may well emerge for the development of equal-opportunities initiatives in which parents play a larger part. She suggests that in the past some LEA and school-based equal-opportunities initiatives may have failed to pay sufficient attention to the role of parents, assuming that they were passive recipients of policies rather than having any active role to play.

A further possibility is that it might have very little impact on the future direction of girls' education, partly because of the enormous number of changes in its form and content which we have seen since 1988. I have already mentioned Kenneth Baker's swift retreat on the issue of overall time allocation. The revision of the amount of time to be spent on science, which was announced in August 1988, has particularly serious impli-cations for girls. An amendment was inserted which allowed for pupils to take a single-award science GCSE, amounting to 10 per cent of time per week rather than 20 per cent which was originally envisaged. This was nominally designed for those pupils 'who may need, for whatever reason, to spend more time on other subjects, for example, to develop a special talent in music or foreign languages'. It was acknowledged in a subse-quent National Curriculum Council consultation report (NCC,

1988) that this alternative model would provide an insufficient basis for 'A' level work, and, in practice, would mean that the career routes of pupils taking this option, most of whom are likely to be girls, will be determined at age 13.

The watering down of the original national curriculum proposals continues. At the end of January 1990, Mr Mac-Gregor passed to the NCC his proposals for the merging of GCSE with the national curriculum, which suggested, amongst other things, that able children be allowed to drop art, geography, history, music and PE after age 14 if they have reached Attainment Level 8 (GCSE B). If this goes ahead, then the gulf between an elite group of middle-class girls on career routes and the majority of working-class girls heading for low skilled work might widen. Further, it appears that a fragmented and diverse range of vocational courses will continue to co-exist alongside the national curriculum as long as these ostensibly allow pupils to comply with attainment targets. In the past, these courses have been taken by working-class pupils and they have generally reinforced traditional notions of masculine and feminine work. It appears that they will continue to do so in the future. Given the complications in determining how vocational subjects and foundation subjects might be combined, it is interesting that at this point Mr MacGregor, Baker's successor as Secretary of State for Education, passed responsibility back to the schools, stating: 'In my judgement, it is right that the schools should be able to make these decisions, not the centre' (quoted in *The Times Educational Supplement*, 2.2.90.) The president of the Secondary Heads Association, Mr John Horne, did not appear to be delighted with this new responsibility, describing it in the same article as 'a curriculum planner's nightmare'. It is interesting to note that a recurring theme in these revisions is a renewed emphasis on the responsibility of schools to organise their own curricula and for pupils to exercise a degree of choice within certain broad parameters. As the national curriculum becomes more complicated, it increasingly resembles the option choice system. One explanation for these constant revisions might be that the government has realised the usefulness of option choice as a legitimating device for profoundly unequal for educational outcomes. It may be against the government's interest that this illusion of freedom be replaced by coercion. Putting choice back into the national curriculum may be yet another manifestation of the government's desperate struggle to win support for a system which is increasingly losing credibility in the eyes of many pupils and parents because of its failure to deliver the promised goods. The changing emphasis also represents unresolved ideological conflicts within the Conservative government, referred to by Maw (1988).

Ultimately, I am sceptical as to whether over the coming years we will see major changes in the sex differentiation of the curriculum. First of all, it is clear that, as reflected in the composition and deliberations of the curriculum working groups, the NCC does not accord very high priority to gender equality (Burton and Weiner, 1990) and this message will certainly be conveyed to teachers. As my own research and that of others indicate, many teachers place low priority on equal opportunities and do not see themselves or the school as part of the problem. There will clearly be ample opportunity within the national curriculum for girls and boys to seek out traditional routes, and it is unlikely that many teachers will have the time, energy or commitment to encourage them to reconsider.

Second, the idea that all pupils will take a similar form of technology up to age 16 seems unworkable. Given the shortage of teachers and the non-existence of facilities in some schools, the government would have to provide a significant injection of cash to ensure that all pupils have access to appropriate materials and equipment. There is currently no indication that they have any intention of making additional resources available. Further, if home economics is to appear on the timetable only as a GCSE option at fourth-year level, then it is highly likely that girls will continue to be overrepresented in this area because of the belief that training in domestic skills is an essential component of female education. It will of course be in the immediate interests of schools to ensure that large numbers of girls continue to take up home economics, for a mass exodus from the subject would produce a large number of redundant teachers. For a range of reasons, it appears likely that technology will continue to mean very different things for girls and boys, and the EOC's concern that the national curriculum may fail to provide equal access to the same curriculum for all pupils is likely to prove well founded. There is also no indication that there will be any systematic national monitoring of the outcome of the new curriculum, and so the effects may be obscured for a number of years. The only exceptions to this no-change situation may be schools who already have consciously formulated equal-opportunities policies and are able to use measures within recent government legislation to further their own agenda with the backing of parents and governors.

CONCLUSION

Although feminists have generally seen gender differentiation in the curriculum as a problem, they have differed in their view of appropriate solutions, some emphasising the importance of a common curriculum and others seeing wider societal changes as an essential precursor to change in school. The debate over science education has revealed the diversity of views with regard to priorities for change. Some writers have seen the provisions of the national curriculum as heralding a new age of democratic education, whilst others have seen it as even better adapted to servicing 'the requirements and the concerns of white middle-class boys and men' (Arnot, 1989a). My own assessment of the national curriculum is that it is highly unlikely to produce very radical changes in gender and class differentiation of the curriculum. Further, it would appear that the national curriculum is not likely to be successful even in the government's own terms of raising standards and producing more school leavers with a narrower range of qualifications to meet the requirements of the labour market in the 1990s. One reason for this is schools' vested interest in maintaining the existing curricular structure and the individualised curriculum as a legitimating device for differential educational outcomes. Given the lack of resources, schools would find it hard to ensure that the same curriculum was being followed by all pupils even if they so wished. Baker deliberately made a decision not to carry out serious consultation with teachers – indeed, for him to do so would have been contradictory, since one of his aims was to diminish their power. However, he did not take account of the fact that, as much research in the area of social policy has demonstrated, the success of innovation depends to a large extent on the support of those at the grass roots who bear prime responsibility for its implementation (Elmore, 1980; Weatherley and Lipsky, 1977). Without the co-operation of teachers, the national curriculum will be no more than a smoke-screen, enabling the government to claim that it is taking radical steps to improve standards, whilst in reality changing very little. Harland (1988) expresses this view very succinctly:

> Put simply, the less we believe parliamentary government capable of resolving our educational problems, the more politicians charged with running an increasingly dis- credited system will seek new ways to demonstrate the legitimacy of their policies. They will find that they need to promise more and hence to control more; but the chances of success may well be slim.
>
> (Harland, 1988, p. 92)

10

GENDER AND THE CURRICULUM

Progressive and conservative elements in the balance

INTRODUCTION

In this final chapter, I summarise the themes which have emerged from the preceding analysis of the management of curricular choice in two schools and will go on to make some suggestions as to possible courses of action which might lead to the achievement of a more democratic curriculum for all pupils.

SCHOOL CULTURE AND THE CONSTRUCTION OF THE GENDERED CURRICULUM

At the start of Part II, I summarised the rather different views of the school's role in the reproduction of gender inequality to emerge from the Australian and British literature. The latter body of work provides a generally depressing picture, summarised by Acker (1987), who suggests that a range of factors hinder the promotion of feminist ideas in school. These range from government apathy to individual teachers' hostility towards feminism and suspicion of innovation generally. From Australia, a more optimistic view emerges. Connell (1986) suggests that although teachers as a group fail to share a common perspective on gender, nevertheless women teachers have acted as important vehicles for feminism. In the Australian literature we also find reports of schools whose culture is increasingly sympathetic to girls' experience and willing to promote their interests.

Crump (1990), for instance, discusses the way in which Australian government policy during the 1970s and 1980s encouraged schools to develop a broad curriculum which presented possibilities for change with regard to gender-differentiated patterns of subject selection. Additional funds were provided through the Disadvantaged Schools Programme and the Participation and Equity Programme with the aim of reducing disadvantage and increasing secondary-school retention rates. Crump's research in one school which had benefited from such additional funding indicated that there was increasing understanding and sympathy between teachers and girls 'who were judged to be responding to a number of policy supported initiatives from the school, for example, ones which aimed to raise female student awareness of career issues' (Crump, 1990).

Data from the Westshire schools generally supported the more depressing picture presented by the British research. The subject choice system produced marked gender and class differentiation. Option choice booklets and the counselling of individual pupils conveyed clear messages about the group for whom each subject was intended, whilst at the same time promoting an ideology of free choice. As Gaskell (1984, 1985) has suggested, the danger of such an approach is that it encourages feelings of guilt and self-blame in individual pupils for their perceived educational failure. Equal opportunities were mentioned in a desultory way by some teachers, but the underlying model was inevitably one of female deficit, with girls and their parents (rather than the school, the curriculum or the option choice system) seen as the root of the problem.

Chapter 4 shed light on the role of teachers in the production of a gender-differentiated curriculum. A cluster of ideologies and operating principles linked with their professional identity often underlay their acceptance of gender divisions as a relatively unimportant fact of life. As mentioned in the previous paragraph, teachers' support for the general principle of free choice within the curriculum, sustained by a belief in the values of child-centred education, prevented them from seeing sex-segregation as a problem. Pupils' superficial acceptance of their chosen subjects was apparently all that mattered, and the examination of group outcomes was neither important nor relevant. Kelly (1988) has been particularly critical of the individualised curriculum because it ignores constraints placed on the individual by his or her social context. Teachers' support for free choice was strangely at odds with another aspect of their professional ideology, a belief in environmental determinism. This led them to the view that rural parents were particularly avid in encouraging sex-stereotyped attitudes among their children, which the school could do little to remediate. The notion that it would be morally wrong for the school to champion political causes, such as equal opportunities, also figured prominently in their thinking. This desire to adopt a non-extremist position is identified by Connell (1986) as another of teachers' key operating principles.

Male teachers in the school often adhered to a traditional ideology of femininity, characterising women's principle role as that of home-maker and mother rather than worker. This was used to justify male dominance of power positions within the teaching profession, but also clearly impacted on their judgement of appropriate curricular and career paths for girls.

Some but by no means all women teachers were angry about the gendered hierarchy in the school. The fact that some women teachers, particularly those who had been promoted or had opted for part-time work, were prepared to justify the status quo demonstrated the difficulty of establishing a common political cause. A minority of male teachers were overtly hostile to feminism and there was a general supicion of promoted women teachers who were seen as unfeminine and asexual. Amidst all this hostility and apathy, a small minority of female teachers identified themselves as active feminists and struggled to bring about improvements in their position. In one school, male hostility was powerfully illustrated by the instant suppression of an independent women's group, perceived as far too subversive. The culture of the schools, then, was generally unhelpful in encouraging feminist ideas to flourish.

GIRLS, THEIR PARENTS AND THE CULTURE OF FEMININITY

In Part III I went on to consider whether girls and their parents were developing and reflecting gender codes which were likely to represent a challenge to that of the schools. First, considering the pupils' perspective, I drew attention to the way in which different commentators have characterised girls and the culture of femininity. Earlier accounts focused on the reproductive qualities of this culture, particularly the prevalence of the ideology of romance among working-class girls (McRobbie,

1978). Anyon (1983) and Valli (1986) stressed the dual elements of accommodation and resistance, as girls challenged patriarchal relations but ultimately sought a way of surviving safely within them. More recently, some accounts of girls' culture in Australia and the United States have emphasised the way in which changing economic conditions (Weis, 1990), liberal educational programmes (Crump, 1990) and the increased impact of feminism (Connell *et al.*, 1982; Connell, 1986) have brought about radical changes in girls' self-perception. The general view emerging from this literature is that girls no longer see themselves as primarily home-makers subordinate to male interests, but place equal or greater emphasis on their role as workers. One of the central aims of my study was to investigate the extent to which radical change could be detected in the ideology of Westshire girls, reflected in their subject choices and their culture more generally.

Overall, what emerged was a diverse pattern of competing elements within the gender codes of Westshire girls. They were clearly sceptical of the school's half-hearted attempts to urge non-traditional subject choices upon them. Like the young women in Griffin's (1985) study, they were unenthusiastic about being the token girl in a male subject, preferring the warmth and security of female areas. Griffin comments: 'This was not a mark of their conservative views, but a pragmatic decision made in a situation of limited available options, an affirmation of the value of female friendship groups' (p. 191). Option choices, then, were still generally traditional, and for working-class girls this often meant spending a significant amount of time on office skills and domestic craft subjects. All girls were notable by their absence from applied science and technology, and physics remained an almost exclusively male preserve. Working-class girls justified their traditional choices in terms of the conditions of the local labour market where work opportunities were severely limited. They also accepted that motherhood and domesticity would play a very important role in their lives, though most girls were unconvinced by romantic visions of these occupations.

Despite these traditional choices, their behaviour and attitudes were far from passively subordinate. They expressed hostility towards sex discrimination, support for equality in the workplace, and prided themselves on choosing subjects autonomously. Some contested teachers' authority in the classroom, at times through an overt expression of sexuality which male teachers found particularly disconcerting.

Middle-class girls were generally pursuing a more academic curriculum than their working-class peers, but were still more likely to opt for arts rather than science subjects. Whereas working-class girls had a clear idea of the sort of job they were likely to get, middle-class girls were vaguer, but were still highly ambitious in terms of educational achievement. A minority of middle-class and working-class girls were developing more radical conceptions of their future lives, opting for non-traditional subjects and career paths and quite explicitly challenging the sexual division of labour in the family. They were also concerned with negotiating acceptance among their peers, aware that espousing feminist ideas too overtly might lead to rejection. Although the girls felt that individual teachers of non-traditional subjects had done their best to encourage them, overall they would have appreciated more support from the school.

It is interesting to compare these versions of femininity with those identified by other commentators. Connell *et al.* (1982) and Connell (1986) characterise working-class Australian girls who challenged teachers' authority as reflecting a form of working-class feminism which is likely to lead to an ongoing challenge of male domination. They comment: 'most of the active school resisters are strong young women who are not about to become doormats to the local boys if they can stand up to parents and schools' (p. 178). Within the Westshire context, I was slightly more sceptical of the potential of working-class girls' contestation of schooling to produce a genuine shift in power relations within the school hierarchy. Despite their rejection of female passivity, these girls were still moving into areas of the curriculum which would undoubtedly lead into typically low-paid female areas of the labour market, effectively precluding future financial autonomy.

At both schools it was possible to identify a group of girls who were adopting a version of femininity which emphasised the importance of educational and career success. This group represented both working-class and middle-class girls, and their form of feminism struck me as offering more potential for long-term change than the more dramatic actions of the working-class school resisters. Connell (1986) points to the danger that women teachers are likely to approve of this version of femininity since it is much closer to their own, and react with hostility to working-class girls' more challenging behaviour. He argues that academic success is in reality only an option for a minority of pupils, but if it is held up as the only approved form of behaviour then those who cannot conform will be pushed into more extreme forms of behaviour. Clearly, this point needs to be taken seriously. I would suggest that whilst it is important to regard academic and career success as legitimate goals for girls, it is equally important for teachers to understand the different forms which working-class feminism may take and to encourage working-class girls to develop active plans for change rather than pursuing purely negative strategies. This might in part be achieved by teachers and pupils working together to develop a critical understanding of the domestic division of labour and the local labour market, so that they can recognise the common elements in their experience.

Among girls, then, there was a range of gender codes which were to some extent informed by class. Parents' versions of femininity were similarly complex. There was a general tendency to endorse conventional gender divisions in the curriculum among all parents, but interview data revealed the diversity of reasons for these opinions. Working-class men were most trenchant in their defence of traditional gender roles in the home and the workplace. Middle-class men claimed to support the general principle of equal opportunities but opposed any positive action. Support for the ideology of fulltime motherhood informed working-class women's defence of traditional gender codes. Like the pupils, a minority of middleclass and working-class women strongly supported changes in women's social and economic status. Teachers' view of a homogeneous group of conservative parents was thus inaccurate, but among certain groups very traditonal attitudes were prevalent.

This brings us back to the fundamental question of whether the picture presented by the Australian and American research – of progressive shifts in the gender codes of female pupils, and, to a lesser extent, schools – might also apply to the Westshire context. It was clear that, in general, women and girls had more radical views on gender issues than men and boys. Indeed, a hallmark of many recent studies is the intransigence of male culture as opposed to the developing nature of female culture. The relatively progressive nature of female gender codes, however, should not blind us to the conservative elements in the culture of Westshire women and girls. This conservatism was underpinned by both ideological and material factors. Thus, although motherhood was no longer romanticised, the sense that women still had prime responsibility for parenting was very strong. In economic terms, the structure of the local labour market led working-class girls in particular to make safe if restricted choices encouraged by their mothers. Getting a job was clearly considered to be more important than breaking out of the established order. Further, the schools, through their adherence to a range of ideologies – including those of free choice and environmental determinism – continued to act as a brake on progressive developments.

The picture, then is both of stagnation and pressure for change in parents' and pupils' gender codes. In this my findings differ from those who suggest that very rapid changes are taking place in the culture of femininity. Reasons for these discrepancies are undoubtedly linked with the specific con- ditions of the local labour market as well as other factors' such as different emphases in government policies and on the general acceptance of feminist ideas in different contexts. There is also the possibility that individual researchers may interpret similar events in different ways. Crump (1990), for instance, questions the common feminist view that male domi- nation of the social space of the classroom is a problem for girls. He comments: 'Though male behaviours and attitudes at Carpenter did rob female students of teacher time in many classrooms, this did not necessarily advantage males.' I would suggest that being robbed of teacher time could not possibly do anything but work to girls' disadvantage. In the present study, I certainly interpreted failure to challenge disruptive male behaviour in an effective way as an indicator of a school ethos which was hostile to girls' intellectual and social development.

THE IMPACT OF THE NATIONAL CURRICULUM ON GENDER DIVISIONS

Finally, in Part IV of the book, I considered the likely impact of the national curriculum in England and Wales on gender divisions. Feminist arguments for and against a national curriculum were discussed, and the strengths and weaknesses of the proposed national curriculum were also assessed. Three distinct views of its possible effects were identified. First was the possibility suggested by Arnot (1989a) that, if rigidly enforced, the national curriculum would have a damaging effect on girls by forcing them to take up a range of subjects designed to meet the interests and needs of middle-class white males. Second was the view put forward by Kelly (1988) that the national curriculum would have an overall democratising effect; in particular, opening up science and technology to girls as well as working-class and minority ethnic pupils. Finally, the outcome which I considered most likely was that the national curriculum, in its final form, would make very little difference to the diverging curricular paths of girls and boys. Since its initial inception, the national curriculum has become increasingly loosely defined and less stringent in its requirements. It is now clear that vocational courses such as secretarial studies will continue, that technology will mean very different things for girls and boys, and girls will be able to take a reduced science course which will not equip them for further study in the area.

Ultimately, it seems that the government has not dared to undermine seriously the ideology of free choice which, as we have seen, has served as a useful legitimating device for differentiated educational outcomes. Further, the lack of commitment to equal opportunities has meant that the government has shrunk from introducing a genuinely common curriculum and tackling sexism within the hidden curriculum. This study shows clearly the complexity of the cultures which currently bring about the divergent curricular paths of girls and boys. In order to change these cultures, teachers, parents and pupils must be convinced in terms of social justice as well as market forces that women and men are entitled to an equal share of responsibility both at work and at home, and an equal education to prepare them for their dual roles. To enable teachers to engage in such discussions, a comprehensive programme of in-service work on equal opportunities would be essential. Parents and governors would also require the opportunity for on-going education in this area. For pupils, equality issues could be studied as cross-curricular themes as well as in personal and social education, which at the moment is in danger of being squeezed off the timetable completely. If such discussion does not take place, then it is very likely that parents, teachers and pupils will both deliberately and unconsciously subvert the idea of a common curriculum, so that divisions based on gender, race and class continue to exist in both the overt and the covert curricula. In response to this situation, I believe that feminists, rather than arguing against the idea of a common curriculum, should point out what needs to be done to make this a reality.

WHERE DO WE GO FROM HERE?

The preceding analysis is clearly critical of the system of subject option choice. To quote Kelly (1988): 'Whenever choice occurs, the disadvantaged use it to disadvantage themselves further' (p. 168). The national curriculum does not hold out much hope that it will bring about a significant change for the better by equalising educational outcomes. There appear to me to be very powerful socialist and feminist arguments for the existence of a common curriculum. Reynolds and Sullivan (1980) are highly critical of the emphasis in child-centred education of allowing pupils control over the content and context of their learning. They argue that it is obviously detrimental to base a pupil's curriculum on their sub-culture if that culture is distorted and limited by political and economic factors beyond their under-standing or control. Such an education, they argue, is ultimately anti-intellectual and fascistic. By way of contrast, they propose that the curriculum should retain 'the rationality and content, but not the values of contemporary bourgeois culture'. Ultimately, they argue, the values of socialism can only flourish in a society 'controlled and developed by the democracy of the universally, compulsorily and excellently schooled' (p. 191). I would support the view that a common curriculum, genuinely informed by equal opportunities princi-ples, is likely to promote greater social justice not only for girls, but also for minority ethnic and working-class pupils.

Although the idea of a common curriculum clearly enjoys

231

widespread support among those who are committed to greater educational equality, its precise nature continues to be disputed. Lawton and Chitty (1987), outlining their recommendations for a national curriculum, draw on the idea of an entitlement curriculum outlined by HMI in the third Red Book (DES, 1983).

> The conviction has grown that all pupils are entitled to a broad compulsory common curriculum up to the age of 16 which introduces them to a range of experiences, makes them aware of the kind of society in which they are going to live and gives them the skills necessary to live in it. Any curriculum which fails to provide this balance and is overweighted in any particular direction, whether vocational, technical or academic, is to be seriously questioned. Any measures which restrict the access of all pupils to a wide-ranging curriculum or which focus too narrowly on specific skills are in direct conflict with the entitlement curriculum envisaged here.

The entitlement curriculum, then, identifies particular areas of knowledge to which all pupils should have access as of right. In *Curriculum 11–16* (DES, 1977) eight areas of experience are identified: the aesthetic and creative; the ethical; the linguistic; the mathematical; the physical; the scientific; the social and political; and the spiritual. Rigid adherence to traditional subject divisions is rejected and the emphasis is on 'the quality of the teaching process and the needs of individual children'.

Lawton and Chitty term such an approach 'the professional curriculum' and contrast it with the national curriculum which they see as essentially bureaucratic, being based on traditionally defined subjects in order to fulfil bureaucratic rather than educational purposes. The obsession with age-related benchmark testing is a clear reflection of this bureaucratic tendency:

> This has all sorts of bureaucratic advantages in terms of presentation of statistics and making comparisons between teachers and schools. But age-related testing makes it extremely difficult to avoid normative procedures, norm-related criteria and judgements about how

a statistically 'normal' child should perform. Age-related, norm-referenced examinations tend to drive everyone (teachers, parents and governors) into thinking of a sizeable proportion of the age group as failures and neglecting to stretch the above-average. It is a recipe for mediocrity and insensitivity.

(Lawton and Chitty, 1987, p. 5)

Lawton and Chitty, then, drawing on the work of HMI, make a strong plea for an entitlement curriculum based on broadly defined areas of knowledge. The problem with this is that it is in many ways very similar to that which the schools in this study already claimed to operate and which produced such unequal outcomes.

Ultimately, it seems to me that to overcome these difficulties it is essential to start from the premise that all areas of the curriculum must be suitable for and taken by a representative cross-section of pupils. I would support the idea of an entitlement curriculum whose aim is to ensure that all pupils gain access to areas of knowledge which are deemed important within the culture. It would then be vital to monitor each area carefully to ensure that pupils within it were not divided by gender, class or race. For instance, if all pupils were ostensibly taking science but in reality girls were absent from physics and most working-class pupils were taking general science, then this should be recognised as a problem requiring investigation and action rather than an inevitable and natural state of affairs. Some subjects would almost certainly require radical overhauling to ensure the equal representation of all groups. In the case of home economics, for example, it is very likely that a new designation would have to be found to dispel the notion implicit in the name that it is about preparing girls for a servicing role in the family. Its content would also have to be rethought, with a new emphasis on helping all pupils to develop self-sufficiency skills, fostering an understanding of food and society, food technology and production and so on. Other subjects such as history and geography, which have less clear-cut gender boundaries, would also have to examine their subject matter to ensure that it reflects an equal concern for girls' and boys' interests. Clearly, emphasising the requirement for equal uptake of subjects would have to be accompanied by a range of other developments, particularly in-service training for teachers.

Despite the heavy-handed bureaucracy and centralised control of the national curriculum, it is unlikely to succeed in terms of improving the situation of girls or in terms of raising standards generally, because it is not informed by a concern for the democratisation of all areas of knowledge. Pupils may perform better in the areas where they are to be tested, but that is not the same thing as raising educational standards in a wider sense. The answer does not lie in the former system of pretending that all pupils are able to operate as entirely free agents and take the consequences of their actions. What is needed as a starting point is a firm commitment to the principle of equal representation of all social groups in all areas of the curriculum. Local Education Authorities are currently encouraging schools to engage in a systematic process of setting goals and monitoring progress towards them in the interests of public accountability. It is vital that equal opportunities feature as a major goal of school improvement.

This book has attempted to shed light on the processes resulting in the production of gender divisions within the curriculum. Although clearly the cultures of pupils and their families are implicated in this process, it is also the case that schools and teachers are active agents. It follows from this that reform of the curriculum has the potential to bring about real change in the construction of masculinity and femininity. The present national curriculum is unlikely to fulfil the extravagent claims made on its behalf, but that does not mean that we should conclude that all curricular reform is doomed.

APPENDIX 1
THE CONDUCT OF THE RESEARCH

THE RESEARCH TIMETABLE

The order in which the different parts of the research were conducted is as follows:

March 1983 – July 1983	Observation at Millbridge.
June 1983	Administration of Millbridge parents' questionnaires (240 distributed, 125 returned, 52 per cent response rate).
June 1983	Administration of Millbridge pupils' questionnaires (150 distributed, 119 returned, 79 per cent response rate).
May 1983 – June 1983	Interviews with Millbridge pupils (10 carried out).
May 1984 – July 1984	Interviews with Millbridge parents (15 sets of parents interviewed).
July 1983 – September 1984	Preliminary analysis of data.
September 1984 – July 1985	Observation at Greenhill.
January – July 1984	Interviews with Greenhill pupils (27 carried out).
May 1985	Questionnaires administered to Greenhill parents (200 distributed, 127 returned, response rate 64 per cent).
May 1985	Questionnaires administered to Greenhill pupils (175 distributed, 132 returned, response rate 75 per cent).

January 1986 – July 1986   Interviews with Greenhill parents
(16 sets of parents interviewed).

Overall, about 200 hours of observation at Millbridge and 400 at Greenhill were carried out. Details of which classes were selected for observation and who was interviewed are given at the start of the appropriate chapters.

DEFINITIONS OF CLASS AND ACHIEVEMENT USED IN THE TEXT

Class is a notoriously difficult term to define. There are not only debates between Marxists and Weberians, but also between those who adhere to a traditional definition of class based on father's occupation (for instance, Goldthorpe, 1983) and those who insist that mother's occupation must also be taken into account (Britten and Heath, 1983; Heath and Britten, 1984). In my study, class was defined on the basis of both the mother's and the father's occupation. Millbridge pupils were defined as working class or middle class on the basis of the information they gave on the questionnaires about their parents' work. For Greenhill pupils this information was derived from pupil admission forms and interviews. Class was assigned to a particular family according to the broad definitions used in the Registrar General's Classification of Occupations. Parents' occupations were grouped thus: (1) professional and managerial; (2) intermediate (semi-professional); (3a) white collar; (3b) skilled manual; (4) semi-skilled manual; (5) unskilled manual. Families were considered middle class if either the father's occupation was 1, 2 or 3a or if the mother's occupation was 1 or 2. The families of women in group 3a were not considered middle class because their pay and status is more comparable with that of manual workers. For some of the analysis, categories 2 and 3a were merged, as were categories 4 and 5. Critics of the Registrar General's Classification of Occupations have argued that it is inadequately theorised, but it is difficult to find any definition of class that pays equal attention to the status of women and men, and so despite its inadequacies it seemed to provide a useful working definition.

Pupils' achievement in both schools was calculated by taking an average of their third-year examination grades awarded in

English and maths, where the highest achievement score was 1 and the lowest was 5. Pupils were then divided into four groups: high achievement (1.0–1.5); above-average achievement (2.0–2.5); below-average achievement (3.0–3.5); and lower achievement (4.0–5.0).

DETAILS OF DATA COLLECTION

Administration of pupils' questionnaire

The questionnaire was distributed to five third-year, mixed-ability English groups at Millbridge Upper School in June 1983, representing an approximate total of 150 pupils. This was about 70 per cent of the year group. I went into each class at the beginning of an English lesson and explained that the overall purpose of the study was to investigate what pupils thought of school and were hoping to do in the future. I emphasised that filling in the questionnaire was voluntary, but almost all of the pupils participated in the study. Three of the teachers allowed pupils to complete the questionnaires in class time and I remained in the classroom to deal with any problems that arose. In the other two classes, the pupils took the questionnaires away with them and were asked to bring them back the next day. Not surprisingly, the response rate amongst this group was slightly lower. Of 150 questionnaires issued at Millbridge, 119 were ultimately returned, representing a response rate of 79 per cent.

At Greenhill, pupil questionnaires were administered during May 1985 to six mixed-ability tutor groups. Most of the pupils managed to complete the questionnaire during the half-hour morning tutor group session, since they were shorter than the questionnaires used at Millbridge. Of the 175 questionnaires which were distributed (this represented approximately 45 per cent of the age group) 132 were returned, a response rate of 75 per cent. At both Millbridge and Greenhill, there were an equal number of girls and boys in the groups to whom the questionnaires were distributed.

Descriptive data from pupils' questionnaires

Of the 119 who replied to the Millbridge pupils' questionnaire, 54 (45 per cent) were boys and 65 (55 per cent) were girls. Of the 132 Greenhill pupils who completed the questionnaire, 68

Table A1 Distribution of boys, girls, working-class and middle-class pupils at Millbridge school in different achievement groups

	Higher achievement	*Above average achievement*	*Below average achievement*	*Lower achievement*	*Totals*
Totals	29 (24)	33 (28)	40 (34)	17 (14)	119 (100)
Boys	10 (18.5)	13 (26.1)	22 (40.7)	9 (16.7)	54 (100)
Girls	19 (29.2)	20 (30.8)	18 (27.7)	8 (12.3)	65 (100)
Working class	17 (21.8)	19 (24.4)	28 (35.9)	14 (17.9)	78 (100)
Middle class	12 (29.3)	14 (34.1)	12 (24.3)	3 (7.3)	41 (100)

Notes: Whole numbers are shown first, followed by percentages in parentheses. (2) Using the Mann–Whitney U test, middle-class girls scored higher than middle-class boys (u = 118.5, z = –2.4800, $p < 0.01$); middle-class girls scored higher than working-class girls (u = 310.0, z = –2.3521, $p < 0.01$)

(51.5 per cent) were boys and 64 (48.5 per cent) were girls. For Millbridge pupils, 75 (66 per cent) were working class and 41 (34 per cent) were middle class, which was about the same proportion as for the parents. For the Greenhill pupils where class could be determined, 71 per cent of pupils were working class and 29 per cent were middle class. This suggests that of the pupils whose class could not be determined, a significant proportion were probably middle class.

Tables A.1 and A.2 show the distribution of boys, girls, working-class and middle-class pupils in these achievement groups at Millbridge and Greenhill respectively. The overall pattern was for middle-class pupils to have higher achievement ratings than working-class pupils and girls to have higher achievement ratings than boys. Although middle-class pupils' academic superiority is well known, it is still widely believed that girls under-achieve in school. However, DES statistics in England and Wales show clearly that over recent years, deficit models are no longer appropriate to describe girls' performance. Achievement levels at Millbridge and Greenhill bear out these general trends.

Administration of parents' questionnaire

At Millbridge, two questionnaires were sent out to each family via pupils, and parents were requested to complete and return

Table A2 Distribution of boys, girls, working-class and middle-class pupils at Greenhill school in different achievement groups

	Higher achievement	Above average achievement	Below average achievement	Lower achievement	Totals
Totals	16 (12)	53 (40)	47 (36)	16 (12)	132 (100)
Boys	11 (16.2)	18 (26.5)	27 (39.7)	12 (17.6)	68 (100)
Girls	5 (7.8)	35 (54.7)	20 (31.2)	4 (6.3)	64 (100)
Working class	2 (3.0)	20 (30.3)	31 (47.0)	13 (19.7)	66 (100)
Middle class	9 (33.3)	16 (59.3)	2 (7.4)	0	27 (100)

Notes: Whole numbers are shown first, followed by percentages in parentheses. (2) Using the Mann–Whitney U test, middle-class girls scored higher than working-class girls ($u = 97.5$, $= -3.8457$, $p < 0.000$); middle-class boys scored higher than working-class boys ($u = 45.0$, $z = -8.7786$, $p < 0.0001$)

either one or both. Questionnaires were sent out to 120 families, thus 240 were distributed in all. After several verbal reminders to the children, 125 questionnaires were finally returned, a response rate of 52 per cent. Some parents might have been deterred by the fact that they had been sent two questionnaires and felt there was not enough time for both parents to complete one. Also, the fact that pupils took the questionnaires home and returned them meant that some wastage was inevitable. Ninety-six of the questionnaires were from families where both parents completed the questionnaire and twenty-nine were from families where only one parent completed the questionnaire.

At Greenhill, parents' questionnaires were given to pupils in four mixed-ability tutor groups at the same time as the pupils were completing their own in May 1985. The pupils were asked to take the questionnaires home to their parents and return them as soon as possible. Again, two questionnaires were sent home to each family and each parent was asked to complete one. Altogether 200 questionnaires were distributed and 127 ultimately returned after one written reminder. This represented a response rate of 64 per cent, rather larger than the Millbridge figure. Ninety were from families where both parents completed the questionnaire and thirty-seven were from families where only one parent completed the questionnaire. An advantage of asking both mother and father to complete a questionnaire was that a reasonable balance of women and men in the sample was obtained (although still more women than men returned questionnaires). A disadvantage was that some families returned two questionnaires and others only one, so that this may have biased the sample.

DESCRIPTIVE DATA FROM PARENTS' QUESTIONNAIRE

The questionnaires were coded and analysed using SPSS. At Millbridge, 51 (42 per cent) of the questionnaires were completed by parents of boys in the third year and 72 (58 per cent) by parents of girls in the third year. This discrepancy might have been because girls identified with the project more closely and put more pressure on their parents to complete the questionnaire. Also, parents of girls may have felt more positive towards the aims of the research. About 44 per cent of respondents were fathers and about 56 per cent were mothers. At Greenhill, 66 questionnaires (52 per cent) were completed by parents of boys and 61 (48 per cent) by parents of girls. Of Greenhill respondents, 56 per cent were women and 44 per cent were men, the same proportion as at Millbridge. Of the Millbridge parents, 80 (64 per cent) were working class and 45 (36 per cent) were middle class and of the Greenhill parents, 67 (63 per cent) were working class, and 39 (37.8 per cent) were middle class. Data on parents' work were obtained from the Millbridge parents' questionnaires, but for Greenhill parents these data had to be extracted from pupil admission forms and interviews and are therefore less reliable. Where it was not possible to determine class with a reasonable degree of certainty, a missing value was assigned.

A further variable that was investigated was the school's definition of the child's achievement. As stated earlier, pupils' report grades for maths and English were averaged to give them an overall score, and these were then divided into four equal groups. Tables A.3 and A.4 show distribution of Millbridge and Greenhill pupils respectively in different achievement groups. Of Millbridge parents who responded, only a

Table A3 Achievement levels of Millbridge parents' children (for girls, boys, working-class and middle-class pupils)

	Higher achievement	Above average achievement	Below average achievement	Lower achievement	Totals
Girls	28 (37.8)	29 (39.2)	11 (14.9)	6 (8.1)	74 (100)
Boys	11 (21.6)	16 (31.4)	18 (35.3)	6 (11.8)	51 (100)
Working class	23 (28.7)	27 (33.7)	19 (23.7)	11 (13.7)	80 (100)
Middle class	16 (35.6)	18 (40.0)	10 (22.2)	1 (2.2)	45 (100)

Note: Whole numbers are shown first, followed by percentages in parentheses

Table A4 Achievement levels of Greenhill parents' children (for girls, boys, working-class and middle-class pupils)

	Higher achievement	Above average achievement	Below average achievement	Lower achievement	Totals
Girls	12 (19.7)	30 (49.2)	17 (27.9)	2 (3.3)	61 (100)
Boys	18 (27.3)	21 (31.8)	21 (31.8)	6 (9.1)	66 (100)
Working class	6 (9.0)	21 (31.3)	32 (47.8)	8 (11.9)	67 (100)
Middle class	20 (51.3)	18 (46.2)	1 (2.6)	0	39 (100)

Note: Whole numbers are shown first, followed by percentages in parentheses

third of the respondents had children of below-average achievement and this might have been because these children and their parents were less keen to participate in the research. At both schools, middle-class parents tended to have higher-achieving children, although on the Mann-Whitney U test this was only statistically significant at Greenhill. Daughters of parents at both Millbridge and Greenhill had higher achievement ratings than sons, although this was only statistically significant at Millbridge.

241

Pupils' interviews

Interviews with Millbridge and Greenhill pupils were semi-structured. Pupils were asked why they were choosing certain subjects and dropping others; why they thought girls and boys often took different subjects; what it would be like to be a girl or a boy in a non-traditional subject area; future educational and work plans; and whether women and men experienced equal treatment at work. The conversation often moved on to a discussion of male and female teachers, and ways in which girls and boys responded in these classes. Pupils were also asked about their friendship groups and the ways they thought girls and boys related to each other inside and outside the classroom. I did not ask directly about relationships with parents because I felt that this might have been too intrusive, but many girls spoke about their relationship with their mothers and their feelings about how their own future might differ.

I interviewed sixty-three pupils, ten at Millbridge and fifty-three at Greenhill. At Millbridge, all pupils were interviewed individually, and at Greenhill interviews were carried out either with individual pupils or with groups of two or three. Interviews with girls tended to be lengthier and to reveal more about personal experience than those with girls.

Pupil observation

At Millbridge, I spent a term and a half, from March to July 1983, observing a third-year, mixed-ability group. They were split up for maths, French and design lessons, and I would follow a different pupil each week to their classes in these subjects. At Greenhill, the period of observation was longer and more intensive. I spent at least three days a week in the school for the academic year 1984–1985. At this school, the third year was divided into five main groups, which were all supposedly mixed ability. In reality, there were more higher-achieving and middle-class pupils in Main Group 1, since it contained all pupils doing two languages. Half the period of observation was spent with a Main Group 1 class and half with a Main Group 5 class.

Parents' interviews

The interview schedules used with Millbridge and Greenhill parents were semi-structured, consisting of questions concerned with parents' accounts of their children's choice of subjects; their views of the importance of design subjects for girls and boys; their explanation of male and female pupils' tendency to be concentrated in different areas of the curriculum; and their opinion of whether the school should intervene to encourage less traditional option choices. Other questions concerned parents' expectations of their child's future educational and occupational paths, their account of their child's domestic and leisure activities and their assessment of how their child was coping with school and responding to teenage culture. A series of questions was included to explore parents' attitudes to the position of women in the labour market and the relationship between motherhood and work. Finally, parents were asked how they felt their child's experience of education differed from their own. A basic list of questions was used in each case, but the wording of questions was not strictly adhered to, and supplementary questions were often used to elicit more detailed information. If I found the conversation moving on to another topic which was interesting and relevant, I made no attempt to return instantly to the interview schedule. In this way, I hoped to obtain enough common ground in the material covered in different interviews to enable comparisons to be made, whilst at the same time allowing those being interviewed to present their own explanations and interpretations of their experiences.

Fifteen sets of parents from Millbridge Upper School were interviewed during the summer of 1984 and sixteen sets of parents from Greenhill Upper School between January and July 1986. Approximately equal numbers of these were working class and middle class. Fourteen of the families lived in either Millbridge, Greenhill or Seatown and seventeen came from the villages and countryside surrounding the small towns, so the balance of town and rural families was about equal. Twenty of the families had daughters in the third year of the Upper School and eleven had sons. The reason for this imbalance was that the major focus of the study was on the creation of girls' educational and occupational disadvantage, and therefore I felt it was important to look at girls' families in particular depth. Parents of boys were included in the study because this was essential for the purposes of comparison. I generally chose parents whose children I had observed in class and whom I had interviewed, so that I could compare children's and parents' accounts. Parents were generally contacted by telephone and only one, a policeman's wife, declined to be interviewed. I made it clear that I was quite happy to talk to either the mother or father alone or else both parents together. Ultimately, thirteen of the interviews were with mothers only, fifteen were with both parents and only three were with fathers only.

Teachers' interviews

Semi-structured interviews were carried out with 19 out of a total of 50 teachers on the staff of Millbridge Upper School in the summer of 1983, ten of whom were men and nine of whom were women. Interviews were carried out with 38 Greenhill teachers out of a total of 100 during the summer of 1985. Twenty-three of these were men and fourteen were women. At both schools, I tried to interview teachers whose classes I had observed, in order to triangulate their accounts of what was happening in their classrooms against pupils' accounts and my own observations. Other teachers whose lessons I had not observed were also interviewed in order to ensure a representative sample of different age groups, subjects taught and positions within the school hierarchy.

The interviews consisted of a series of questions about the third- and fourth-year curriculum, the option choice system, the performance and attitudes of girls and boys in particular subjects and their responses to male and female teachers. At the end of the interview, teachers were asked about their views of whether women and men had equal chances of promotion in teaching. At Greenhill, this was particularly apposite, since an HMI report on the school published in 1984 had criticised the fact that a relatively small proportion of women teachers were in positions of responsibility in the school and had recommended that the school should redress the balance.

APPENDIX 2
OPTION CHOICE SCHEMES
AT THE TWO SCHOOLS

MILLBRIDGE UPPER SCHOOL FOURTH-YEAR
COURSES 1983-4
Notes for guidance to students

These notes give an outline of the courses to be offered in the fourth year but are all dependent on adequate staffing being available and a sufficient number of students choosing the course to make it viable. Please read them, ask for help if there is anything you do not understand, and think about them carefully. At the beginning of the summer term you will discuss your ideas with staff and your parents, and suggest six, seven or eight courses you would like to do in addition to English, mathematics, physical education, religious education and careers.

English – Everyone will take the basic English course
Mathematics – Everyone will take a basic mathematics course

Options

Modern languages – If you are making good progress with a language you should continue to study it
    1 French
    2 German
Sciences – You should choose *at least one*
    3 Physics
    4 Chemistry
    5 Biology
    6 (General) Science
Humanities – You should choose *at least one*

    7 History
    8 Geography
    9 Religious and social studies
Design and creative arts – You should choose *at least one*
    10 Technical drawinag
    11 Woodwork
    12 Metalwork
    13 Combined technical courses
    14 Music
    15 Art
    16 Pottery
    17 Home economics
    18 Needlework
Additional courses
    19 Use of English
    20 Computer studies
    21 Electronics
    22 Rural studies
    23 Commerce
    24 Community service
    25 Typewriting
    26 Parentcraft

NAME

TUTOR GROUP

INTERMEDIATE YEAR – PROVISIONAL OPTIONS SCHEME 1985–86. GREENHILL UPPER SCHOOL

CORE	1	2	3	4	5	6	NOTES
	Latin 'O'	French	Geography	Physics	Secretarial studies →	(arrow up)	(a) One subject to be ticked in each column.
English 4	Music 'O'/C.S.E. Drama C.S.E. Art	German History Classical St.	Biology Chemistry E.P.A.	Biology Computer studies Community Services	French History	German Geography	(b) Colum 1 = non exam. except where indicated. (2 periods).
Maths 4	H.E. Pre catering Needlework Metalwork	R.E. (C.S.E.) Electronics Art/Tex. Metalwork	Tex./Dress Pottery Technology H.E.	H.E. Art/Tex. Art	Geography Geology Chemistry Tex./Dress	History Drama Physics	(c) Columns 2–6 = 'O' Level/C.S.E. subjects. (3 periods).
P.E. 3							
R.E./Careers 2	Woodwork Computer studies Keyboarding Outdoor pursuits	Humanities →	Pre Catering	Pottery Technology	Tech. graphics	Tech. graphics Computer studies	(d) 'O' Level R.E. available in core time.
Soc. Ed./ 2	T.D. Secretarial studies → Engineering technology →	Home & family studies →		Metalwork Woodwork	Science	Woodwork Science	(e) Latin & Music groups miss one period of P.E.
Computing 2 ___ 13					Applied engineering		(f) Arrows indicate where subjects spread over more than one option.

REFERENCES

Acker, S. (1987) 'Feminist theory and the study of gender and education' *International Review of Education* special issue on Women and Education.
—— (1988) 'Teachers, gender and resistance' *British Journal of Sociology of Education* 9, 3: 307–23.
Aggleton, P.J. and Whitty, G. (1985) 'Rebels without a cause? Socialisation and subcultural style among the children of the new middle classes' *Sociology of Education* 58: 60–72.
Althusser, L. (1971) 'Ideology and ideological state apparatuses' in *Lenin and Philosophy and Other Essays* London: New Left Books.
Anyon, J. (1983) 'Intersections of gender and class: accommodation and resistance by working class and affluent females to contradictory sex-role ideologies' in S. Walker, and L. Barton, (eds) *Gender, Class and Education* Lewes: Falmer Press.
Arnot, M. (1982) 'Male hegemony, social class and women's education' *Journal of Education* 164: 64–89.
—— (1984) 'How shall we educate our sons?' in R. Deem, (ed.) *Coeducation Reconsidered* Milton Keynes: Open University Press.
—— (1989a) 'Crisis or challenge: equal opportunities and the national curriculum' *NUT Education Review* 3, 2: 7–14.
—— (1989b) 'Consultation or legitimation? Race and gender politics and the making of the national cirriculum' *Journal of Criticial Social Policy* 27: 20–38.
—— and Whitty, G. (1982) 'From reproduction to transformation: recent radical perspectives in the curriculum from the USA' *British Journal of Sociology of Education* 3: 93–103.
Ashburner, L. (1988) 'Just inside the counting house: women in finance' in A. Coyle and J. Skinner (eds) *Women and Work: Positive Action for Change* London: Macmillan.
Ball, S.J. (1981) *Beachside Comprehensive: A Case Study of Secondary Schooling* Cambridge and London: Cambridge University Press.
—— (1987) *The Micro-Politics of the School: Towards a Theory of School Organisation* London: Methuen.
Bell, C. and Newby, H. (1977) (eds) *Doing Sociological Research* London: George Allen and Unwin.

REFERENCES

Bennett, N. (1976) *Teaching Styles and Pupil Progress* London: Open Books.

Bently, D. and Watts, M. (1987) 'Courting the positive virtues: a case for feminist science', in A. Kelly (ed.) *Science for Girls?* Milton Keynes: Open University Press.

Bernstein, B. (1975) *Class, Codes and Control* vol. 3, London: Routledge & Kegan Paul.

Black, E. (1987) 'Brave new world? Aspects of office skills training in a college of further education', paper delivered to St Hilda's Conference, Oxford, on Ethnography and Inequality, 14th–16th September 1987.

Bourdieu, P. (1977) 'Cultural reproduction and social reproduction' in J. Karabel and A.H. Halsey (eds) *Power and Ideology in Education* Oxford: Oxford University Press.

Bowles, G. and Duelli Klein, R. (eds) (1983) *Theories of Women's Studies* London: Routledge & Kegan Paul.

Bowles, S. and Gintis, H. (1976) *Schooling in Capitalist America* London: Routledge & Kegan Paul.

Britten, N. and Heath, A. (1983) 'Women, men and social class' in E. Garmarnikow, D. Morgan, J. Purvis, and D. Taylerson (eds) *Gender, Class and Work* London: Heinemann.

Burgess, R.G. (1984) *In the Field: An Introduction to Field Research* London: George Allen & Unwin.

—— (ed.) (1985) *Issues in Educational Research: Qualitative Methods* Lewes: Falmer Press.

Burton, L. and Weiner, R. (1990) 'Social justice and the national curriculum' *Research Papers in Education* 5, 3: 203–7.

Buswell, C. (1984) 'Sponsoring and stereotyping in a working class comprehensive school in the north of England' in S. Acker, *et al.* (eds) *World Yearbook of Education 1984: Women and Education* London: Kogan Page.

Byrne, E. (1985) 'Equity or equality: a European overview' in M. Arnot (ed.) *Race and Gender: Equal Opportunities Policies in Education* Oxford: Pergamon Press in association with the Open University.

Carrington, B. and Short, G. (1987) 'Breakthrough to political literacy: political education, antiracist teaching and the primary school' *Journal of Education Policy* 2, 1: 1–13.

Chadwick, V. (1989) 'Equal opportunities in the teaching profession: the myth and the reality' in H. De Lyon, and F.W. Migniuolo, (eds) *Women Teachers: Issues and Experiences* Milton Keynes: Open University Press.

Chamberlain M. (1983) *Fenwomen: A Portrait of Women in an English Village* London: Routledge & Kegan Paul.

Chodorow, N. (1978) *The Reproduction of Mothering: Family Structure and Feminine Personality* California: University of California Press.

Clarricoates, K. (1980) 'The importance of being Ernest . . . Emma . . . Tom . . . Jane' in R. Deem, (ed.) *Schooling for Women's Work* London: Routledge & Kegan Paul.

Coffield, F., Borrill, C. and Marshall, S. (1986) *Growing Up at the Margins* Milton Keynes: Open University Press.

Cohen, A. (1982) 'Belonging: the experience of culture' in A. Cohen (ed.) *Belonging: Identity and Social Organisation* Manchester: Manchester University Press.

Comber, L.C. *et al.* (1981) *The Social Effects of Rural Primary School Reorganisation* a study on behalf of the Department of the Environment and the Department of Education and Science, Final Report, London: HMSO.

Connell, R.W. (1986) *Teachers' Work* Sydney: George Allen & Unwin.

—— Ashenden, D.J., Kessler, S. and Dowsett, G.W. (1982) *Making the Difference: Schools, Families and Social Divisions* Sydney: George Allen & Unwin.

Corrigan, P. (1979) *Schooling the Smash Street Kids* London: Macmillan.

Cowie, C. and S. Lees, (1981) 'Slags or drags' *Feminist Review* 9: 17–31.

Coyle, A. (1988) 'Behind the scenes: women in television' in A. Coyle, and J. Skinner, (eds) *Women and Work: Positive Action for Change* London: Macmillan.

—— and Skinner, J. (1988) (eds) *Women and Work: Positive Action for Change* London: Macmillan.

Crowther Report (1959) *15–18*, a report of the Central Advisory Council for Education London: HMSO.

Crump, S.J. (1990) 'Gender and the curriculum: power and being female' *British Journal of Sociology of Education* 11, 4 365–87.

Cunnison, S. (1984) 'Macho culture in the school and the response of women teachers: the case of a mixed single sex high school', paper delivered to Girl Friendly Schooling Conference, Didsbury College, Manchester Polytechnic, 1984.

—— (1985) *Making it in a Man's World: Women Teachers in a Senior High School*, occasional paper no 1, Hull: University of Hull Department of Sociology and Anthropology.

—— (1989) 'Gender joking in the staffroom' in Acker, S. (Ed.) *Teachers, Gender and Careers*, Lewes: Falmer Press.

David, M.E. (1981) *The State, Family and Education* London: Routledge & Kegan Paul.

Davies, L. (1984) *Pupil Power: Deviance and Gender in School* Lewes: Falmer Press.

Deem, R. (1981) 'State policy and ideology in the education of women, 1944–1980' *British Journal of Sociology of Education* 2, 2: 131–43.

—— (1988) 'The great Education Reform Bill 1988 – some issues and implications' *Journal of Education Policy* 3, 2: 181–9.

—— (1989) 'The reform of school governing bodies; the power of the consumer over the producer?' in M. Flude, and M. Hammer, (Eds) *The 1988 Education Act*, Barcombe: Falmer Press.

Delmar, R. (1986) 'What is feminism?' in A. Oakley, and J. Mitchell, (eds) *What is Feminism?* Oxford: Basil Blackwell.

Denscombe, M. (1980) ' "Keeping 'em quiet": The significance of noise for the practical activity of teaching' in P. Woods, *Pupil/Strategies* London: Croom Helm.

Denzin, N. (1970) *The Research Act* Chicago: Aldine.

DES (1977) *Curriculum 11–16: A Review of Progress* (HMI Red Book One)

London: HMSO.

—— (1981) *Statistics of Education, Vol 1, Schools* London: HMSO.

—— (1983) *Curriculum 11–16: Towards a statement of entitlement* (HMI Red Book Three) London: HMSO.

—— (1984) *Initial Teacher Training: Approval of Courses*, Circular 3/84, London: DES.

—— (1987) *The National Curriculum 5–16 : A Consultation Document* London: DES, July.

Dex, S. (1985) *The Sexual Division of Work: Conceptual Revolutions in the Social Sciences* Brighton: Harvester Press.

Dorset County Council (1986) *Abstract of Statistics for Dorset* Dorchester: Dorset County Council.

Duelli Klein, R. (1983) 'How to do what we want to do: thoughts about feminist methodology' in G. Bowles and R. Duelli Klein, (eds) *Theories of Women's Studies* London: Routledge & Kegan Paul.

Elliott, J. and Powell, C. (1987) 'Young women and science: do we need more science? *British Journal of Sociology of Education* 8, 3: 277–86.

Elmore, R (1980) 'Backward mapping: implementation, research and policy decisions' *Political Science Quarterly* 94, 4: 601–16.

Equal Opportunities Commission (EOC) (1987) *The Response of the Equal Opportunities Commission to the Consultative Document: The National Curriculum 5–16* Manchester: Equal Opportunities Commission.

Finch, J. (1984) 'It's great to have someone to talk to: the ethics and politics of interviewing women' in C. Bell and H. Roberts (eds) *Social Researching: Politics, Problems, Practice* London: Routledge & Kegan Paul.

Fullan (1982) *The Meaning of Educational Change* Ontario: OISE Press.

Fuller, M. (1983) 'Qualified criticism, critical qualifications' in L. Barton, and S. Walker, (eds) *Race, Class and Education* London: Croom Helm.

Gambetta, D. (1987) *Were They Pushed or Did They Jump? Individual Decision Mechanisms in Education* Cambridge and London: Cambridge University Press.

Gaskell, J. (1984) 'Gender and course choice: the orientation of male and female students' *Boston University Journal of Education* 166, 1: 89–102.

—— (1985) 'Course enrolment in the high school: the perspective of working-class females' *Sociology of Education* 58 (January): 48–59.

Giddens, A. (1979) *Central Problems in Social Theory* London: Macmillan.

Goldthorpe, J. M. (1983) 'Women and class analysis: In defence of the conventional view' *Sociology* 17, 4: 467–89.

Griffin, C. (1985) *Typical Girls? Young Women From School to the Full-time Labour Market* London: Routledge & Kegan Paul.

Harding, J. and Sutoris, M. (1987) 'An object relations account of the differential involvement of boys and girls in science and technology' in A. Kelly (ed.) *Science for Girls?* Milton Keynes: Open University Press.

Hargreaves, A. (1978) 'The significance of classroom coping strategies' in L. Barton and R. Meighan (eds) *Sociological Interpretations of Schooling and Classrooms* Driffield: Nafferton Books.

—— (1982) 'Resistance and relative autonomy theory: Problems of distortion and incoherence in recent Marxist analyses of education, *British Journal ofSociology of Education* 3, 2: 107–26.

Harland, J. (1988) 'Running up the down escalator: crisis management as curriculum management' in D. Lawton and C. Chitty, (eds) *The National Curriculum* Bedford Way Papers 33, London: Kogan Page.

Heath, A. and Britten, N. (1984) 'Women's jobs do make a difference: a reply to Goldthorpe' *Sociology* 18: 4.

Holly, L. (ed.) (1987) *Girls and Sexuality* Milton Keynes: Open University Press.

Kamin, L.J. (1974) *The Science and Politics of IQ* Harmondsworth: Penguin.

Kelly, A. (1982) 'Gender roles at home and at school' *British Journal of Sociology* 3, 3: 281–95.

—— (1986) 'Gender differences in teacher-pupil interaction: A meta-analytic review' paper presented to British Educational Research Association Conference, University of Bristol, 1986.

—— (ed.) (1987) *Science for Girls?* Milton Keynes: Open University Press.

—— (1988) 'Towards a democratic science education' in H. Lauder and P. Brown (eds) *Education in Search of a Future* Lewes: Falmer Press.

—— *et al.* (1985) 'Traditionalists and trendies: Teachers' attitudes to educational issues' *British Educational Research Journal* 11, 2: 91–104.

Kessler, S., Ashenden, D., Connell, R.W. and Dowsett, G.W. 'Gender relations in secondary schooling' *Sociology of Education* 58: 34–48.

King, R. (1978) *All Things Bright and Beautiful? A Sociological Study of Infants' Classrooms* London: Wiley.

Kohlberg (1966) 'A cognitive developmental analysis of children's sex-role concepts and attitudes' in E.E. Maccoby (ed.) *The Development of Sex Differences* Stanford: Stanford University Press.

Lawton, D. and Chitty, C (1987) 'Towards a national curriculum' *Forum for the Discussion of New Ideas in Education* 30, 1: 4–6.

—— (eds) (1988) *The National Curriculum* Bedford Way Papers 33, London: Kogan Page.

Lees, S. (1986) *Losing Out: Sexuality and Adolescent Girls* London: Hutchinson.

Lynd, R.S. and Lynd, H.M. (1964) *Middletown in Transition* London: Constable.

MacDonald, M. (1980) 'Socio-cultural reproduction and women's education' in R. Deem (ed.) (1980) *Schooling for Women's Work* London: Routledge & Kegan Paul.

McRobbie, A. (1978) 'Working class girls and the culture of femininity', in Women's Studies Group, Centre for Contemporary Cultural Studies *Women Take Issue* London: Hutchinson.

—— and Garber, J. (1976) 'Girls and subculture' in S. Hall and T. Jefferson (eds) *Resistance Through Rituals* London: Hutchinson CCCS.

Mahony, P. (1985) *Schools for the Boys? Co-education Reassessed* London: Hutchinson.

Martin, J. and Roberts, C. (1984) *Women and Employment: A Lifetime Perspective* The report of the 1980 DE/OPCS Women and Employment Survey, London: HMSO.

Mason, K.M. (1987) *Schoolgirls in a rural context* unpublished PhD thesis, University of Aston, Birmingham.

Maw, J. (1988) 'National curriculum policy: coherence and progression?' in D. Lawton and L. Chitty (eds) *The National Curriculum* Bedford Way Papers 33 London: Kogan Page.

Measor, L (1983) 'Gender and the sciences', in M. Hammersley and A. Hargreaves (eds) *Sociology of Curriculum Practice* Barcombe: Falmer Press.

Menter, I. (1989) 'Teaching practice stasis: racism, sexism and school experience in initial teacher education' *British Journal of Sociology of Education* 10, 4: 459–75.

Mies, M. (1983) 'Towards a methodology for feminist research' in G. Bowles and R. Duelli Klein (eds) *Theories of Women's Studies* London: Routledge & Kegan Paul.

Miles, S. and Middleton, C. (1990) 'Girls' education in the balance: the ERA and inequality' in M. Flude and M. Hammer (eds) *The Education Reform Act 1988: its origins and implications* Lewes: Falmer Press.

Mitchell, J. (1986) 'Reflections on twenty years of feminism' in J. Mitchell and A. Oakley (eds) *What is Feminism?* Oxford: Basil Blackwell.

—— Mitchell, J. and Oakley, A. (eds) (1986) *What is Feminism?* Oxford: Basil Blackwell

Mortimore, P., Sammons, P., Stoll, L., Lewis, D. and Ecob, R. (1988) *School Matters: The Junior Years* Wells: Open Books

Myers, K. (1989) 'High heels in the market place' *Education* 16th June 559–60.

National Curriculum Council (NCC) (1988) *NCC Consultation Document: Science* London: NCC

Newby, H. (1977) *The Deferential Worker* London: Allen Lane.

—— (1980) *Green and Pleasant Land: Social Change in Rural England* London: Wildwood House.

—— et al. (1978) *Property, Paternalism and Power* London: Hutchinson.

Newson Report (1963) *Half Our Future* a report to the Central Advisory Council for Education, London: HMSO.

Norwood Report (1943) *Curriculum and Examinations in Secondary Schools* a report to the Secondary Schools Examination Council, London: HMSO.

Oakley, A. (1972) *Sex, Gender and Society* London: Temple Smith.

—— (1974) *The Sociology of Housework* Oxford: Martin Robertson.

—— (1981) 'Interviewing women: a contradiction in terms' in H. Roberts (ed.)

Payne, G., Hustler, D. and Cuff, T. (1984) 'GIST or PIST: teachers' perceptions of the project Girls Into Science and Technology', Manchester: Manchester Polytechnic.

Pratt, J. (1985) 'The attitudes of teachers', R. Deem, L. Kant and M. Cruickshank in J. Whyte (eds) *Girl Friendly Schooling* London: Methuen.

—— Bloomfield, J. and Seale, S. (1984) *Option Choice: A Question of Equal*

Opportunities Windsor: NFER–Nelson.

Prendergast, S. (1987) 'Girls' experience of menstruation in school' in Holly, L. (ed.) *Girls and Sexuality* Milton Keynes: Open University Press.

Prendergast, S. and Prout, A. (1980) 'What will I do . . .?' Teenage girls and the construction of motherhood' *Sociological Review* 28, 3: 517–35.

Rendal, M. (1985) 'The winning of the Sex Discrimination Act' in M. Arnot, (ed.) *Race and Gender: Equal Opportunities Policies in Education* Oxford: Pergamon Press in association with Open University Press.

Reynolds, D. (1982) 'The search for effective schools' *School Organisation* 2, 3: 215–37.

Reynolds, D. and Sullivan, M. (1980) 'Towards a new socialist sociology of education' in L. Barton, R. Meighan and S. Walker (eds) *Schooling, Ideology and the Curriculum* Lewes: The Falmer Press.

—— (1981) 'The comprehensive experience' in L. Barton and S. Walker (eds) *Schools, Teachers and Teaching* Lewes: Falmer Press.

Rich, A. (1972) 'When we dead awaken: writing as re-vision' *College English* 34: 18–25.

Riddell, S. (1988) *Gender and Option Choice in Two Rural Comprehensive Schools* unpublished PhD thesis, University of Bristol.

—— (1989) 'Exploiting the exploited? The ethics of feminist educational research' in R. G. Burgess, (ed.) *The Ethics of Educational Research* Lewes: Falmer Press.

Rosenfeld, S.A. *et al.* (1985) 'Rural women and girls' in S. Klein (ed.) *Handbook For Achieving Sex Equity Through Education* Baltimore: Johns Hopkins University Press.

Rutter, M., Maughan, B., Mortimore, P., and Ouston, J. (1979) *Fifteen Thousand Hours: Secondary Schools and Their Effects on Children* London: Open Books.

Ryrie, A.C., Furst, A. and Lauder, M. (1979) *Choices and Chances: A Study of Pupils' Subject Choices and Future Career Intentions* London: Hodder & Stoughton, for The Scottish Council for Research in Education.

Scott, S. (1985) 'Feminist research and qualitative methods: a discussion of some of the issues' in R.G. Burgess (ed.) *Issues in Educational Research: Qualitiative Methods* Lewes: Falmer Press.

Segal, S. (1987) 'Is the future feminine? The separate world of Dale Spender' *New Socialist*, January 1987.

Shaw, J. (1980) 'Education of the individual: schooling for girls or mixed shcooling – a mixed blessing?' in R. Deem (ed.) *Schooling for Women's Work* London: Routlege & Kegan Paul.

Sieber, S. D. (1982) 'The integration of fieldwork and survey methods' in R. G. Burgess (ed.) *Field Research: A Sourcebook and Field Manual* London: Allen & Unwin.

Skelton, C. and Hanson, J (1989) 'Schooling the teachers: gender and initial teacher education' in S. Acher (ed.) *Teachers, Gender and Careers* Lewes, The Falmer Press.

Spender, D. and Sarah, E. (1980) *Learning to Lose: Sexism and Education* London: The Women's Press.

REFERENCES

Stanley, J. (1986) 'Sex and the quiet schoolgirl' *British Journal of Sociology of Education* 7, 3: 275–86.

—— (1989) *Marks on the Memory: Experiencing Education* Milton Keynes: Open University Press.

Touraine, A. (1981) *The Voice and the Ear: An Analysis of Social Movements* New York: Cambridge University Press.

Valli, L. (1983) 'Becoming clerical workers: business education and the culture of femininity' in Apple, M. and Weis, L. (eds) *Ideology and Practice in Society* Philadelphia: Temple University Press.

Valli, L. (1986) *Becoming Clerical Workers* New York: Routledge.

Walden, R. and Walkerdine, V. (1982) *Girls and Mathematics: The Early Years* Bedford Way Papers 8, London: University of London Institute of Education.

—— (1985) *Girls and Mathematics: From Primary to Secondary Schooling* Bedford Way Papers 24, London: University of London Institute of Education.

Walkerdine, V. (1981) 'Sex, power and pedagogy' *Screen Education* 38: 14–23.

Wallace, C. (1987) *For Richer For Poorer: Growing Up in and out of Work* London: Tavistock.

Weatherley, R. and Lipsky, M. (1979) 'Street-level bureaucrats and institutional innovation implementing special education reform' *Harvard Educational Review* 7, 2: 171–97.

Weiner, G. (1986) 'Feminist education and equal opportunities: unity or discord?' *British Journal of Sociology of Education* 7, 3: 265–75.

Weis, L. (1990) *Working Class Without Work: High School Students in a Deindustrializing Economy* New York: Routledge.

Whitehead, A. (1976) 'Sexual antagonism in Herefordshire' in D. Leonard Barker and S. Allen, (eds) *Dependence and Exploitation in Work and Marriage* Longman: London.

Whyte, J. (1986) *Girls Into Science and Technology* London: Routledge & Kegan Paul.

Whyte, J., Deem, R., Kant, L. and Cruickshank, M. (eds.) (1985) *Girl Friendly Schooling* London: Methuen.

Willis, P. (1977) *Learning to Labour: How Working Class Kids Get Working Class Jobs* London: Saxon House Books.

Wolpe, A.M. (1974) 'The official ideology of education for girls' in M. Flude and J. Ahier (eds) *Educability, Schools and Ideology* London: Croom Helm.

Wolpe, A.M. (1988) *Within School Walls: The Role of Discipline, Sexuality and the Curriculum* London: Routledge.

Woods, P. (1976) 'The myth of subject option choice' *British Journal of Sociology* 27, 2: 130–49.

—— (1979) *The Divided School* London: Routledge & Kegan Paul.

INDEX

academic success 228
achievement: definition of 236–7;
    differences in 48, 42, 238, 240–1
Acker, S. 35, 67, 223
age-related testing 232–3
Aggleton, P.J. 162
aggression 152, 155–6, 160
Althusser, L. 10
Anyon, J. 11, 94, 143, 161, 226
Arnot, M. 11, 15, 35, 98, 165, 216,
    218, 230
attention seeking, by boys 147–8
Australia: feminist teachers in 223;
    gender-differentiated curriculum
    in 223–4; girls' self-perception in
    226

Baker, K. 211, 218, 221
Ball, S.J. 37, 85
behaviour, in the classroom 147–8
Bentley, D. 213, 214
Bernstein, B. 10
biological determinism 79–80, 87,
    174
biology 38, 39, 41, 74, 96, 144
Black, E. 162
Bourdieu, P. 10
Bowles, S. 10
boys: career choices of 10, 60, 61,
    116; coercive sanctions against
    152–3; lesson content to appeal
    to 148–50; manipulation of
    gender codes by 98, 154–6; as
    negative

reference group 106–8; subject
    choices of 59–60, 67, 96; and
    teacher authority 146–8, 155;
    teachers' typifications of 143–6
Burgess, R.G. 7
Burton, L. 216
Buswell, C. 60, 154
Byrne, E. 212

career choices 227–8; of boys 10,
    60, 61, 116; of girls 12, 61, 116,
    124–5, 128–9, 227–8; see also job
    aspirations
career women 183–4
careers 165, 170, 217
Chadwick, V. 86
Chamberlain, M. 31
chemistry 39, 96, 165, 166;
    presentation of by schools 51
chold-centred education 80–1, 87,
    231
childcare, girls' view of 133–4
Chitty, C. 232–3
Chodorow, N. 215
Clarricoates, K. 143, 146
class 12, 238; definition of 12–13,
    236; and option choices 38–9, 48–
    9, 64; and parental aspirations
    for children 186–7; and
    perception of subject importance
    170, 173; see also middle class;
    working class
coercive sanctions 152–4
Coffield, F. 128

Comber, L.C. 26
commercial subjects 38, 39, 48; *see also* secretarial studies
common curriculum 214–15, 217, 231–2; *see also* national curriculum
Connell, R.W. 11, 13, 36, 66, 69, 71, 77, 86–7, 88, 94, 142, 160, 161, 207, 223, 225, 227, 228
Corrigan P. 142
Cowie, C. 110, 160
Coyle, A. 25
craft *see* domestic crafts; technical crafts
Crowther Report (1959) 79
Crump, S.J. 223–4, 229
Cunnison, S. 83, 151, 153, 156
curriculum 1, 207, 231; gender differentiation in 9, 10, 76–7, 79, 111–12, 221; *see also* entitlement curriculum; national curriculum
curriculum content 72, 75, 114

David, M.E. 165
Davies, L. 142
Deem, R. 79, 209, 210
discipline 142, 152–4
discrimination, girls' attitude to 111–12, 114
disruptive behaviour 58, 61, 143, 162; by boys 154–5; by girls 157–61; teachers' methods of dealing with 146–54
domestic crafts 38, 39, 48, 51, 60, 226; *see also* home economics needlework
domestic division of labour 106, 164; children and 177–80; parents' attitudes to 181–2, 202; pupils' views of 129–31
domesticity, culture of 52
drama, and challenging gender codes 150

economics 39
Education Reform Act, 1988 209, 210, 211
educational aspirations 115–16
Elliott, J. 215, 216

English 95, 165
entitlement curriculum 232–3
environmental determinism 68, 73, 74, 75, 78–9, 174–5, 224–5
Equal Opportunities Commission 217
equal opportunity 35, 37, 50, 71, 88, 230, 234; national curriculum and 219–21, 230; and option choices 62–4, 76–7; parents'view of 173, 191–8; teachers and 15, 78, 80–1, 220, 224, 230
family, sex-stereotyping in 174, 175, 177; *see also* domestic division of labour
female solidarity 151–2
female subcultures 93–4
feminine science 213–14
feminism: in schools 35–6; of teachers 77, 84, 88, 223, 225; of working-class girls 94, 160, 226–8
feminist methodology 14, 17
feminist science 214
femininity 131–6, 137, 142; and career success 227–8; and control of girls 153; cultural definitions of 143, 146; exploitation of by girls 157–61, 162; girls' construction of 9–10, 93, 94 225–6; male teachers 225; parents' versions of 228; and teachers' resistance to gender equality policies 81–7; traditional conceptions of 143, 146; women teachers' use of 151–2
free choice 35, 50, 53–62, 230; teachers and 70, 71, 80, 224
Fuller, M. 161

Garber, J. 19
Gaskell, J. 14, 38, 128, 224
gender: definition of 12; and option choice 9–10, 38–9
gender boundaries, crossing 106–7, 112–13
gender codes 15, 35; competing 143–63; at home 165, 228; manipulation of, as means of contestation 154–61; parents' 228, 229; pupils' 226–7, 229;